Folk Tales
and Legends

Folk Tales and Legends

Retold by
Michaela Tvrdíková

Translated by
Vera Gissing

Illustrations by
Vojtěch Kubašta

Cathay Books

First published 1981 by
Cathay Books
59 Grosvenor Street
London WI

Retold by Michaela Tvrdíková
Translated by Vera Gissing
Graphic design by Aleš Krejča
Illustrations © Vojtěch Kubašta
This edition © Artia 1981

ISBN 0 86178 056 6

Printed in Czechoslovakia
1/20/02/51-01

Contents

In ancient times there lived in the land of Greece a blind poet called Homer. He travelled from city to city, telling people about ancient heroes, such as brave Achilles and clever Odysseus, Paris and his beautiful wife Helen, mighty Hercules and daring Hector. His poems exalted Greek battles for the city of Troy and told of the strange fate of Greek heroes after the Trojan war. Many other poets came before and after Homer, who, like him, told of legendary heroes and wise seers, of clever tricksters and mysterious magicians, of gruesome battles, great loves and incredible adventures. These poets were to be found not only among the Greeks, but among the ancient Sumerians and Indians and in almost every other country in the world. Many of the legends they told are now forgotten, but others have been handed down from generation to generation and are preserved to this day.

The best known and loved legends are to be found in this book. Read them therefore as if you were listening to ancient songs, or admiring antique paintings and statues, for they are the precious remnants of the ancient past, the bygone glory of our ancestors.

How Gilgamesh Sought Immortality

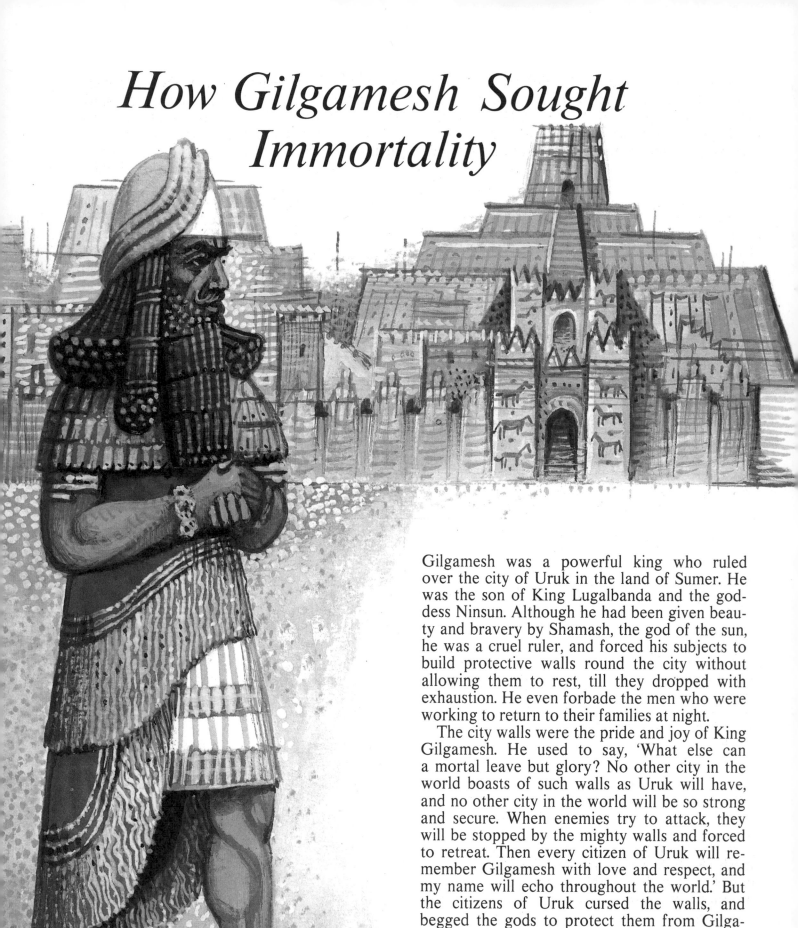

Gilgamesh was a powerful king who ruled over the city of Uruk in the land of Sumer. He was the son of King Lugalbanda and the goddess Ninsun. Although he had been given beauty and bravery by Shamash, the god of the sun, he was a cruel ruler, and forced his subjects to build protective walls round the city without allowing them to rest, till they dropped with exhaustion. He even forbade the men who were working to return to their families at night.

The city walls were the pride and joy of King Gilgamesh. He used to say, 'What else can a mortal leave but glory? No other city in the world boasts of such walls as Uruk will have, and no other city in the world will be so strong and secure. When enemies try to attack, they will be stopped by the mighty walls and forced to retreat. Then every citizen of Uruk will remember Gilgamesh with love and respect, and my name will echo throughout the world.' But the citizens of Uruk cursed the walls, and begged the gods to protect them from Gilgamesh's cruelty. Their pleas were heard by Anu, the highest and the most powerful of gods, who was the protector of Uruk. Anu told Aruru, the creator of men and beasts, to make a strong clay giant who would be able to tame Gilgamesh.

And so the strange giant Enkidu was born. His body was covered with hair and he lived with the wild beasts in the desert. He ate grass with gazelles and drank river water with lions. He wrecked the snares and traps of hunters and chased them away. Rumours of the new master of the desert reached the city of Uruk. When they came to Gilgamesh's ears, he grew angry and made up his mind to humiliate Enkidu.

'A beautiful woman might win where strong hunters have failed,' he said to himself. So he sent the lovely Shamchata to Enkidu. Shamchata was as clever as she was beautiful. She took bread and beer with her, and when the hunters left her in Enkidu's desert, she sat in the shade of the cedar trees and sang a sweet song. Enkidu heard it, and came to her. 'Sit by me,' she said with a smile. 'Take some bread and drink the beer.' Enkidu could not resist. He liked the woman, he enjoyed the bread, and the beer made him merry.

'He who has not tasted beer, does not know what he is missing,' said Shamchata laughing. 'Beer creates good humour among people.' When the wild beasts saw Enkidu eat bread, drink beer and talk with the woman, they fled from him.

'Why are my friends running away?' asked the giant, and Shamchata replied, 'You have eaten man's food and drank his drink. You are no longer a beast, but one of us. Come with me to Uruk. I will take you to our King Gilgamesh. He is as strong and courageous as you, so you will be friends.'

When Enkidu entered Uruk, he marvelled at the magnificent buildings and huge market squares. The citizens stared at the hairy giant with wonder. 'He is as big as Gilgamesh,' they said. 'If not bigger.'

The king met Enkidu on his way to the temple of Ishtar, goddess of fertility. Gilgamesh recognized the giant from the desert, and stormed. 'So you are the wild man who lives with beasts and stops my hunters from killing beasts! You will be severely punished for that.'

Without replying, Enkidu pounced on Gilgamesh. Both heroes wrestled fiercely, without either of them being able to bring the other to his knees. But in the end Enkidu proved himself the stronger of the two, and was pronounced the winner.

'I did not think there was a man on earth who could beat me,' the king muttered. 'So let us not be enemies, but friends.' The two embraced and sealed their pact of friendship.

Some days later Gilgamesh said to Enkidu. 'In the distant Lebanese mountains there is a cedar forest which the monstrous Khumbaba guards. He is the creator of all evil and injustice. Come, let us go after this monster. Let us kill him, and then cut down the cedar trees and use them to make doors for the temple of the god Enlil at Nippur.'

Enkidu was startled to hear such talk. 'Oh brother, I know the whereabouts of this cedar forest. I have often wandered near it with beasts, but I have never dared enter it, for Khumbaba is the most terrible creature. His mouth is a fire, his voice a tempest, and his breath is death.'

'Very well then,' Gilgamesh said curtly, 'I shall go alone.' 'You surely do not think me a coward?' Enkidu cried. 'If I cannot sway you, I shall come too.' So both the heroes set out to the mountains.

Gilgamesh's mother, goddess Ninsun, always worried about her son. She hastened to the sun god Shamash and begged him to help the two giants to kill Khumbaba.

'I shall help them,' Shamash promised, 'because Khumbaba is truly evil and deserves to die.'

When Gilgamesh and Enkidu entered the cedar forest and came face to face with the terrible Khumbaba, Shamash let loose eight hurricane winds against the guard of the cedar forest. Khumbaba was blinded and fell to his knees crying, 'Oh, Gilgamesh! Ask the mighty god Shamash to calm the winds, and I in turn will leave this place and never again sow the seeds of evil and hate.'

'Do not trust him but cut off his head!' Enkidu cried. Gilgamesh listened to his friend and killed the evil creature. Then they cut down the cedar trees to make the large doors for the temple of god Enlil. They took the severed head of Khumbaba back to Uruk with them.

Gilgamesh's fame spread far and wide, until it reached the ears of the beautiful Ishtar, the goddess of love and fertility. She fell in love with him and offered marriage. But the proud Gilgamesh refused her. 'I was not born to marry, but to seek eternal fame for myself. What use would a wife be, even if she were a goddess? She would only distract me from my task.'

Ishtar was very offended by this and ran to her father Anu, who was the most powerful of all the gods. She told him what had happened. 'You must send the celestial bull against him!' she pleaded. 'Let it pierce Gilgamesh's heart with its horns and trample his body with its hooves. Let it avenge my shame!'

Mighty Anu granted his daughter's request, and Ishtar led the celestial bull to Uruk.

The first time the bull panted a huge hole opened in the ground and a hundred Uruk citizens fell into it. The second time it panted another huge hole opened and two hundred Uruk citizens fell into it. And the third time it panted a bigger hole still appeared in the ground and Enkidu fell into it. But he leapt out again and

seizing the beast by the horns, jumped on his back and rode him round the city. The bull resisted, rearing and snorting at Enkidu, and lashing him with his powerful tail, but still he could not shake him off. Gilgamesh then came to his friend's aid, and wedged his sword in the bull's throat. Then they tore the bull's heart out of its body and offered it to the sun god Shamash as a sacrifice. The enraged Ishtar watched and cried, 'Beware, Gilgamesh! You will be punished for shaming me and for slaying the celestial bull!'

Hearing Ishtar's words, Enkidu tore a hind leg off the bull and threw it at her. 'You deserve the same fate as this bull,' he shouted. The death of the celestial bull and the new complaints from the goddess Ishtar angered the gods, and they decided that Gilgamesh and Enkidu should be severely punished. This time Ninsun pleaded in vain for her son. The gods Enlil and Shamash promised to do what they could to help, but Anu, the king of gods was unbending. 'We cannot allow Gilgamesh and Enkidu to do exactly

as they like. Enkidu was created to tame Gilgamesh, but instead he has become his friend. Together they have destroyed a whole cedar forest in the Lebanese mountains, killed its guard Khumbaba, shamed the goddess Ishtar, and slain the celestial bull. One of them must die.'

Shamash disagreed. 'It is true that Gilgamesh and Enkidu killed Khumbaba, but they did so with my help, because Khumbaba sowed only evil and injustice. It is true that they also slew the celestial bull, but they offered its heart as an offering to me.' Enlil added, 'It is true they cut down a whole cedar forest in the Lebanese mountains, but they did so to use the trees to make doors for my temple at Nippur.'

Anu frowned and said, 'It is your fault that you were drawn into it. Nevertheless, one of them has to die.'

'Then let it be Enkidu,' said Enlil.

As soon as Enlil had spoken, Enkidu took to his bed. No matter how Gilgamesh tried to cure his friend, after three days he was dead.

Gilgamesh was brokenhearted at the death of

his friend. He mourned for him for six days and nights, and when he had no more tears left, he cried, 'What use is strength, beauty, courage and wisdom to a man, when death can come and turn everything to dust. My dear Enkidu has died, tomorrow may be my turn. Oh, how wretched it is to be a poor mortal!'

Then he remembered there was just one man living, who had been given immortality by the gods. He was an old ancestor called Uta Napishtim and he lived in the middle of the sea on the Island of the Blessed.

'I shall go to Uta Napishtim to find out how I can become immortal,' Gilgamesh decided. Instead of a robe he put on the skin of the celestial bull, and set out on the long journey.

He travelled to the east, till he came to Mount Mashu, where the sun always sought repose. This mountain was guarded by awsome giants who looked like scorpions. They were terrible to behold, and no one dared go near them. Yet Gilgamesh walked bravely to one of the scorpion men and said, 'Please let me climb Mount Mashu! I must reach the coast on the other side, and then travel by sea to the Island of the Blessed, where my ancestor Uta Napishtim lives.'

The guard replied, 'Man in the bull's skin, do not climb Mount Mashu! The rocks are impassable and the darkness is impenetrable. It will take you many hours, if you are lucky enough to survive. So far no one has, with the exception of the sun god Shamash, who passes through here daily on his way to the sky.'

But Gilgamesh stood his ground. 'I am Gilgamesh, the king of Uruk, and I must get through, come what may.' 'In that case, go!' the scorpion guardman cried.

Gilgamesh climbed and soon found himself in a narrow pass, surrounded by complete darkness. His feet and hands were torn by sharp stones, but he climbed on relentlessly until he saw the first signs of dawn. Climbing still further he found himself before the rising sun. As the sun rose he was enveloped in a dazzling glow and he stepped into a beautiful garden with magnificent trees which bore jewels, and lazurite instead of fruit. Soon after he reached the sea shore.

At the edge of the sea lived Siduri, a female innkeeper to the gods. At the sight of Gilgamesh, clad in the skin of a wild animal and covered by a layer of dust, Siduri took fright and locked herself in her house. But Gilgamesh hammered on the door and cried, 'Foolish Siduri, why do you lock yourself in? I am the one

who cut down a whole cedar forest and slew Khumbaba, its guard! I am the one who killed the celestial bull — it is his skin I wear instead of a robe. Your lock would be an easy thing to break.'

Siduri replied, 'If what you say is true, then you are no other but the king of Uruk. Why are you travelling this hard path? Why are your cheeks so sunken with grief? Why are your eyes without fire?'

'I had a friend called Enkidu, but he has died,' Gilgamesh explained. 'I mourned him for six days and nights, and when I had no tears left, I decided to call on Uta Napishtim, who is my ancestor and lives on the Island of the Blessed. He alone knows the secret of immortality. I must know this secret. I too want to be immortal. I do not want to die like Enkidu.' 'You are a fool, Gilgamesh,' Siduri said with a laugh, and opened the door. 'You will never pass across the Waters of Death, which surround the Island of the Blessed. You are rich, you are handsome, you are famous. Is not that enough? Enjoy life, feast, drink, be merry, be happy with your wife and children. That is the true meaning of life. Do not waste time and effort in searching for something which in any case you will never find.' The exhausted Gilgamesh sat down in Siduri's house, drank her wine and said, 'I cannot do as you say. Please advise me how I can reach the Island of the Blessed.'

'You will never reach it, unless you persuade Uta Napishtim's boatman Urshanabi to row you across,' Siduri replied. 'He has magic amulets, which protect him from the Waters of Death. He lives nearby in a wood.'

Gilgamesh then went to find Urshanabi. The boatman's hut was empty, the hearth cold, his bed long deserted. But from a shelf several clay statues sneered at him. The impatient Gilgamesh crossly knocked them to the floor. As they smashed to pieces, an old man came in. 'Who are you and what do you want here?' he asked sternly.

Gilgamesh replied, 'I am the one who cut down a whole cedar forest in the Lebanese mountains and killed the guard Khumbaba. I am the one who slew the celestial bull and who wears his skin instead of a robe. I am Gilgamesh, King of Uruk.'

The old man nodded and said, 'But why make this hard dangerous journey? Why are your cheeks sunken with grief? Why are your eyes without fire and without tears?'

'I had a friend called Enkidu and he died,' Gilgamesh replied. 'For six days and nights

he found the plant he ripped it from the sea bed and carried it to the boat, paying no attention to the unbearable pain the thorns were causing him.

'I have gained immortality after all,' Gilgamesh cried joyfully. Urshanabi too was content that their mission had been successful. When they came ashore, Gilgamesh thanked the kind boatman and set out to the city of Uruk. As he was very tired and thirsty, when he saw a well with clean, cool water, he was glad to stop for a drink and a rest. Unfortunately he fell asleep, and a snake slithered by and swallowed the magic plant of life. So Gilgamesh did not get his immortality after all. But snakes are now immortal, and they shed their skins instead of dying.

Gilgamesh returned home sad and empty-handed.

But as he neared Uruk and saw the towering city walls reaching to the skies, he said to himself. 'What else can a mortal being leave, but fame! No other city in the world boasts of such massive walls as my Uruk, no other city in the world is as strong and secure. When enemies attack and are stopped by the mighty walls, and forced to retreat, every citizen of Uruk will remember Gilgamesh with love and respect, and my fame will echo throughout the world.'

The Death and Resurrection of Osiris

The moment Typhon had spoken, his seventy-two mighty allies rushed and slammed the lid, hammered in nails and sealed it with lead. Before Isis and her loyal subjects realized what had happened, Typhon and his comrades were on their way with the chest to the mouth of the River Nile, where they cast it into the sea.

The heartbroken Isis cut off a lock of her hair, and wrapped in the robe of mourning she set out to search for the chest containing her husband. Accompanied by faithful Anubis, the god with the head of a dog, she searched hard

It is said that Osiris was the god who taught the Egyptians how to cultivate fields, build houses, make pots, utensils and weapons. He also taught them how to worship gods, sing songs, read, write and count.

In return, all the Egyptian people respected and loved their wise sovereign and his beautiful wife Isis and were overjoyed when their son Horus was born. The baby was given to the priests of Buta to raise.

Osiris' stepbrother Typhon envied Osiris his success, and decided to destroy him. Typhon then joined forces with the Ethiopian queen Aso and seventy-two powerful Egyptian princes. Together they schemed to bring about Osiris' death.

One day, when Typhon and Osiris were bathing in the sea, Typhon measured the imprint of Osiris' huge body where it had rested on the soft sand.

Then Typhon had a magnificent chest made, decorated with gold and jewels, to the exact size of Osiris.

Soon afterwards Osiris held a splendid banquet, whereto the chest was brought. Everyone admired it, and Typhon remarked, as if joking, 'I shall give this chest to the person, who fits into it the best.'

All the guests tried the chest, but it was too large for them all, except for Osiris. It was a perfect fit for him.

'The chest is yours,' Typhon announced. 'But you shall never leave it!'

and long before finding the place where Typhon had thrown the chest into the sea. But then, after further investigation, Isis discovered that the chest had been cast out by the sea and had come to rest at the base of a tamarisk tree near the city of Byblos. The tree grew rapidly to a gigantic size, completely enclosing the chest.

Malcandre, the king of the city of Byblos, admired the massive trunk and had the tamarisk tree cut down to serve as a pillar in his palace.

'Alas, alas,' Isis cried, when she learned all this. 'How can I reach the chest which imprisons my unfortunate husband?'

Clad in simple clothes, Isis made her way to the well by the king's palace. Here she sat alone, day after day, talking to no one, but being friendly to the royal servants, combing their hair, spraying them with exquisite perfumes, such as the queen herself did not even use. Eventually Queen Astarte, curious to meet this strange woman, asked her into the palace. Isis entered and soon became the nurse to the king's son.

At night, while everyone was sleeping, Isis bathed the little body of the prince in purificatory flames. While the child lay in the fire, Isis turned into a swallow and flew around the pillar which held the chest with the body of her beloved Osiris.

One night Queen Astarte woke up, and saw her child in the flames. She cried out in terror, and cursed Isis, who immediately changed back from swallow to woman.

'Wait,' Isis called out. 'You do not know what you are saying. I am goddess Isis, and if you had not meddled in matters you do not understand, the fire would have burned all mortal substances out of the prince's body. Now you have deprived him of immortality.'

The queen gasped and said, 'Oh, mighty goddess, forgive me! I did not know who you were.'

Isis then asked for the tamarisk pillar. She freed the chest and had it carried to the sea, where she opened it and bathed her husband's body in her tears.

Osiris, of course, was a god, and was therefore immortal. He could not remain dead for ever. Though his soul had entered the underworld, it returned into his body when Isis kissed his mouth, and Osiris came to life again.

Isis was overjoyed, but her husband said, 'What use is life to me, when treacherous Typhon rules my land? First I must humiliate him.'

'It should not be you, but our son Horus should avenge his father,' Isis pronounced. Osiris agreed and so they set off to the city of Buta, where Horus lived.

Their son had grown into a handsome young man, as strong as a wrestler and as wise as the priests who had raised him. After so long, he was very pleased to see his parents, but Osiris wasted no time in testing him whether he was ready to fight his uncle. 'What is the most important thing in the world?' the father asked.

'To avenge one's father', Horus replied without hesitation.

Satisfied with the answer, Osiris continued, 'What animal does a man need most in battle?'

'A horse,' was the prompt reply.

'Why a horse?' Osiris wondered. 'Why not a lion, for instance?'

'A weak man needs a lion to help him. But if a strong warrior wishes to chase the enemy, a horse serves him best.'

Osiris was content. He could see that his son was ready to fight Typhon.

His confidence was well founded, for when Horus and his followers marched against Typhon, the sight filled Typhon's heart with such terror, that he turned heel and fled with his seventy-two allies out of Egypt into Ethiopia.

After this Osiris and Isis took up the reign over the Egyptian people once again.

Daring Rama

The city of Ayodhya stood on the banks of the river Saragu in distant India. King Dasaratha was its sovereign. He had three wives, as was the custom of that country. Kausalya, with whom he had a son, Rama, was the first. Then came Kaikeya, who bore him another son Bharata, whilst Sumitra, the youngest wife, presented him with twins, Lakshmana and Satrughna. Kausalya was the king's favourite, though he owed his life to Kaikeya, who once had healed his mortal wounds. For this he promised to fulfil any two of her wishes.

Time was passing and King Dasaratha was growing old. He decided therefore to hand the reign of the country over to his eldest son Rama. He announced this decision to his councillors and his people. The kingdom rejoiced, for Rama was known to be a brave, wise man, whose wife Sita was as good as she was beautiful.

Only Manthara, the hunch-back maid of Queen Kaikeya, was discontent. 'Can you not see how your son has been humiliated?' she said to her mistress. 'Did not the king promise to grant two of your wishes? Why not ask for Bharata to be chosen as his successor and for Rama to be exiled into the jungle for fourteen years?'

Kaikeya thought it over. Having decided, she took to her bed and pretended to be gravely ill. The worried king hastened to her chamber and cried, 'What is wrong, dear Kaikeya?'

'I am very sick and can only be cured if you fulfil my two wishes,' she replied.

'Years ago, when you healed my mortal wounds, I vowed I would grant you two wishes,' said the king. 'The promise still stands.'

'Good,' Kaikeya whispered. 'Then hand the reign over to Bharata and send Rama into the jungle for fourteen years to do penitence.'

The request grieved King Dasaratha. Nevertheless he sent for the two sons and said, 'I announced that I shall hand over the rule of my kingdom to Rama. But Kaikeya desires Bharata to reign and asks that Rama goes into the jungle for fourteen years to do penitence. Years ago I promised to grant her any two wishes, so I have to stand by my promise.'

'But father, I do not wish to rule instead of Rama!' Bharata protested, but Rama said, 'Our father is right, brother, and we must obey him. I shall go into the jungle for fourteen years and you shall reign.'

'I agree if you insist,' Bharata sighed, 'but after fourteen years, when you return, you will be the ruler of this kingdom.'

With that both the princes left their crestfallen father.

When beautiful Sita heard of the unhappy fate of her husband, she wept and vowed, 'I shall go with you, Rama! I shall never desert you!'

'You cannot come,' Rama objected. 'The jungle is full of wild beasts, with dangers lurking everywhere. It is not a fit place for a woman raised in luxury.'

Yet Sita stood firm. And when Lakshmana, not wishing to desert his half-brother, insisted on coming too, Rama had to give in and take them both.

The three of them walked sadly towards the jungle. Clad in the rough robes of penitents, the two brothers were protected by armoured breastplates which no spear could penetrate. At the waist they carried magic swords, which dealt only mortal blows, and on their backs were magic bows and quivers holding arrows which never missed their target. The quivers never ran out of arrows. Sita carried the jewels Rama had given her.

They travelled for a long time, cutting their way through dense thicket, crossing brooks and rivers, hills and mountains, until at last they came to Mount Chitrakutu, the home of the holy hermits. The aged Valkimi, their noble leader, greeted them warmly. 'Prince Rama and Prince Lakshmana, I welcome you both! And you too, lovely Sita! Build yourselves a hermitage and live with us here in this lovely spot. There is ample beast and fruit, plenty of honey, and good, healthy fresh water from the springs. You will live well.'

The brothers thanked Valkimi for such a kind reception, and soon the three newcomers settled in. They built a simple hut and lived in contentment with the other hermits. Their happiness lasted for many years. One day, the sister of the master demon wandered near their hut. Shurpanakha was a stupid, ugly woman and she took a fancy to the handsome Rama.

'Be my husband, hero!' she said to him. 'I am the sister of the master demon and you will be happy with me.'

Rama laughed, and jokingly replied, 'I am already married, and you would hardly wish to put up with my wife. But I have a younger brother. He is handsome and brave. Why not court him?'

Shurpanakha therefore turned her attentions to Lakshmana, but he turned her down too. 'I am just my elder brother's servant. Surely you would not wish to be the wife of a slave.'

The fearsome demons, on their way to the hut where the princes lived, crashed to the ground when struck by the deadly arrows fired from the brothers' magic bows. The same fate awaited Khara and his fourteen thousand demons, when they, too, came to attack. It was a vicious battle, for the demons were very strong, but Rama and Lakshmana stood their ground, bringing down one demon after another with their arrows. The invincible Khara was eventually killed by Rama's magic sword. Shurpanakha, wild with despair, fled from the battlefield to Ravana, the king of the demons. On hearing what had happened he cried angrily, 'I shall have my revenge on both the princes!'

His advisors tried to talk him out of it. 'Rama and his brothers are formidable enemies. If you fight them, you will perish, even with all the demons at your side. Do not open the gate of Death, or you yourself will enter!'

Ravana's son then said, 'The cruellest punishment for both the princes, father, would be to carry off Rama's beautiful wife, Sita. You will not kill them in battle, but this way they will die of grief.'

The king praised his son for his clever advice, and travelled with him to the hut on Mount Chitrakutu. In silence they waited for the brothers to depart, when Sita would be alone at home. But the princes guarded her well and she was never without them.

Then the demon king's crafty son came up with another idea. 'We shall have to trick them.'

One morning, when Rama went hunting in the forest and Sita was alone with Lakshmana, Ravana's son, hidden by a nearby bush, called for help in Valmiki's voice. Lakshmana ran out, but did not find the old man. Ravana, in the meantime, crept into the hut, and abducted the astonished Sita.

The brothers were overcome with grief when they realized that Sita had disappeared. They searched for her in vain, they waited for her return in vain. The wise Valmiki then said, 'I am sure Sita was abducted by one of your enemies. It must have been him who called you from the bushes, imitating my voice. Go to Mount Rshyamuku to see Sugriva, the king of the monkeys, and his wise counsellor Hanuman. They may be able to help you.' The brothers set off once more with renewed hope. They reached Mount Rshyamuku, after crossing many rivers and many hills. Sugriva, the king of the monkeys, welcomed them kindly. After listening to their story, he said, 'I know, Rama, where your wife has been taken and I will help you!'

Then the hideous Shurpanakha pounced on Rama and Sita, threatening, 'I shall devour your horrible wife and then you will be mine!'

Sita was terrified of the vile Shurpanakha, whose ugly hands were already reaching for her. Lakshmana drew his sword and cut the nose and ears off that hideous creature. Screeching with pain, Shurpanakha fled to her mighty brother Khara, the master of the demons. Khara grew extremely angry when his disfigured sister told him how she had been shamed, and he immediately sent fourteen thousand demons to kill Lakshmana.

He entered a cave and came out again, carrying Sita's jewellery. 'I saw a demon carrying Sita. She dropped the jewels nearby. But I cannot tell you where the demon hid her. I shall send my monkeys to search the whole world. They will be led by the wise, brave Hanuman. He is sure to find her.'

Sugriva summoned Hanuman, who said, 'I know, my king, where the demons live. Their home is a hundred miles from here, on the Isle of Lanka. They say there is a magnificent city there with houses built of gold, and that it is ruled by the mighty Ravana, the king of the demons. I shall try to get there.'

Hanuman then left with the monkeys.

Many days passed before Hanuman reached the coast. When at last he saw the glow of the Isle of Lanka reflected in the sea, he wondered how to reach it. The demons guarded their city well and drowned anyone daring to cross the water. 'If there is no way to get there by sea, we will try the air,' Hanuman said to his monkeys.

Using a sheer rock jutting out over the sea as a springboard, he took a running jump, so that with one immense leap he was in the air. Waving his enormous tail like a wing, he rose into the clouds and flew like a bird, falling into the bushes right by the city walls. There he waited for the dark night to cover Lanka.

When the sun set and the moon rose into the sky, Hanuman leapt over the walls and crept into the royal palace. No mortal being had ever witnessed such magnificence. The walls were of pure gold, the stairs and floors of crystal, the pillars of jewels and the ceilings of pearls. Hanuman quickly scanned the whole palace. He saw many hideous demons, including Ravana and his son. He entered the kitchens, pantries and cellars. He did not miss a single chamber or a single hall, but it seemed as if the beautiful Sita had disappeared from the earth.

Hanuman ran out of the palace to search the large garden, when Sita suddenly appeared before him. She was clad in dirty, torn clothes, her face was smeared with tears, yet she still looked so exquisite, that her beauty took Hanuman's breath away. She was strolling towards a lake strewn with water lilies, gazing in silence upon its surface. Hanuman approached her, and said gently, 'I bring you greetings from the valiant Rama, noble Sita!' The astonished Sita gaped at the monkey, while Hanuman continued, 'Have no fear! Hanuman will come with a great army

and will set you free. Do not lose hope, but bear your humiliation a little longer!'

Sita whispered, 'Tell Rama and his brother Lakshmana that I think of them constantly. Ravana is pressing me to be his wife, but I keep refusing him. I can bear my suffering another month, but after that no one shall find me amongst the living.'

Hanuman bade the unhappy Sita goodbye, and hastened back to Sugriva, his king.

The earth trembled with fear when Rama, Lakshmana, Sugriva and Hanuman, heading a million monkeys, marched to save Sita. Everything that stood in their path was brushed aside like a speck of dust. No barrier stood up to the vast army, no power could stop its incredible strength.

'How can we cross the sea, how can we get to the Isle of Lanka?' Rama worried on the way. Sugriva tried to cheer him. 'Do not be afraid, prince. My monkeys will win even over the sea.'

He was right. The moment the monkey army reached the shore, Hanuman issued orders, and the monkeys collected trees and rocks, till a strong, firm bridge started rising above the sea.

At first Ravana laughed to see the monkeys' efforts. 'I will knock down the bridge and the monkeys with one smite', he boasted. But in the morning, when the bridge reached the island, and millions of monkeys headed by the two princes were rushing towards him, Ravana grew frightened. He hid in his palace and sent his son to lead his army.

A cruel battle followed. The monkeys, like possessed creatures, pounced upon the strong demons. They crawled into everything, and penetrated everywhere. They were on trees, walls, towers, and roofs, astride the hideous demons' heads, on their backs, under their feet. Though hundreds of them died, thousands more crossed the bridge from the mainland. Rama, Lakshmana, Sugriva and Hanuman fought in front like lions.

The demons were now on the retreat. Even Ravana's son was hiding in one of the palace towers, from where he fired poisoned arrows at Rama and Lakshmana. The princes were struck and fell unconscious to the ground in a pool of blood. Life slowly ebbed away from their bodies. Ravana's son ran to his father and cried, 'Rama and Lakshmana are dead! I killed them with my poisoned arrows!'

Ravana shouted for joy, and summoned the unhappy Sita to tell her of the death of her husband and his brother. Sita sank to the floor and begged, 'Please kill me too, fearsome Ravana! Then you will accomplish your one good deed in life if you permit me to die with my beloved Rama.'

But Ravana turned a deaf ear to her pleas.

As night cloaked the city, the monkeys gath-

ered together outside its walls. Sugriva and Hanuman sadly carried the corpses of the two princes to their burial. Suddenly Hanuman said, 'I have heard, my king, that high up in the Himalayan mountains four magic herbs are to be found. One joins limbs to the body, another heals wounds, the third gives life back to the corpse and the fourth gives it a golden glow. I shall go there immediately. Perhaps I shall be able to revive the princes.'

'You are wise and brave. Go!' said Sugriva, embracing the loyal Hanuman. 'If only you are successful!' With that blessing Hanuman left swiftly.

The following day the battle started afresh. 'Rama and Lakshmana may be dead, but we shall not retreat until we have rescued the lovely Sita and destroyed Ravana's repulsive kingdom,' Sugriva pronounced.

The death of Rama and Lakshmana gave the demons courage and hope, and for a time it looked as if they were going to be the victors. Ravana joined the fight this time and it seemed as though the city would not be conquered. But suddenly there was a golden glow in the midst of the monkeys' army and to the demons' astonishment, Rama and Lakshmana appeared, resurrected from the dead by the valiant Hanuman. The princes threw themselves into the fight, and a terrible battle broke out. The demons were mowed down, one after the other and Ravana's son was amongst the victims. When the fighting was at its most vicious, Ravana and Rama met. The duel was short. The mighty demon king could not avoid the blows of the prince's magic sword. He dropped his weapon, shielded his eyes with his hands, but before he could beg for mercy, he fell dead to the ground. And Lanka, the city of the demons, was destroyed.

How joyful was the reunion of Rama, Lakshmana and Sita! King Sugriva and the valiant Hanuman could not hide their tears when they saw the happiness they had brought their friends. They all turned for home with gladness filling their hearts.

As they neared the river Saragu, they met a magnificent procession led by king Bharata. Seeing his brother Rama, the king dismounted, knelt before him and said, 'It is fourteen years to the day since you were sent into the jungle to do penitence. Our father, King Dasaratha, had died long ago, and so had my mother. I am keeping my promise, and handing back to you the reign of our kingdom, which is yours by right.'

Rama, greatly moved, embraced his brother. Then he bade Sugriva, Hanuman and all the monkeys a friendly goodbye, and turned towards the city of Ayodhya, to take up the rule there. He reigned for many years with the loyal Sita at his side, and his reign was as happy and wise as it was long.

How Prometheus Gave Men Fire

There was a time, long ago, when peace reigned on earth. In those days mighty Zeus and other gods lived on Mount Olympus. Lively fish swam in clear streams, bright coloured birds chirped happily as they flew through the air and herds of cattle grazed contentedly on grassy plains. But there was no one to catch the fish, no one to hear the birds' song, and no one to tend the cattle. Man was not yet on earth. Prometheus, who saw into the future, and Epimetheus, who was always wiser after the event, were brothers from the Titan race of gods. Sadly they roamed the earth searching for beings like themselves. They knew that soil gave life to grass and trees, and that without water they could not stay alive. In regions where it had not rained for some time the soil was dry and plants and trees withered and died. Birds and beasts abandoned these places. Only the fish were trapped and often perished in dried-up river beds.

'Soil and water are life,' Prometheus stated. 'We shall use clay and water to make creatures who will resemble the gods and ourselves — we shall create men.'

'Yes!' cried Epimetheus, who was rather hasty by nature. 'I will make the men and you can supervise my work.'

Prometheus agreed and went to see Pallas Athene, the goddess of wisdom and intelligence to ask for help. She was not very willing, but she returned with Prometheus to his brother.

Epimetheus had been hard at work and had already made from clay a whole generation of people. Some looked very nice, but mostly they were ugly, even repulsive. And though Athene breathed life into their bodies, she did not give many much intelligence.

Prometheus lived with the ugly, rather clumsy people, using his wisdom to teach them to hunt,

plough fields, grow corn, cook and bake, build carts and harness cattle, build boats and work the sails. He taught them various trades, to mine copper, silver, gold and other metals and to turn these into many useful objects. He taught them to count, read and write, to understand nature and to cure sickness. But he did not teach them obedience and respect towards the gods. The gods on Mount Olympus viewed the behaviour of men with distrust and anger. 'We shall punish the people for not bringing sacrifices to our altars by depriving them of fire,' mighty Zeus decided. And he sent torrential rain to earth, which put out all fires, and terrible gales which blew the ashes and the red hot cinders right out to sea. Life was difficult without fire. People could not bake bread, nor make implements and they could not keep warm. But Prometheus did not forsake them. He knew that in the palace on Mount Olympus he would find the eternal flame which blazed night and day, and that he could bring a part of it to his people.

In a forest he broke off a thick branch and hollowed it out. He climbed Mount Olympus and filled the hollow with some of the red hot cinders from the eternal fire. The following day Zeus noticed smoke pouring from people's dwellings and workshops and he guessed that Prometheus must have come to their aid. 'He must be punished,' Zeus said angrily, and he im-

mediately ordered his brother Hephaestus, the god of fire and forge, to arrest Prometheus and to chain him to the rocky peak of Mount Caucasus.

The unfortunate Prometheus went through terrible torture. Burned by the fierce sun and whipped by rain and snow, he craved for water and food. And every morning he was attacked by a giant eagle who gnawed his liver with his sharp beak. His liver always grew again by the following night providing fresh nourishment for the winged monster. It was an agonizing punishment, but Prometheus stood up to the torture bravely and proudly. He felt no guilt, for all he did was to help his beloved people.

Finally the gods themselves had pity on him. Mighty Zeus let his heroic son Hercules slay the eagle and set the victim free. From that day he has never again deprived men of fire, which had been bought at such a terrible price.

Daedalus, the Inventor and Icarus, his Son

Daedalus was the cleverest craftsman not just in Athens, but in the whole of Greece. The churches and palaces he built were like the works of the gods, and his statues were incredibly lifelike. Only one man, Talus, the son of Daedalus' sister, could match his artistry. He was the inventor of the potter's wheel and the saw and he could carve marble statues to match those of his instructor Daedalus. But Daedalus never allowed him to build churches and palaces, and one dark evening, in a fit of jealousy, he threw his brilliant nephew of a high Athenian wall. But Talus did not die. The goddess Pallas Athene liked the talented young man, so she caught him before he hit the ground and turned him into a bird.

Daedalus' shameful deed did not remain a secret. He escaped just punishment only because his nephew's corpse was never found. Afraid of staying on in Athens, Daedalus fled to the Island of Crete, taking Icarus, his son, with him.

Minos, the King of Crete, welcomed the skilful inventor warmly. His wife, Queen Pasiphae, had just given birth to a monster child, half human, half bull, and so he ordered Daedalus to build a palace in which no one would find his hideous son.

'I will carry out your wish,' Daedalus agreed, 'if you promise me that you will allow me to return home after five years. By then Athens will have forgotten about Talus.'

The king agreed, and Daedalus built an enormous labyrinth to hide Minotaur, the monster child, who was taken to live in the centre of the building, surrounded by a maze of twisting passages.

Nobody knew their way about the palace and anyone who entered the labyrinth became so lost, they never found their way out again.

It had taken exactly five years for Minotaur's palace to be completed. But though King Minos praised Daedalus' work and rewarded him generously, he turned a deaf ear to his pleas to return to Athens.

'You have everything you need here and you miss nothing. In Athens you would only have to answer for murdering your nephew Talus, whereas here you are safe. Be thankful you are in Crete.'

Daedalus realized he would not be allowed to leave the island openly. To escape by way of the sea was impossible, for the shores were well guarded.

'So the sea belongs to the king,' said he. 'But the sky is mine. I shall escape like a bird.'

The inventor then set to work. From countless feathers, long and short, he made two pairs of wings, glueing them with wax. One pair was for himself, the other for his son Icarus.

'You are not to fly too low,' Daedalus warned him. 'Your wing could catch on a rock or a high tree. Neither must you fly too high, otherwise the warmth of the sun would melt the wax and your wings would fall apart.'

With that warning they flew up into the sky and headed home. But the young, excited Icarus did not heed his father's warning nor his cries. He rose higher and higher, till the burning sun slowly began to melt the wax. Large yellow spots fell into the sea and feather after feather followed them.

Finally the body of the unfortunate Icarus plunged headlong into the waves and only the scattered plumage on the sea surface showed the grief-stricken father his son's grave.

Daedalus never returned to his own country. He flew to Sicily instead, and built many fine temples and palaces. But he never recovered his peace of mind.

How Theseus Slew Minotaur

The war between Aegeus, the king of Athens, and Minos, the king of Crete, ended with Aegeus' defeat, for which he had to pay dearly. He was ordered to send, every nine years, seven youths and seven maidens as a sacrifice to Minotaur, Minos' monster son. When the third payment was due, Theseus persuaded his father Aegeus to let him accompany the victims to Crete. 'If I slay Minotaur, I shall put an end to this murder,' he said in justification.

'Old men are as impatient as children,' the old king remarked in parting. 'When the ship is bound homeward, if you are victorious, hoist your white sails instead of the black ones. Then I shall see from afar whether I should cheer your victory or cry for your defeat.'

Minos, with his wife and daughter Ariadne at his side, was waiting impatiently for the Athenians. He was surprised to see Theseus among the victims, but Theseus explained, 'I have not come to be fed to Minotaur, but to slay the beast and so free my country from having to make such a shameful and cruel payment.'

The king remained silent, and Ariadne's eyes never left the youth's face. She had fallen in love with him at first sight and had made up her mind to help him as best as she could. When the Athenians were locked up in prison, where they were to spend their very last night, Ariadne unlocked the back door and whispered to Theseus, 'Listen to what I have to say. You will never kill Minotaur without my aid. He is invulnerable. He can only be slain with my father's magic sword.' And she handed Theseus the sword and a ball of twine. 'When you enter the labyrinth,' she continued, 'tie the end of the twine to a pillar and unroll the ball as you walk. Then you will be able to find your way out again.'

Theseus thanked the princess and fell asleep, knowing he would be the victor.

The following day the guards took the Athenian youths and maidens to Minotaur's palace and locked them inside. Theseus told the others to stay by the entrance, then he tied the end of the twine to a pillar and, alone, went in search of Minotaur. He walked on and on through the maze of passages, until he heard a deafening

roar, and found himself face to face with Minotaur, the hairy giant with the bull's head. Theseus hurled himself at the monster and drove the sword right through his heart. Then holding fast to the twine, he returned to his own kind.

There was much joy, laughter and happy tears among the young Athenians, when Theseus reappeared. But the worried-looking Ariadne burst in. 'Alas!' she cried, 'Father has found out I gave you the magic sword. You must flee swiftly and take me with you.' Ariadne then led them through a secret door to the shore, where the Athenian ship lay anchored. Before the king's guards reached Minotaur's palace, the boat was far out at sea.

As night approached, the Island of Naxos appeared on the horizon, and the travellers decided to sleep there. In her sleep Ariadne had the strangest dream. She saw Dionysus, god of wine and revelry, who said, 'You are not destined to be the wife of Theseus. It is the will of my father Zeus that you be mine. Therefore do not leave with the Athenians, but remain on this island.'

Ariadne was sad, but she did not dare argue with the gods. She bid the unhappy Theseus goodbye and tearfully gazed at his boat as it sailed away towards Greece.

The silence around her was suddenly broken by loud singing and clatter. A fine carriage, covered with ivy and vine, and pulled by a pair of tigers, was being driven towards her. Young Dionysus was the driver. He lifted Ariadne to his side and carried her away . . .

Theseus' boat was speeding towards Athens. Grieved at having to leave Ariadne behind, he forgot in his sorrow to order the black sails to be replaced by white ones to show his father that all was well.

King Aegeus was standing on a cliff, anxiously watching out for the boat's return. When he saw the black sails in the distance, with a cry of despair, he flung himself into the sea. Ever since then this sea is called the Aegean Sea.

The Adventurous Argonauts

Once upon a time King Athamus ruled in Orchomenus, the wealthy, important city of Boeotia. With his wife Nephele, the goddess of clouds, he had two children, a son Phryxus and a daughter Helle.

Athamus had every reason to be happy and content, yet he drove his true wife away and married the proud Ino. She turned out to be a wicked stepmother to Phryxus and Helle, particularly after she gave birth to children of her own. From then on she had only one thought in mind: how to be rid of her stepchildren. Then she had a monstrous idea. She called all the women of the kingdom together and said, 'Do you want the harvest in your fields to be doubly rich? Then listen to me! You must roast the corn before sowing it. Then you will have crops such as you've dreamed of. But you must not tell your husbands nor anyone else about this.'

The simple women believed their queen, and when it was time to sow the seeds, they secretly roasted them first. Naturally enough not a single stalk of corn came up.

Terrible hunger and poverty spread throughout the land and nobody knew the cause, for the normally talkative women kept silent, as if they had lost their tongues. The king therefore sent a messenger to the Delphic Oracle to ask how to appease the gods and bring prosperity back to his land.

But the sly queen said to the messenger, 'You must not go to the prophet! Say instead that the gods demand the king's children, Phryxus and Helle, as a sacrifice. If you obey me, I will reward you well, if not, I shall avenge myself most cruelly.'

The messenger was too terrified to disobey, so the whole kingdom was told that the king's children were the cause of its misfortune.

The grief-stricken king fought hard against sacrificing his beloved children, but he feared the anger of his people and of the gods, so in the end he had to give in.

The night before the sacrifice, as Phryxus and Helle were peacefully asleep and unaware of their cruel fate their real, holy mother sent a golden-fleeced winged ram to their aid. 'Sit on the golden ram,' she whispered as they slept. 'It will carry you to safety. Only death awaits you while you remain here.'

The children awoke and followed their mother's advice. They mounted the golden ram and it flew high up, carrying them across the sea. After they had been flying for quite some time, Helle looked down; her head started to spin, and she lost her balance and fell. The sea closed over her and the little girl drowned. Since that day this sea has been called Hellespont.

Phryxus held on firmly and finally landed in distant Colchis, ruled by King Aeetes. The king received the little rider kindly and Phryxus, grateful to be saved, offered the ram to the gods who protect fugitives. But he gave the golden fleece to King Aeetes.

The king was overjoyed with such a valuable gift and had the fleece nailed to a holy tree dedicated to Ares, the god of war. A dragon who never fell asleep was set to guard it. He did this not only because the fleece was real gold, but mainly because a wise seer had visited him and said, 'You shall continue to rule and to stay alive and well only while you have the golden fleece.'

Even in those days people wanted to live long and enjoy their life and power. King Aeetes was no exception.

When Phryxus grew up, he married Chalciope, the king's eldest daughter, and they lived happily at the royal court. But his father, King Athamas, was cruelly punished by the gods. He and his wife Ino and their children all perished. His nephew, Aeson, next ruled Orchomenus, until he was overthrown by his brother Pelias. Aeson then went into seclusion, and fearing for his son Jason's life, he declared him dead. But

Jason was very much alive. He was put in the care of the wise Centaur, Chiron, who lived in the mountains. Chiron was half man, half horse, but he was renowned far and wide for his great knowledge and kindness. He made an excellent teacher for young Jason.

When Jason had grown into a handsome

wards the city. He did not even notice that he had lost one of his sandals in the water.

As soon as King Pelias saw Jason at the royal palace, he gasped and turned as white as a sheet. He had noticed that Jason's sandal was missing and recalled that a prophet had told him to beware of a man wearing one sandal.

'Who are you? Where do you come from? Who are your parents? What do you want here?' he cried bombarding Jason with questions. The youth replied, 'I am your nephew Jason, the son of Aeson. I have come to claim the throne which is mine by right.'

The king was horrified. He realized that the prophecy was about to come true and that he would not escape his fate. But he was not going to give up the throne willingly and was determined to fight his destiny. So he said to Jason, 'Son of my brother, be welcomed! I shall be happy to hand over the reign of the kingdom, which is rightly yours. But first I want you to accomplish a difficult task. Phryxus, one of our kin, has died in the distant land of Colchis. Night

youth, drilled in defence and wisdom, his tutor Chiron said, 'I shall be grieved to part from you, but there is nothing else I can teach you. You are wise and knowledgeable, you are brave and an excellent warrior. The time has come for you to seize the throne which your uncle unjustly holds.'

Jason was sad to part from his guardian, but he obeyed him as always and he set out to the city. Though only clad in a panther skin, with a spear in his hand and sandles on his feet, he resembled a young god. After some time he came to a river and noticed an old woman standing with her eyes downcast. 'How pleased I am you have come, young man,' she cried happily. 'I have been waiting here so long for someone to carry me across this river.' Jason gathered the old woman in his arms. She was as light as a feather, and in a trice they were on the other side.

'Thank you, young man! I shall never forget your kindness,' she said and then disappeared. Jason had no idea that he had carried Hera, the queen of heaven, across the river.

For a while Jason looked around, wondering where the old woman had disappeared to. Then with a shrug of the shoulders, he hurried on to-

after night his spirit appears before me and begs me to recover the golden fleece of the ram which had once carried him to Colchis. His spirit cannot rest in peace until the golden fleece is in our land. Bring it to me and then take up the reign! I am getting old and my son does not hanker after power. There won't be any argument between you.'

Jason agreed. He was happy to go. Such an adventure would be more exciting than staying with the king. And the king was content, for he believed that Jason would perish on the dangerous journey.

Jason assembled a band of the bravest and wisest men to accompany him, including strong Hercules, Orpheus the musician, Theseus, who had slain Minotaur, Peleus, Meleager, Idmon the seer, Polydeuces the wrestler, Tiphys, Ancaeus, and the sons of Boreas, Zetes and Calais, who had wings on their shoulders. Hera, the goddess of heaven was to keep vigil over them. Argus, the noted ship-builder built them a magnificent vessel with a figurehead carved out of the holy oak from the sacred grove of Dodona to ensure a safe and successful journey. They named the ship the Argo, which means swift, after Argus, the craftsman who made her and the crew were called the Argonauts.

The day came at last when all was ready to set sail across the sea. Crowds of people came to wave them off. Even the aged Chiron had climbed down the mountain, with his wife by his side. She was holding a babe in her arms — little Achilles, the son of the sea nymph Thetis and of Peleus.

The passage proved long and full of trouble. Luck was with them at first. They passed safely through Hellespont, where unfortunate Helle had perished, then sailed to a barren, rocky coast. Idmon the seer ordered them to cast anchor and go ashore. There they came upon the blind, aged Phineus, a gifted prophet who was once a powerful king. As he had revealed to his people the intentions of the gods, Zeus had punished him by taking away his sight. But his persecution did not end there, for whenever he was about to eat, two winged monsters, the Harpies, swooped down on the food, devouring every morsel. Only a dreadful stench remained when they left.

Phineus was expecting the Argonauts, for it was his destiny to be freed from his sufferings by the two sons of Boreas, who were in the crew.

The Argonauts gave food to the aged man, but as he was about to eat, the monstrous Har-

neus.' Boreas' sons flew down to their companions and related what had happened. Fresh food was prepared for the aged man. This time the Harpies did not appear. The grateful Phineus said in warning, 'There are many other trials waiting for you on your route, my friends. You must particularly beware of the Symplegades, the rocks which guard the entrance into the Black Sea. Nobody has sailed through yet without a calamity. These rocks move, and spread apart, then crash together. They would smash your ship to a pulp. Send a dove ahead. If she passes through safely, you will too. And you must remember to cast anchor by a small island

pies swooped down, tore the food from his hands and flew away again. But Zetes and Calais, the two winged Argonauts, soared after them and attacked the hideous creatures with swords. They would have killed them, but Iris, the messenger of the gods, who was the goddess of the rainbow, stopped them by saying, 'Do not harm the Harpies, for they are the swift dogs of the gods themselves! The gods' wrath would follow you. Let them be, and I promise you that they will never again pester blind Phi-

beyond the land of the Amazons. It is called Aretias and is the home of vulturous birds with metal beaks and talons. Even their feathers are of metal and they can fire them as arrows. You must chase these birds away — then you will see.'

The Argonauts thanked the old man for all the advice and continued their journey. Phineus gazed after them with his sightless eyes, a lonely figure on the rocky shore.

Other eyes were also carefully watching the vessel. The goddess Pallas Athene had come to help the daring seafarers, to save them from the treacherous Symplegades. They were indeed a terrifying sight with water whirling madly round them, the waves crashing, and the rocks

clashing with a deafening roar. Fear gripped the Argonauts' hearts. At that moment Ancaeus let the dove go. The rocks parted swiftly and the dove flew towards them with the speed of an arrow. By then the rocks were closing again. The dove only just got through before they closed and clashed with a thunderous crash.

'Row for your life,' Jason cried and Tiphys held tight to the helm. The rocks parted and the vessel slipped between them. The crew rowed with all their might, but huge waves rose before them, forcing the ship to a stop. And the rocks were closing in on them ... it seemed destruction could not be avoided. But Pallas Athene stepped in. With her hands she held the rocks apart, and the ship slipped into safe waters. The Symplegades calmed down and remained apart. The Argonauts heaved a sigh of relief and sailed on in a happy frame of mind. They did not know that their joy would soon turn to deep sorrow.

After a while the voyagers were in need of fresh water and meat. When they sighted land, they went ashore, not realizing that a monstrous boar was lying in wait in the high reeds. Idmon the seer headed in its direction and the boar pounced on him, tearing his leg. Friends rushed to Idmon's side and slew the beast, but they were too late to save the seer's life.

The Argonauts were grief-stricken at the loss of the wise and good Idmon. But as often happens, misfortune does not come singly. The clever Tiphys, who steered the Argo so ably and had saved the ship from disaster many times, went to sleep that night with a headache and never rose again. The seafarers left their comrades' fresh graves with heavy hearts. Ancaeus now took over the helm and he steered the Argo capably and safely.

Some time later, when the Argonauts had passed the kingdom of the warlike Amazones, they came to a small island. A strange bird suddenly appeared above the ship. He spread his huge wings, and fired a feather towards the ship. The metal quill stabbed a sailor in his shoulder. Everyone recalled the words of the blind old Phineus.

'Let us think,' Jason said to his comrades, 'how to scare away these dreadful birds. We cannot shoot them all down with arrows. We must chase them away, as Phineus told us.'

The Argonauts finally came upon an idea to trick the birds. A few members of the crew raised their spears and balanced their shields upon them, so forming a protective roof. Under this the rest of the men rowed swiftly towards

the shore, whilst the metal bird feathers showered down into the shields and bounced off again like hailstones. Once by the shore, the men lowered their shields and started to scream and to beat onto the shields with their swords, waving their spears above their birdlike helmets. The birds, hearing the piercing noise and seeing the strange figures right by their nests, grew frightened and flew off to some distant region, never to return to that island.

The Argonauts sighed with relief and wondered why wise Phineus wanted them to anchor at such an inhospitable island, where they were almost destroyed by the dreadful birds. Then suddenly the sky darkened and a raging storm, such as they had never experienced, bore down upon them. Lightning zigzagged constantly through the sky and streams of rain poured down from the clouds. If caught in such a storm on the open sea, the Argonauts would have hardly escaped with their lives. How glad they were now to have heeded Phineus' advice!

Next morning, as the sun rose, the seafarers decided to sail on, but then they noticed four young men, dressed in rags, waving madly to them from the shore. As they came nearer, they sank to their knees and begged, 'Please save us! A vicious storm brought us to this inhospitable island. We are lucky to have escaped with our bare lives. But we stand to lose those too, for this is the home of monstrous birds who spear people with their feathers and peck them to death with their beaks.'

Jason replied, 'Do not be afraid, for we have chased away the horrific birds. They will never come back. But we shall take you with us. Tell us first who you are and where you are heading.'

One of the young men stepped in front and said, 'Perhaps you have heard of Phryxus, who flew to Colchis on a golden fleeced ram. He gave the golden fleece to King Aeetes, who in return gave him his daughter Chalciope for a wife. We are their sons. Our father is dead, but our mother is still alive. From his deathbed our

father bade us to go to the city of Orchomenus in Greece, for that is our native land. That is where we were heading, but the gods did not favour our journey, and we were shipwrecked. Now we should at least like to get back to Colchis.'

Jason was amazed at this unbelievable coincidence. Now he knew why the blind Phineus urged them not to miss the island of Aretias. He explained with sincerity to the sons of Phryxus who he was and why he was making this voyage. Now it was their turn to be surprised. 'King Aeetes is tough and cruel,' they said to Jason. 'He will refuse to give you the golden fleece, and you will not be able to take it secretly.' Jason only shrugged his shoulders. 'We shall sail to Colchis all the same.'

Not long afterwards the Argo entered Colchis harbour at the mouth of the River Phasis. When goddess Hera saw that Jason and his comrades had reached their goal safely, she went to Pallas Athene, to discuss how she could help Jason to obtain the golden fleece. Clever Athene said, 'King Aeetes has a beautiful young daughter Medea. She is a wise sorceress, gifted with foresight. If my sister Aphrodite, the god-

dess of love, were to instruct her mischievous son Eros to awake in her the feeling of love towards Jason, she would be sure to help him.'

Hera wasted no time and sought out Aphrodite, who only shook her head and said, 'Eros is such a rascal. He would rather listen to anyone than to his own mother. At this very moment he is in the meadow playing dice with Ganymede. Ganymede is a very capable waiter when he pours nectar into Zeus' cup, but he is no good at throwing dice.'

This was true. Eros had a pile of dice in front of him, whereas poor Ganymede had only two. And those he lost too, just as the goddess approached. He was almost in tears, but Eros was hopping happily on one foot. He did not even notice the two goddesses as they drew near.

'What have you done now?' Aphrodite scolded her naughty son. 'You've robbed poor Ganymede of all his dice. On your feet now! You are to fly to Colchis and shoot your arrow right through the heart of King Aeetes' daughter Medea. Make sure the arrow goes deep, so she falls in love with the hero Jason, who has just arrived there. When you come back I shall give you a beautiful new toy, a ball, with which

Zeus himself used to play when he was a little boy on Mount Olympus.'

Eros did not feel like going and tried to persuade his mother to give him the ball there and then, but Aphrodite stood her ground. Finally Eros flew off.

Jason, in the meantime, was discussing with his comrades what should be done. In the end he suggested, 'You stay here near the ship. I shall go with Phryxus' sons to the king. Perhaps we can come to some amicable arrangement. If not, we'll think again.' Everyone was in favour of the idea, so Jason left with his relatives. The king welcomed his grandsons and Jason kindly. He listened to them attentively, but when Jason explained why he had come, the king grew angry and stormed, 'Out of my sight at once! How dare you! You ask for the golden fleece? You might as well ask for my life and my kingdom!' But Jason was not afraid. 'I have come because it is the wish of the gods and the command of my king. I and my comrades are the descendants of the gods. You would be wise to give the golden fleece to us.'

The king looked startled as he replied, 'If you are true descendants of the gods, I shall let you have the golden fleece. But first you must convince me that you speak the truth, so you must accomplish the following feat. I have a field which is dedicated to Ares, the god of war. I plough this field with two bulls, who have metal horns; I sow dragons' teeth in this field and reap armed men who grow there. If you accomplish this, the golden fleece will be yours!'

Jason nodded and left with his new friends. On their way out, Chalciope, the mother of Phryxus' sons ran to them with outstretched arms. She embraced her children, and thanked Jason for saving their lives. His eyes, however, were glued to the beautiful sorceress Medea. She too could hardly hide her excitement, for she fell in love with Jason at first sight. The arrow of Eros had not missed its target.

Phryxus' sons begged their mother to ask her younger sister to help Jason. How can a mother refuse her children and how can a woman refuse a man with whom she is in love? When Jason met Medea in a secret hideout that night, he was given the magic ointment, to protect him against the monstrous bulls and the armed men.

'Smear it over your whole body, and you will be as strong as the eternal god,' Medea said. 'You will then perform the task the king has set you quite easily. When you return home, think of me sometimes. I too will remember.'

'I shall never forget you,' Jason promised.

'I should be very happy if you came with me to my country. Nothing would part us then but death.'

Medea was overjoyed. 'I shall come with you, Jason, even to the end of this earth! My father will realize that I helped you and he would punish me cruelly, if I remained.'

The next day a huge crowd assembled at the field dedicated to Ares. When Jason arrived, dressed in his high helmet and golden armour, protected by a round shield and armed with a spear and a sword, everyone gasped with anxiety. They felt so sorry for the magnificent hero. Two fearsome bulls with metal horns, their nostrils spitting fire rushed out of an underground passage. They pounced on Jason, but he stood his ground. At first he protected himself with the shield, then he tossed it aside, and, grasping the bulls by their horns, proceeded to harness them to the plough. The bulls realized that Jason was too strong for them and they ploughed the whole field for him as meekly as lambs. When that was done, Jason unharnessed them and they trotted back underground. Everyone gazed with admiration at the young hero. Jason was then handed a helmet with dragon teeth, which he sowed in deep furrows. Then he walked to his friends to rest.

Before very long helmets sprouted through the soil, followed by spears, and then by a swarm of warriors. Jason picked up a stone and threw it among them. This caused a terrible uproar. The warriors were at each other's throats, fighting for the stone so viciously, that dozens were left dead on the ground. The few who remained alive made an easy target for Jason's sword.

Jason stepped before the king and said, 'I have fulfilled the task you set me, oh king, so let me have the golden fleece!'

The king was furious. He guessed quite rightly that Medea had helped Jason, though her face gave nothing away. But he smiled and said, 'Yes, you have performed all the feats I asked of you. Tomorrow the golden fleece shall be yours.'

The clever Medea also guessed that her father was aware that she had aided Jason. Knowing his cruel nature all too well, she realized that her efforts could come to a bitter end. So that evening she ran to the Greek ship and said to Jason, 'Be ready to depart! I have helped you once and will do so again, though I act against my father and against Colchis. But promise me, Jason, that you will take me with you and that you will marry me.'

'I have already given my promise,' Jason replied, 'and shall be only too happy to keep my word.'

Medea then led him to Ares' holy copse, where the golden fleece was nailed to a huge oak. In the late darkness the fleece shone like a huge lantern, its light falling on a horrific dragon, who sat under the oak welcoming intruders with menacing hisses. But Medea approached the dragon without fear and touched his head with a magic herb; instantly the dragon fell asleep. After keeping guard for so many years, he slept very deeply.

Jason pulled the golden fleece off the holy oak and hastened with his sweetheart to the ship which was ready to sail. It left the shore the moment they were aboard.

The king did not find out till the next day that Jason had sailed off with the golden fleece and his daughter. In a rage, he, immediately, sent his fastest ships in pursuit. By then Jason and his men were well on the way to the land of the Phaecians.

Alcinous, the king of Phaecia, and Queen Arete, welcomed the Argonauts warmly. They were pleased to see Jason with his faithful men, and glad to hear how they had outsmarted King Aeetes, who was much feared and much disliked.

Soon after the Argonauts' arrival at Alcinous' palace, the fleet from Colchis anchored in the harbour. The pursuers demanded Jason, the golden fleece and Medea.

This time, however, with Jason present, the king was unafraid and said to Aeetes's messengers, 'Jason and his comrades are my guests. I cannot hand him over to you. Jason has earned the golden fleece and it is his by right. And Medea? If she is already Jason's wife, she belongs to him. If not, she must return to her father.'

The Queen Arete heard his words and hurriedly called together prominent citizens to witness Jason's and Medea's wedding. Whilst the others were still negotiating, Medea became Jason's wife. The pursuers were too afraid to return to Colchis empty-handed, so they remained in Phaecia.

The Argonauts were, at last, nearing their native land and Medea said,

'Our troubles are not yet over. The old king Pelias will not be eager to hand over his kingdom, though you have fulfilled the task he set you. But do not fear, I shall help you again.'

As Medea stepped ashore, she turned herself into an aged woman. So disguised, she hobbled into the palace and asked for an audience with Pelias' daughters. 'What do you want?' they asked her.

'I wish to show you what I can do,' Medea said. As they watched she put boiled water in a huge pan, adding a few drops from a bottle. Next she asked for an old ram to be thrown in.

They all expected the ram to stew but instead it changed into a lovely young lamb, which bleated sweetly.

King Pelias heard of this miracle. As he was old and ill, he yearned for his lost youth, so he decided to take the magic bath. But as soon as he was in, he cried despairingly and died. The daughters searched vainly for the old woman but she had disappeared.

By the time the Argonauts entered the city with the golden fleece, the old King Pelias was already dead. There was now nothing to stop Jason from becoming the new king and wise Medea the new queen.

So the prophecy which long ago foretold that a youth wearing one sandle would deprive Pelias of his kingdom and his life, came true.

Heroic Achilles

There was once a sea nymph called Thetis, who was the most beautiful daughter of the aged Nereus. She was so lovely that even Zeus, the king of the gods, courted her. It was predicted that Thetis would bear a son who would prove himself braver than all others. And if he happened to have a god for a father, then he would be greater than all the gods and would deprive Zeus of his heavenly throne. Zeus feared this and so decided that Thetis should wed the best of all the mortals — none other than Peleus, king of the Myrmidons in the province of Thessaly. Peleus often saw Thetis riding her dolphin in the sea, or disappearing in her cave in the cove of the myrtle copse. He tried in vain to approach her. The nymph was timid and always escaped, either by turning herself into a bird, or into a snake.

One day mighty Zeus appeared in Peleus' dream and said, 'If you want to take Thetis, you must wait till she falls asleep in her cave. Then you must bind her firmly with a strong rope and hold on tightly, no matter what she may change into.'

Peleus followed the god's advice and managed to tie Thetis in her cave. She turned into a bird, a snake, fire, water, but Peleus did not let her go. Finally she changed back into the lovely nymph and said, 'You must have been advised by one of the gods. I therefore accept it must be their will that I should become your wife. But remember this: if just once you turn on me in anger, I shall disappear and you will never see me again.'

Their wedding was a most ceremonious occasion. Hera, Zeus' wife, invited all the gods. Apollo, the god of music, played the lyre, and the nine Muses, the goddesses of the arts, sang to his music. The divine godmothers, the Moerae, predicted the fate of the descendant which would be born to the newlyweds.

'Your son will be brave. He will have no equal in battle and will become famous for his part in the seige of Troy.' Peleus was overjoyed to hear he was destined to have such a son, but Thetis was not as happy. She feared all the dangers ahead of the yet unborn infant. Yet she hid her fears and smiled at the guests. Everyone present was glad that Hera had not invited Eris, the goddess of discord, to the wedding. But Eris was sly. She was well aware that all the goddesses were by nature rather vain, so she picked a golden apple and wrote on it, 'For the loveliest of you!' and threw it into the banqueting hall through the window. As she had guessed, three goddesses immediately started fighting over the apple — Hera, Pallas Athene and Aphrodite. Eventually, they turned to Zeus, and asked him to decide who deserved it. The prudent Zeus, not wishing to turn any of the goddesses against him, said, 'Paris, the son of Priam, the king of Troy, is a better judge than I. He is, however, unaware of his noble birth and works for his father as a simple shepherd in the mountains. Let him decide!'

The goddesses hastened to Paris. He was very surprised to see the three divine creatures approaching. When he heard their request, he was too afraid to reply.

'Have no fear, young man,' Hera said. 'If your decision favours me, I shall give you riches and the reign over many large kingdoms.'

'I shall give you wisdom and skill, in which no one vill be your equal. Furthermore, you will become famous in battle,' Pallas Athene cried, interrupting Hera.

Aphrodite only whispered, 'All I shall give

you will be the most beautiful woman in the world.' Without any hesitation, Paris gave the apple to Aphrodite.

The months passed, and Peleus and Thetis became the parents of an infant who was destined to become a great hero. They named him Achilles. Thetis cared for her little son well, bathing him in the magic waters of the river Styx to make him invulnerable, and dipping him in holy fire, to make him immortal. She always held little Achilles by his heel, which remained his one vulnerable spot.

One night Peleus caught Thetis plunging Achilles into the fire and he was shocked and terrified to see his little son in the flames. Shouting angrily, he turned on Thetis. She looked at her husband, with sadness and reproach in her eyes and placed the infant on his bed. Then she disappeared like steam, as she had once warned him, never to return. Peleus was at a loss what to do with motherless baby son. He decided to take him to the wise Centaur Chiron, who had raised many children to become wise and valiant. Chiron was happy to have the little Achilles and gave all his time to him. As the boy grew, he taught him to hunt and to fight, to sing and to play the lyre. He taught him how to heal, and all basic principles, so necessary for life. The loving Thetis often visited Chiron's cave, to spend a few happy hours with her son and to witness his fast progress.

When Achilles' education was completed, Chiron took him back to the royal palace. Achilles missed the wise Chiron, but soon became firm friends with the kind Patroclus, who, to some degree, took the place of his dear old tutor. Then something happened which was to direct the fate of Achilles and the fate of many other heroes.

Aphrodite, the goddess of beauty and love came to Paris, and said, 'I promised you the most beautiful woman in the world in exchange for the golden apple. Her name is Helen and she is the wife of Menelaus, the king of Sparta.

Paris was no longer tending herds. He had returned to the city, leaving the mountains where he had been sent as an infant, because the Fates had foretold that he would bring destruction of Troy. Once the king was reunited with his son, he put the ominous prophecy out of his mind and kept Paris at his side. But Paris, anxious to find the woman he had been promised, grew restless. He turned a deaf ear to his mother's pleas and his father's warning, and sailed to Sparta. The Spartan king, Menelaus, made the youth very welcome, not guessing he would be repaid in a most treacherous manner. From the moment Paris saw the beautiful Helen, he fell in love. She was, in truth, the loveliest of all mortal women. And when Menelaus had to go away for a while, young Paris carried Helen off to Troy.

When the deceived King found his wife had fled with their guest, his fury knew no bounds. He sent for all the Greek kings, princes and warriors and asked them to accompany him to Troy, to get Helen back. They all agreed, wishing to help him to wipe out his shame.

Young Achilles was also preparing to leave for Troy with the others, but his divine mother Thetis was doing her best to stop him. When arguments and pleas were of no avail, she turned to cunning. That night, as Achilles lay fast asleep, she sat him upon her dolphin and

rode with him in the night's darkness to the Island of Skyros, ruled by Lycomedes, her good and loyal friend.

When Achilles awoke and saw the fertile flat land surrounded by sea, instead of his native mountains and deep forests, he was astonished and grieved. But eventually he gave in to his mother's reasoning and promised to stay on the island instead of going to fight in Troy. Thetis disguised him as a girl and took him to King Lycomedes. 'Dear friend,' she said, 'I have brought you my daughter, for she has been wanting to live as one of the warlike Amazones, fighting and hunting in the forests. I am sure that among your sweet daughters such manly whims will soon leave her. I beg you therefore to look after her!'

The king was happy to oblige and his daughters were pleased too. But young Achilles, brought up to fight and hunt, was terribly embarrassed to find himself in the company of the gentle daughters of the king of Skyros. He put up with the indignity only to please his mother.

The disappearance of Achilles created panic among the Greek ranks, for Calchas the soothsayer had predicted that Troy would fall only if Achilles was present. So Odysseus, the clever king of Ithaca, offered to search for the young man. In his travels he came to the shores of the Island of Skyros and called on King Lycomedes.

As soon as the experienced Odysseus saw Thetis' daughter, he noticed that she behaved differently from the other maidens. It occurred to him immediately that she could be Achilles in disguise. To test Achilles, he placed many beautiful, feminine gifts, before the maidens, and just one shield and one spear. Without thinking, Achilles automatically reached for these weapons.

'I have found you at last! You are Peleus' son! Odysseus cried, and Achilles did not argue. So Thetis had not succeeded in keeping Achilles away from the Trojan War. She could not alter his destiny.

At last the Greeks sailed for Troy, led by Agamemnon, the king of Mycenae. With Achilles, there were many other famous heroes, but Troy too had valiant warriors, such as Paris' brother, Hector, who was the leader of the Trojans. The two sides were well matched.

The battle of Troy went on for nine long years without the Greeks having any success though Achilles and the other warriors performed many deeds of bravery. The tenth year was to decide the war.

At that time there was a big dispute in the Greek camp. The Greeks had captured a beautiful Trojan maiden named Briseis. Achilles fell in love with her and wished to marry her, but Agamemnon, the leader, insisted that Achilles must give up the girl. The young man obeyed, but pined for the lovely Briseis and was hurt by Agamemnon's command. In wrath he said, 'My men and I will refuse to join Agamemnon in battle, until he atones for the insult he has inflicted on me.'

The Trojans soon noticed that the feared Achilles was avoiding the fighting, and this gave them courage again. They attacked from the city with greater frequency and always unexpectedly.

Once they cut off the Greeks from their ships and were about to set their vessels alight. Achilles' faithful and loyal friend Patroclus then pleaded earnestly with the offended youth,

'Achilles, you must stop bearing a grudge. Our best warriors are dying because of you. The Trojans are forcing us to retreat. They have even reached our vessels and are trying to burn them. At least put on your armour and brandish your sword. If the Trojans see you are part of us again, they will panic and run away.'

But Achilles refused to give in. He just said, 'I am not going anywhere. If you think it enough for the Trojans to see my armour, then take it and put it on yourself! Chase the enemies away from our ships, but I warn you, do not pursue them further!'

Patroclus put on his friend's armour and sped towards the Greek vessels. And in truth, as soon as the Trojans saw Achilles' helmet and shield glittering in the sun, they turned and fled in disorder.

But Patroclus did not heed Achilles' warning and advice and went in pursuit. Heading the Greek troops, he speared every warrior he

overtook, galloping right to the walls of the city of Troy. It now seemed certain that this time the city would finally be conquered. But he was stopped by the voice of Apollo, who cried, 'Wait, Patroclus! Troy is not destined to fall by your hand!'

Hearing these words, Patroclus hesitated and in that unguarded moment Hector, the most daring Trojan, hurled himself at him and plunged his sword through his heart.

Both sides now fought viciously for Patroclus' corpse. The Greeks were losing. Hector had already stripped the dead Patroclus of Achilles' armour and had thrown it into his chariot. He was tying the corpse to the back of the chariot, to be dragged in dishonour through the dust to the city.

But all of a sudden the real Achilles himself appeared amid the Greeks. Unarmed and without a helmet or shield, yet he appeared as menacing as Ares, the god of war.

When the Trojan warriors saw the heroic figure of Achilles and heard his fearful voice, they scattered in panic. Patroclus' corpse was

left behind on the battlefield, but Achilles' magnificent armour was still in Hector's chariot on its way to Troy.

Achilles and all his comrades mourned deeply the loss of the loyal Patroclus, who was liked and admired by everyone. They burned Patroclus' dead body with all the ceremonial rites and buried his ashes in Trojan soil far from his homeland.

Patroclus' death ended Achilles' anger. All he yearned for now was to avenge the death of his most loyal friend. Forgetting completely about his dispute with Agamemnon, he waited with impatience for his mother Thetis to bring him new armour. She was having it made by Hephaestus, god of fire and forge, who applied all his skill to ensure it was truly magnificent. No

mortal on earth could boast of such a shield, helmet, sword or spear.

Everyone who saw Achilles in his new armour gasped — the sight of him was enough to put fear into the heart of any enemy and to make anyone run away in terror.

Thus splendidly attired, Achilles rode at the head of the Greek army to the plain surrounding the walls of Troy.

When the Trojans saw the hero in his new armour, their courage withered and they took to their heels. They thought they would only be safe behind the city walls. Brave Hector alone remained outside, but when Achilles confronted him, he, too, lost his courage. He ran for his life with Achilles not far behind him. They circled the walls of Troy three times before Hector was caught. The duel was short. Hector was unable to withstand the blows from the enraged Achilles and soon fell dead to the ground.

Achilles then cut a hole through each of Hector's ankles, threaded a strap through the holes and tied the corpse to his chariot. Then he dragged it disgracefully through the dust to the Greek camp.

The gods, however, took pity on the fallen hero, whom Achilles, in his great anger, had so degradingly shamed.

Zeus himself sent Priam, the old king of Troy, and Hermes, the messenger of the gods, to fetch Hector's corpse. Hermes cloaked Priam's carriage in a cloud, so no one could see him and no one could hurt him. Soon the Trojan king found himself in Achilles' tent. The aged man fell to his knees, kissed Achilles' hands and feet and pleaded,

'Think of your poor father, whom you shall not see again, for the Fates fortell that you will die soon after the death of my son Hector. Imagine how he will weep and suffer when he learns that your ashes are far from your homeland. At least he will know that you have been buried with all the rituals due to a hero. How much unhappier am I! You have slain my dearest son, the leader of the Trojan warriors, but his corpse lies in shame in the dust by your tent. Therefore have mercy on a feeble old man. Give me Hector's corpse, and let me bury him with the dignity due to him.'

Hearing these words, Achilles began to weep. He let Priam put Hector's corpse in the car-riage, and promised not to continue with the fighting until Hector had been buried with due rites.

The men and women of Troy wept for many days and nights for their beloved hero. But when the funeral was over, the fierce fighting started again.

Achilles was aware that Death was waiting for him by the Trojan walls, yet he did not avoid any battle. As the missiles, the swords and the spears just bounced off his body, it seemed as though the prophecy would be proved to be untrue.

There was but one spot on Achilles' body which was vulnerable — his heel, which was not protected by the holy magic.

Yet one day, when Achilles was riding at the head of the Myrmidons towards Troy, an arrow pierced his heel. The arrow had been fired by the notable marksman Paris, but it is also said that Apollo himself directed his hand. Achilles died from this wound.

This is how valiant Achilles, the greatest hero of the famous battle of Troy, was slain.

The Wanderings of Odysseus

When valiant Achilles fell by the city walls, the Greeks were grieved and afraid. There was not a man among them as brave and as strong as the heroic son of Peleus and Thetis. Their hope that Troy would fall died with him. But as the kings conferred, Odysseus, the clever king of Ithaca, rose and said, 'When strength and courage are not enough, we must add cunning. We will take Troy by guile.'

The Greeks accepted Odysseus' proposal. That night they built a gigantic wooden horse and hid their bravest warriors in its body. The rest of the men sailed to a nearby island, and anchored out of sight. Only one soldier was left in the deserted camp — a man called Sinon. The next morning the Trojans were amazed to see the empty enemy camp, and they went to investigate. They found no trace of the Greek army nor of the fleet, only the gigantic wooden horse was left standing.

'Do not touch it,' warned the Trojan priest, Laocoon. 'Who knows what Greek trickery this may be.'

Then they found Sinon trembling like a leaf. He begged for his life to be spared and explained that the Greeks, after ten years, finally realizing they could never conquer Troy, had sailed for home.

'I was left behind because I had an argument with King Agamemnon,' Sinon added. 'The wooden horse is an offering to Athene, so that she would grant them a safe return. They made sure you would not be able to drag it through any of your gates into the city, by making it so gigantic.'

While Sinon was telling these lies, Poseidon, the god of the sea, who favoured the Greeks,

sent two serpents after Laocoon to strangle the priest and his two sons. The Trojans thought this was a sign from the gods and believed Sinon had spoken the truth. Overjoyed that the long war was at last happily over, they dragged the enormous horse into the city. They did not care that parts of the walls had to be knocked down to get it through.

All Troy celebrated the retreat of the Greeks into the early hours. Towards morning, when everyone was asleep, Sinon opened the secret trapdoor on the horse, and released the Greek warriors concealed inside. Soon fires were burning on the city walls, signalling to the other Greek warriors, who had sailed back to Troy under the cloak of darkness. The Greeks attacked the unsuspecting, sleeping city and soon all Troy was aflame and all her citizens either dead or taken prisoner.

So ended the Trojan war.

Odysseus, whose wit and cunning brought the Greeks their triumph, was doomed not to have an easy voyage home. As his fleet of twelve ships, laden with rich booty, put out to sea, he did not dream he would not reach his destination for another ten years, and would arrive alone.

It was Poseidon, the god of the sea, whom Odysseus had angered, who caused this anguish. On their return voyage they sighted a rocky headland with signs of smoke. 'Anchor here,' Odysseus instructed his men. 'I shall go with a small party to the island to see what kind of people live there. Who knows, perhaps they will invite us to share their roast mutton or fish.'

Taking a cask of choice wine, Odysseus and some of his best men rowed to the shore. But it was not the home of hospitable fishermen and shepherds, but of brutal Cyclops, the giants, who only had one eye in the middle of their forehead. They were a wild and lawless tribe, with each giant living in his own huge cave, rearing goats and sheep.

Odysseus left some of the crew on the shore, and travelled inland with twelve of his men. Soon they came upon an enormous cave, where they found baskets of cheese and great pots of milk, but not a living soul.

'Let us get out of here!' the men begged Odysseus. 'Nothing good will come of it if we stay in this eerie place.'

But Odysseus did not listen to their pleas, for his curiosity was aroused. 'Have a rest, men,' he said, 'and let us see who comes in.'

A little while later a giant Cyclops entered the cave, driving his flock of lambs and goats. He

barred the entrance with a heavy rock, then milked the flock. As he was finishing his work, he noticed the strangers.

'What do you want here?' he roared in a thunderous voice.

'We have been shipwrecked near this shore. We need help,' Odysseus lied.

Polyphemus, the giant Cyclops, roared with laughter, seized two of the crew and swallowed them as if they were raspberries. Odysseus and his companions stood by, helpless and horrified. The giant smacked his lips and said to Odysseus, 'What is your name?'

'I am called No-one,' clever Odysseus readily replied.

'Remember this, No-one: I adore human flesh and I shall eat you all, one by one.'

After that he went to sleep.

The terrified men tried to think of a way to escape from the Cyclops' cave. They could of course kill the giant in his sleep, but then they would never get out into the daylight again, for

they were not strong enough to move the rock which blocked the entrance.

Next morning Polyphemus breakfasted on another two Greeks and then drove out his flock, blocking the entrance again.

Odysseus was seething with anger and was determined to have his revenge. He worked out a plan. They would blind the giant.

They found a long wooden club in the cave, and sharpened one end to a point. Then they waited for the return of the terrible Cyclops.

When at dusk Polyphemus drove his flock back into the cave, Odysseus said, 'Let us go! I will give you this cask of wine if you do. Wine is tastier than human flesh.'

Polyphemus took a sip and liked it. 'You are right,' he agreed. 'But when I have drunk all the wine, I will want to eat more human flesh. I will not let you go!'

Then he finished the whole cask of wine in one swallow, tumbled to the ground and fell instantly asleep.

Odysseus was waiting for just that. Thrusting the pointed end of the wooden club into the fire, he and his helpers drove the red hot, sizzling point into the giant's one eye. The Cyclops, maddened with pain, tore the club out of his eye, but he was blind and helpless. Hearing his screams, his neighbours, the Cyclops who lived near, ran to his cave and cried, 'Why are you making so much noise, Polyphemus? Has someone hurt you?'

'No-one! No-one is killing me,' Polyphemus hollered.

And hearing this the other Cyclops went back to bed, muttering, 'What is he shouting about, the fool, when no one is hurting him.'

When morning came, the giant rolled away the rock and let out his sheep and goats one by one, his hands groping over their backs, to make sure not one of the Greeks could slip out.

Odysseus tricked him all the same. He bound his remaining companions to the bellies of some of the largest rams with the thickest coats, and he himself escaped by clinging fast to the ram's belly with his hands. The Cyclops never realized that the Greeks were escaping.

'We are not out of danger yet,' Odysseus whispered.

'Keep quiet, all of you, so the giant will think we are still in the cave. Otherwise he may send some of the other Cyclops after us and that would be the end of us.'

The Greeks then drove the flock to the boat and soon were on board their ship, sailing safely away. Odysseus then shouted with all his might to Polyphemus, who was vainly groping for his lost lambs,

'If anyone asks who blinded you, tell him it was Odysseus.'

'The fool that I am!' cried the giant. 'A seer told me once I should lose my sight at the hands of a man of that name. But I was expecting another giant, not a weak human worm! Do not rejoice too soon, Odysseus! My father Poseidon rules the seas and he will make sure that you shall never reach home again!'

The vessels sailed across the calm sea, but the men felt uneasy, fearing that Poseidon would avenge their attack on his son.

They next stopped at a strange little island. It floated like a ship and was the home of Aeolus,

the ruler of the winds, who was loved by all the gods. He and his wife and their twelve children were friendly and kind to the travellers who remained their guests for several weeks.

Aeolus, who had heard their tale from the very beginning to end with attention, said in parting,

'I shall gladly help you. Take this sack, but never untie it, for it contains all the unfavourable winds which would blow you off your course. Now you should sail home safely.'

Odysseus thanked kind Aeolus gratefully and put out to sea once more. Aeolus had ordered the gentle western breeze to accompany them and it drove them towards their native land.

Nine days and nights they sailed, and on the tenth day they could see the shores of Ithaca on the horizon.

Happy Odysseus, who for nine days and nights did not close an eye, but stood guard over the precious sack, allowed himself to sleep at last. But his men were curious to see what was inside the sack, so they untied the knot and released the winds. At once a terrible gale seized the ships and whirled them far from their native land.

When at last the storm was over, Odysseus sailed into a narrow creek surrounded by towering cliffs. After casting anchor, he and his men climbed the cliff and saw a large town nearby. Walking towards it, they met a very tall girl who was on her way to a well.

'What is that town and who lives there?' Odysseus asked.

'It is the home of the Laestrygones,' the girl replied. 'My father is their king. If you wish, I will take you to him.' Odysseus gladly agreed and they followed the maiden to the palace. Imagine their horror when they discovered that the Laestrygones were giant cannibals! The king at once snatched up one of the Greeks and ate him for his supper, just as Polyphemus had done. The others took to their heels and fled back to the ships, the giants in pursuit. They showered the ships with rocks and speared the men like fish. It was a terrible disaster for Odysseus and his expedition. Only his own ship escaped to the open sea. All the others were wrecked by the monsters and their crews drowned.

Saddened by the loss of so many brave companions, Odysseus and the few survivors came to a small island.

They went ashore, but stayed near their ship, afraid to wander too far. But on the third day Eurylochus, Odysseus' rebellious cousin, decided to explore further and took a few men with him. Soon they came upon a pretty cottage, with wolves and lions roaming round it, but behaving in a tame and friendly fashion, as though they were pets.

Just then, a beautiful woman came out of the cottage, welcomed the strangers warmly and asked them in. They all entered willingly, except Eurylochus, who fearing some kind of trick, stayed outside looking in through the window.

The woman appeared most hospitable to his comrades, but she, secretly, slipped some magic powder into their wine, which changed them one and all into swine. Then she drove the loudly grunting animals into the pigsty and poured acorns and mast into the trough for them to eat.

It was then Eurylochus realized the woman was the powerful enchantress Circe, and he hastened back to Odysseus. Anxious to help his men, Odysseus rushed into the cottage, brandishing his sword as if wanting to slay her.

Circe was startled. 'Who are you, stranger, and why are you not afraid of me?' she cried. 'Could you be the cunning Odysseus, the man who is not afraid of anything? The gods told me he would stop here on his way from Troy.'

'It is I,' Odysseus answered.

Circe's behaviour changed immediately. She gave his men back their human form, and said,

'It is my duty to help you on your journey home. Listen, Odysseus, to my sound advice. You must descend into the Kingdom of the

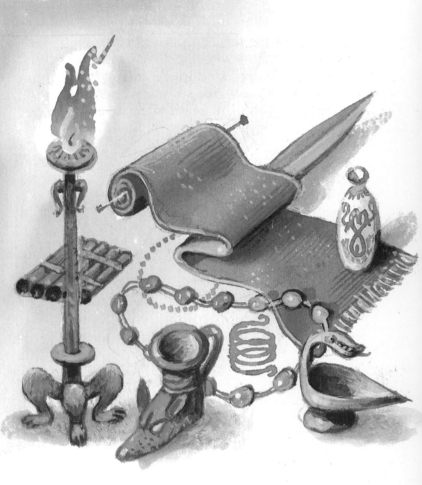

Dead to see wise old Tiresias, the renowned seer. He is the only one who knows what Fate has in store for you. Then you can continue your voyage.'

'How do I reach that awesome Kingdom of the Dead?' the startled Odysseus asked.

'Do not worry,' Circe comforted him. 'Board your ship and the wind will take you there. At the entrance you must make offerings to the gods of the underworld. After that everything will go well.'

In parting, Circe gave Odysseus a black ram and a black ewe and he sailed away. At dusk they passed by another strange, gloomy shore. It was a sad, eerie land, cloaked in dense fog, through which the rays of the sun never penetrated. Odysseus made the sacrifices, slaying the black ram and the black ewe, and, quite alone, entered the Kingdom of the Dead.

The moment he entered, the ghosts of the dead crowded round him, making a terrible din, but Odysseus paid no attention to them.

He quietly waited for old Tiresias. At last he appeared, with a golden sceptre in his hand, and asked, 'Why have you come to these inhospitable parts?'

'To find out from you how to get safely home,' Odysseus replied.

hurried back to join his friends and to launch his ship again.

They sailed on with renewed hope, and eventually came near the island on which Helios' herds grazed. Odysseus wanted to sail past this land, but the rebellious Eurylochus said, 'We are tired and weary. Let us rest on the island. We shall not harm the herd.'

Hearing the cheers with which his men greet-

The seer looked thoughtful and then said, 'Powerful Poseidon is very angry with you for blinding his son. But other gods favour your return. Continue your journey, but do not touch cattle belonging to Helios, the mighty king of the sun, when you land on his island. There are as many oxen grazing on that isle as there are days in a year, and as many sheep as there are nights. Helios sees everything from above. If he catches you stealing, nothing will save you. Leave his herd in peace, then you will reach home safely.'

Odysseus thanked Tiresias and when the aged seer went away, Odysseus stayed a while longer to talk to the spirits of the warriors who had fallen in the battle of Troy.

He spoke to Achilles and Patroclus, to the spirit of his own mother, who had died from grief when her son failed to return. At last he

ed Eurylochus' words Odysseus had to give way. Perhaps his men would have kept their word if a sudden storm had not broken the next day, whipping the seas for seven nights and days. Their food supply was gone, they could not fish and terrible hunger gnawed at them. Eurolochus then said,

'Why should we die a slow death of hunger? I cannot think of a worse way to die. Let us slay a few oxen. We are in dire need, so perhaps Helios will forgive us. And if he does not, then it is better to perish quickly at sea than to slowly starve to death here.'

Odysseus tried hard to argue with his men, begging them to change their minds, but it was of no use. Eurylochus slew several of the sacred cattle and gave them to the men to roast and eat. Odysseus was the only one who did not touch the meat.

When the storm finally abated and the Greeks were able to sail away from the land, a gigantic wave rose suddenly. It lifted the ship and flung her against a rock where she broke like a delicate shell. Everyone perished except Odysseus, who gripped the ship's keel and stayed afloat.

This was how Helios punished the disobedient men.

Unfortunate Odysseus floated for nine days and nights, till the sea cast him out onto the shore of a lonely isle— the isle of the nymph Calypso. Neither gods, nor men visited her, and loneliness made the nymph very unhappy. She was overjoyed when she saw that the sea had brought Odysseus to her, and her kindness to him was boundless.

But Odysseus was far from happy, for he longed for home. Though well cared for by the nymph, he spent many hours on the shore, yearning to see at least the smoke from his home island of Ithaca on the horizon. This vigil went on for several years.

'Why are you so sad?' Calypso would ask. 'Why are you always so homesick? Here you

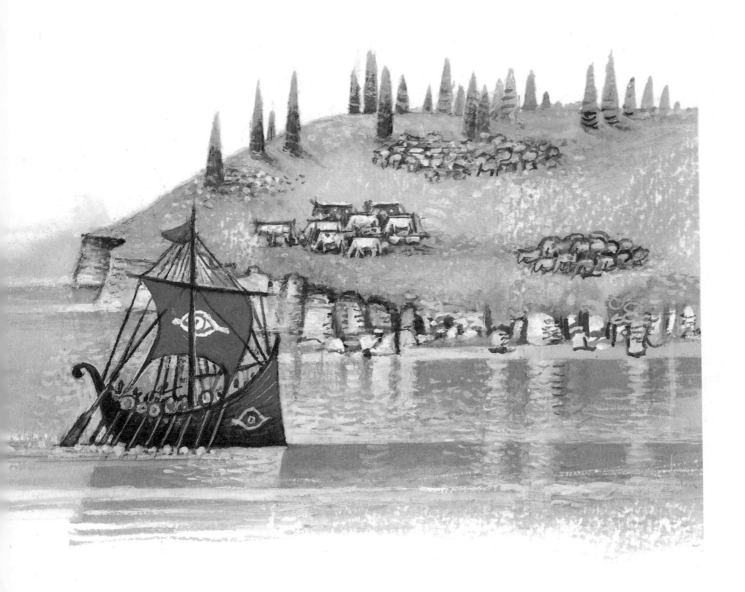

have everything you can possibly want. Who knows what trials await you at home?'

But homesickness is a kind of malady no one can cure.

Finally the gods took pity on the unhappy hero. Pallas Athene begged Zeus to send Hermes to Calypso to tell her to let Odysseus leave. The nymph was very sad to hear Zeus' message, but she dared not anger the gods by disobeying. So she said to Odysseus,

'There is no longer any need for you to be unhappy! Take an axe, cut down some strong trees and build a raft from them. I will supply you with food and drink for the journey, and

will send a favourable wind to take you home. You should get there safely.'

Odysseus, overjoyed at hearing such news, swiftly built a raft and set out for home once again.

He had been sailing on the sea for quite some time and nothing bad had happened. He was beginning to believe that his wanderings were at an end and that soon he would be home. Almost ten years had passed from the day he had left burning Troy.

It was his bad luck that just then he was seen by Poseidon, the god of the sea, who was on his way back from a feast with the Cyclops. Remembering his poor blind son, Polyphemus, he sent the most vicious storm upon the lone sailor. The raft disintegrated and Odysseus, clinging onto a long beam, was tossed ashore on an island far from his homeland.

The Phaeacians lived on this island. They were peaceloving people, gay and hospitable. Moreover, they were excellent sailors who owned magic ships with minds of their own, which could steer themselves. They sailed only by night and were faster than a bird. Alcinous, the king of Phaeacia, had a most beautiful daughter Nausicaa.

The princess had just gone with her friends to play in the river mouth. They were playing with a ball in the bright sunshine, and it rolled into the water. The maidens cried out, and Odysseus, who was asleep nearby, woke instantly. Delighted to hear human voices, he rose, but as his clothes had been lost in the storm, he covered his nakedness with a large leaf. The maidens ran away frightened by the sight of the dishevelled, unshaven, naked man. Only Nausicaa remained.

'Please hear me out, whether you are a goddess or a mortal woman,' Odysseus said to the maiden. 'I have been caught in a raging storm which after nineteen long days finally broke my raft. I am battered and weary, more dead than alive. Please tell me where I am and please help me!'

The lovely princess was sorry for the unfortunate man, so she said,

'You have come to the Phaeacian island, which lies at the very end of the earth. I am the daughter of Alcinous, the king. I will fetch some clothes and take you to the town to see my father who will surely help you.'

Odysseus, washed and dressed proved to be a splendid, handsome man and Nausicaa looked at him admiringly. Alcinous, too, received him

kindly and assured him of his help. 'Tell us, stranger,' he said later, 'who you are and what disaster struck you.' Odysseus shook his head. 'Honourable king, it is such a long story. Most probably no other mortal has suffered such agonies as I. And I am still too weary to relate it all now.'

'You are right,' the king agreed. 'Rest and listen to our musican, who sings wondrous songs of legendary heroes.'

A blind aged man was led in. He sat down, his fingers skimming the strings of the lyre, whilst he sang a long song about the Greek attack of Troy. He sang about Agamemnon, Menelaus, Achilles and Patroclus. He even sang about Odysseus, how he told the Greeks to build a wooden horse and how they then conquered Troy.

Odysseus could not help it. Tears trickled from his eyes.

'Why are you so moved, stranger?' the king asked. 'Could it be that some of your relatives perished at Troy?'

'I am Odysseus,' said the king of Ithaca.

An excited murmur spread through the hall. Odysseus now had to relate his adventures and tell of his troublestrewn voyage home.

'You poor man,' Alcinous cried, embracing Odysseus. 'Now all your troubles will be over.'

The very next day he ordered one of their finest ships to be prepared, and loaded it with precious gifts. The next day at sunset the ship put out to sea with Odysseus on board. Before the break of dawn, it was already coming in to the Ithacan harbour. Odysseus was in a deep sleep, so the Phaeacian crew carried him gently to the shore. They placed his rich gifts by his side and then returned to their ship and sailed away.

When Odysseus awoke, he could hardly believe that he was home again after twenty long years. Filled with emotion he gazed at the familiar hills and green meadows, soft woods and fertile fields. He hid the precious gifts in a nearby cave, and purposely smeared and tore his clothes, ruffled his hair and beard, so he would look like a beggar. In this disguise he entered the palace, and stood in a dark corner to observe what was going on.

He did not see anything pleasing. The palace was full of suitors, courting his own wife Penelope and urging her to choose one of them for a husband. Penelope kept on refusing but still they kept insisting. Even Telemachus, Odysseus' young son, was unable to help his mother. He was too inexperienced to deal with all of the impudent suitors. Penelope excused herself, saying that before she could think of a wedding, she would first have to weave a funeral shroud for the aged Laertes, Odysseus' father. Whatever she wove in the day, she undid at night, and so the shroud was never finished. But the suitors discovered her trick and finally forced Penelope to promise that the next day she would choose one of them.

In the morning she said, 'Listen, all of you who have come to woo me. I will choose the man who is as strong as Odysseus. Here is his bow, with which he could shoot through a dozen axes in one go. I will marry the one who can do it.'

The suitors lined up but not one of them could even bend the bow. Odysseus, still disguised as a beggar, then came forward. He gripped the bow, and bent it easily, sending his arrow flying through the whole line of the axes.

The suitors paled and gaped dumbly, as the marksman cried, 'I am Odysseus!' With that he let fly another arrow and the first suitor fell down dead, shot through the throat. Then came flying a second, and a third arrow. By then Telemachus had drawn his sword and hurled himself, followed by other loyal servants, at the remaining suitors. A fierce battle developed, but soon all the impudent suitors were sprawled on the ground in pools of their own blood.

Odysseus put his bow aside and hastened to his faithful wife. They embraced lovingly, shedding tears of happiness and joy, because they were together again after twenty long years of lonely separation.

So at last the troublestrewn wanderings of Odysseus, the Ithacan king, were safely and happily over and he could live in peace.

The Founding of Rome

King Amulius was the cruel ruler of Alba in Italy. He drove the rightful King Numitor from the throne and forced his daughter Silvia to become Vestal virgin, a priestess, who had to guard the eternal fire in the temple of Vesta — the goddess of fire and family hearth. Amulius did this because Vestal virgins were not allowed to marry, so Numitor's family would have no more descendants to endanger the power he had wilfully gained.

One day, when Silvia had gone to the River Tiber to wash the holy urns, she was seen by Mars, the god of war, who instantly fell in love with her. Being a god, he did not worry about the fact that Vestal virgins were not allowed to marry. And Silvia did not dare oppose the god's will. After some time, twins were born to her and she named them Romulus and Remus.

When the jealous King Amulius found this out, he ordered his servants to seize both the baby boys and drown them in the river. The servants took Romulus and Remus from the heart-broken Silvia, but they could not bring themselves to end their lives. Instead they placed the babes on the river bank, and went away. Mars did not let his baby sons die. He sent a she-wolf to care for them and a woodpecker to bring them food. The royal babes stayed with the wolves and grew into big, strong boys.

One day the shepherd Faustulus saw the boys and caught them. He took them home to his wife Acca Laurentia, and together they brought them up. The way the boys grew and flourished was a joy to behold. When they reached their eighteenth year, there was no shepherd who could match their strength, courage and ability, nor their intelligence and foresight. Their reputation spread far and wide, and eventually reached the ears of the servants, who long ago had been ordered to drown the twins. Realizing immediately that the two fine youths were none other than Romulus and Remus, they went to Silvia and owned up to everything.

'You are kind men for having spared my childrens' lives,' Silvia said with tears of joy in her eyes. 'Mars will reward you.'

How joyful was the reunion between Romulus, Remus and their mother! The kind Faustulus, his wife and the other shepherds were happy too. One shepherd said, 'Romulus and Remus, be our leaders! We shall go with you to the royal palace, and you can be sure every man who meets us will join us too. The wicked Amulius has ruled us far too long. The time has come for the kingdom to return to the rightful hands.' So with Romulus and Remus at their head, the shepherds marched to the city.

The news flew before them and they were joined by farmers, potmakers, shopkeepers, blacksmiths, and all the men who met them on their journey. When the terrified Amulius saw the enormous, angry crowd approaching, he jumped out of the window in despair and was instantly killed.

Romulus and Remus restored their old grandfather Numitor to the throne, who then reigned in Alba wisely and justly for many years. The followers of Romulus and Remus wanted to found a new city which would be ruled by both brothers. The wise King Numitor favoured the idea and so they departed to a region surrounding the River Tiber to build their city. A dispute arose between the brothers over who should be the founder and after whom the city should be named. They agreed that Romulus would climb the hill Palatinus, and Remus the hill Aventinus. The one who saw the bigger flock of birds would be the founder. Remus saw six birds, Romulus twelve.

Romulus wasted no time in starting to build his city. As the supervisor he chose a most capable man named Celer, who also happened to be most violent. First came the walls. Before long they towered round what would be the future city. Remus was upset that the gods had determined his brother to be the founder of the new city, so he started to ridicule the work.

'Do you call this a wall?' he sneered. 'Any enemy could jump over it quite easily.'

'Let him just try!' Celer cried angrily. 'If anyone dared to leap across it, I would kill him with my own hands.'

Remus laughed, ran to the wall and jumped over it. The quick-tempered Celer raised his spade and split Remus' head.

When the city had been completed, it was named Rome after Romulus, who then reigned there for many years, until his father Mars came to fetch him in his chariot to take him away to heaven to live with him.

Sampo the Magic Mill

Two brothers lived in the distant land of Kalevala. Vainamoinen, the eldest, was a musician and Ilmarinen, the youngest, a skilful blacksmith. Far and wide there was no other man who could strum the kantele so wondrously, sing ancient songs so melodiously, or advise as wisely as Vainamoinen; and far and wide there was no one who could make such excellent swords and farm implements as Ilmarinen did.

One day Ilmarinen decided to travel to the far north, to desolate, dismal Pohjola, to court the lovely Aino, the daughter of the powerful but evil Queen Louhi.

'Do not go to Pohjola, dear brother!' Vainamoinen warned. 'Queen Louhi is as cruel as the sea. You will fare badly.'

'I know what she is like,' Ilmarinen snapped back. 'But why should I listen to your advice? I know what you are up to! You are after the lovely Aino yourself and are worried she may choose me!'

Vainamoinen shrugged his shoulders and strolled to the sea shore. He was wondering whether to go on foot, or to harness the horses to the sledge, or to put out to sea in a boat. Suddenly he heard the sounds of weeping from the reeds. Stepping nearer, he saw a lone boat.

'Why are you crying, little boat?' he asked.

'Because all the other boats have sailed away long ago to fish for salmon and herring, or to bring goods from foreign lands; but I have been left behind and forgotten.'

Vainamoinen said happily, 'Do not weep, little boat! No longer will you rot by the shore! The wind will stop tearing your red sails, the birds will stop building nests on your masts, fishes will stop darting under your keel. We shall sail together to desolate, dismal Pohjola, for the beautiful daughter of Queen Louhi.'

The boat stopped crying and said, 'I will be happy to sail with you and will help you if you are ever in need.'

So Vainamoinen sailed away on the little boat.

Blacksmith Ilmarinen harnessed the horses to the sledge and off he drove through the snow. The brothers travelled their separate ways, unaware of each other's whereabouts, but they both arrived in Pohjola at the very same time.

Queen Louhi was sitting with Aino in a room not in an ivory castle, nor in a stone castle, but in a wooden castle. Their dogs Halli and Lukki, who were always on guard and never fell asleep, suddenly started to bark. Louhi tossed a log on the fire and said, 'I wonder who is visiting us? If blood flows from the log, there will be war, if water, there will be peace.' But a drop of honey fell from the log.

'Suitors are coming to court you, dear Aino,' Louhi laughed, as Vainamoinen and Ilmarinen entered the wooden castle 'Come in! Sit down! Drink and eat and tell us what brings you here,' she said in welcome.

'Oh, mighty queen,' Vainamoinen then said, 'We have come to your icy kingdom, to desolate, dismal Pohjola, to court your lovely daughter Aino. We are brothers from the land of Kalevala. Let her choose one of us for a husband.'

Aino lowered her blue eyes and Queen Louhi shook her head. 'It will not be an easy choice to make between two fine youths like you. Let us wait till the morning. Tomorrow is always wiser than yesterday. Now we shall sit at the oak table and entertain one another, as is fitting for friends to do. I know who you are: you are Vainamoinen, the musician, and you Ilmarinen, the blacksmith. Pick up your kantele, Vainamoinen! Play and sing some nice songs for us!'

They sat at the oak table, drinking beer, eating venison, singing and laughing till it was almost dawn. As they were preparing for bed, Louhi asked her daughter, 'What do you think of your suitors? Do you like either of them?'

'I like Ilmarinen,' Aino replied.

Early next morning Louhi said to the brothers, 'I shall give the hand of my daughter to the one who fulfils the task I set him. You, Vainamoinen, must build from this spindle a ship six hundred feet long, which will sail without wind, without a crew, without losing her way or coming to grief. And you, Ilmarinen, must make from this ring a mill with three sets: the first must grind flour, the second grind salt and the third grind gold.'

The brothers nodded in silence. Ilmarinen then went to prepare his tools, whilst Vainamoinen decided to talk things over with his boat.

'That certainly is not an easy task,' remarked the boat when it heard what he had to say. 'You can do it only by casting a spell on the spindle by saying three magic words.'

'What are those words?' Vainamoinen asked.

'That I cannot tell you. They are known only to the old giant, Antero Vipunen, who sleeps in a meadow seven miles from here. Three paths will take you there; the first is strewn with sharp needles, the second with pointed swords, the third with blades of axes.'

Vainamoinen thanked the boat for the advice and went to see his brother.

'Please make me iron boots so I can walk along paths strewn with sharp needles, pointed swords and blades of axes,' he begged. 'Whilst you are at it, please make me a steel bludgeon so I can wake old Antero Vipunen. I want him to tell me three magic words. And make me

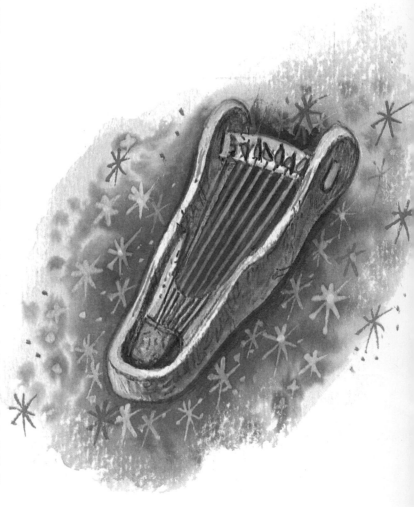

69

a smal golden chain on which I can thread the three words.'

Ilmarinen dismissed him with a wave of the hand. 'I shall not make you anything, brother. I have much work to do and no time to waste helping you.'

Vainamoinen did not argue, but walked over the sharp needles, the pointed swords and the blades of axes, till he came to the old giant. Antero Vipunen was sprawled in a green meadow, an aspen growing from his chest, a birch from his hair, and a pine from his nose. He had been asleep there, winter and summer, for three hundred years.

Vainamoinen tore the aspen from the giant's chest with one mighty pull. Vipunen shuddered and went on snoring. When the musician pulled the pine from his nose, the giant sneezed, till there was a crash of thunder in the distance, and went on sleeping. Tearing the birch from his hair did not make him even wince, so Vaina-

moinen crawled into the giant's giant mouth, and then into his stomach. There he began with his axe to strike mighty blows at the giant's belly. At last Antero Vipunen awoke and wailed, 'Alas! What is this awful pain in my belly? Wind, or indigestion?'

'It is I, Vainamoinen! And I shall keep on hurting you until you tell me the three magic words.'

'Alas!' wailed the giant once more. 'I cannot tell you the three magic words. I myself need them.'

Vainamoinen wedged the axe deeper into the belly and cried, 'What do you need the magic words for, when all you do is sleep?'

'That is true,' agreed Antero, whilst Vaina-moinen struck once more.

'Auch! That hurt! Come on out and I will tell you the three cursed words. But remember, you can use them only once. Then they lose their power and become useless.'

Vainamoinen crawled out of Vipunen's belly and he told him the three magic words.

As soon as the giant uttered the first word, lightning flashed thrice over the forests; as he uttered the second word, thunder roared thrice over the sea, and as he uttered the third word, a violent storm and a fierce gale broke round them, throwing the young man off his feet and carrying him all the way back to Queen Louhi's castle.

Meanwhile Ilmarinen was busily beating iron. His work was almost finished, but he was unable to make the three sets, one for grinding out flour, the second for grinding out salt, the third for grinding out gold.

Vainamoinen smirked when he saw his brother working away at his mill; he wedged the axe into the spindle, but it slipped out and cut into his knee. Blood spurted out onto the white snow, and Vainamoinen could not stop the flow, no matter how he tried.

He limped to Ilmarinen and begged, 'Please help me, brother! You are the master of iron, and iron will obey you. An iron axe has slashed my knee and I cannot stop the blood from gushing out.'

Ilmarinen, startled to see so much blood spurting out, started to chant,

'Now, iron axe
why do you hack
a brother of mine?
Why not choose pine
or slash another tree!
Heal the wound and let him be!'

But the wound did not heal and the blood kept spurting out.

'That iron is not doing what it is told,' Ilmarinen remarked. 'Someone else has power over it now. Do you know who?'

'I think I do. It must be Queen Louhi. She

'Oh, iron axe
you have no choice
so hear my voice
or there'll be the devil to pay!
This minute you must obey
for if my brother gets worse
I will put on you a terrible curse.
So stop the blood spurting
and the wound hurting.
Heal him now!
Or hear how
I will burn you till you scream
throw you in an icy stream
with a hammer you I'll beat
that is the fate you will meet.'

The minute Ilmarinen had spoken, the axe jumped to Vainamoinen's side and healed his terrible wound.

'Thank you, dear brother,' Vainamoinen said and then whispered the three magic words to Ilmarinen.

When he uttered the first magic word, Ilmarinen struck the mill with the hammer and it began to grind out flour. When he uttered the second magic word, Ilmarinen struck the mill once again and it started to grind out salt. And when he uttered the third word, Ilmarinen struck the mill for the third time and it started to grind out gold. At that moment the sun set.

'You have won, Ilmarinen,' Louhi said. 'My lovely Aino will be your bride.'

Ilmarinen returned home safely with his beautiful wife Aino, but his happiness was short-lived. One day the lovely Aino fell ill; for three nights and days she was delirious and on the fourth day she died. Wise Vainamoinen vainly tried to cure her with many health-giving herbs and please her with his music but nothing seemed to cure her of her illness.

'Aino was not meant for you, dear brother,' he said to Ilmarinen. The three magic words could have helped her but they have now lost their power.'

After this the two brothers lived together as before. Ilmarinen did not marry again, and Vainamoinen remained a bachelor. So ten long years passed by.

One evening, as the brothers sat by the fireside, someone knocked on the door. The brothers bade the caller enter, and a man, not too old and not too young, came in out of the snowy night. Knocking the snow off his boots, he said in greeting to them,

'Good evening, one and all! May I rest a while and warm myself?'

ordered the axe to hurt me. She does not want me to win her daughter Aino. You see, I have learned the three magic words from Antero Vipunen. They will help me to fulfil the task she set me.'

'Oh, brother!' Ilmarinen cried. 'Tell me the three magic words and I shall gladly heal you. It is evening now, so you cannot finish your task, come what may. Mine is almost finished. But I need to know those very words.'

Vainamoinen frowned and replied, 'When I asked you this morning to make me iron boots, a steel bludgeon and a golden chain, you refused. Yet now you ask me to help you?' Ilmarinen blushed with shame.

'Forgive me, dear brother. I shall heal your knee whether you tell me the three magic words or not.'

Once more he started to chant:

'You are most welcome! Do sit down!' the brothers cried in unison, and passed him bread, venison and beer. Then they asked, 'Who are you? Where are you from and whereto are you going?'

'It matters not who I am,' the wanderer replied with a smile. 'I come from a far, distant land. I wanted to travel to find out how people lived elsewhere and to learn something from them.'

'How wise,' Vainamoinen nodded. 'Tell us then what you have seen and which is the best place to live in.'

The traveller laughed. 'Where else but in desolate Pohjola! The region may be most inhospitable, but it is ruled by the clever Queen Louhi; she gave the hand of her daughter to a blacksmith called Ilmarinen after he had made her a magic mill with three sets: the first for grinding out flour, the second for grinding out salt, the third for grinding out gold. They call this mill the sampo, and they think very highly of it. No wonder too, for the little mill grinds out far more than they need. What they do not use, they exchange with merchants for various

a strange rock this is, smooth, yet scaly, and it has fins.'

Vainamoinen laughed. 'That is no rock, but an enormous fish. Take your sword and kill it, so we can go on.'

Ilmarinen severed the fish's head with one swift blow. They dragged the head into the boat, remarking, 'What a huge pike this is!'

When they came ashore, they cooked the head. There was enough fish for them and for all the villagers who gathered round. When there was nothing left except the white bones, Vainamoinen said, 'The pike's jaws will make an excellent kantele. I can use the intestines for strings.'

Soon he had made the kantele, and when he played it and sang, everyone marvelled at the beautiful sound. 'I have never known a kantele to play so beautifully,' Vainamoinen remarked. 'It truly is a magic instrument.'

Queen Louhi sat in a room of her castle—not the wooden castle, nor the stone castle, but the ivory castle, when her dogs Halli and Lukki, the two who were always on guard and never fell asleep, started to bark.

Louhi then tossed a log on the fire and said, 'I wonder who is visiting us? If blood flows from the log, there will be war, if water, there will be peace.'

A drop of blood fell from the log as Vainamoinen and Ilmarinen entered.

'Come in, sit down, drink and eat a little and tell me what brings you here,' Louhi welcomed them.

The wise Vainamoinen then spoke, 'We come to your kingdom, mighty queen, for the magic mill, the sampo. For ten years now it has ground you flour, salt and gold. For ten years now it has brought prosperity to Pohjola. It is high time for my people to be blessed with such prosperity. Return the mill to us! After all, Ilmarinen made it and I helped with the three magic words.'

Queen Louhi laughed. 'You have come all this way in wain — for nothing. The sampo is mine. No-one else shall have it. If you remember well, Ilmarinen exchanged it for my lovely daughter Aino.'

'But Aino has died long ago.'

'That I know, and I have shed many tears for her. But that is not my fault. Why don't you make another mil?' Louhi suggested.

Ilmarinen dismissed Lueen Louhi's idea with a wave of his hand. 'You know, dear queen, that it would be impossible to make another like it. For that I would need another three magic

goods. Nowhere in the world are people so well off as in dark Pohjola.'

The mysterious wanderer had long been gone, but his words remained to haunt the brothers. 'That would be something, to own the magic mill, the sampo,' Ilmarinen often remarked, 'I shall never be able to make anything like it! But it is not fair: I have lost my wife long ago, yet Pohjola goes on thriving because of me.'

Vainamoinen agreed. 'We shall return to Queen Louhi and ask for the mill. In these past ten years she's had more than her fair share of ground flour, salt and gold.'

So one fine day the brothers set out again in Vainamoinen's little boat to desolate Pohjola. They sailed along the blue sea, till the boat came to a sudden stop, as if it hit a rock. Ilmarinen put his hand in the water and said, 'What

words, for the ones I had have lost their power.'

His brother Vainamoinen then said, 'We have come with good will to distant Pohjola, and with good will we shall depart. If you refuse to part with the sampo, we will leave without.'

'You have spoken wisely,' Louhi remarked, and invited them to join her at the supper table.

The sun had risen and was peeping into the room, when Vainamoinen downed the last jug of the beer he had been drinking all through the night, and said,

'Mighty queen, would you be kind enough to show us at least how the sampo grinds out flour,

salt and gold? We would be so happy to see it operating.'

Louhi replied, 'That can be done. But do not get any ideas that you will be able to steal it. It is guarded by one thousand guards. And if you managed to overpower the thousand armed men, you could never beat Halli and Lukki, the dogs who are always on guard and never fall asleep. And if you did, you could not beat me. But that you know.'

Louhi led the brothers into a large room locked with seven locks and guarded by the dogs Halli and Lukki.

Sampo the magic mill stood there on a silver table; with one set it ground out flour, with the second salt, with the third gold. One thousand armed men stood round it, whilst servants came and went, bringing empty sacks, filling them with the flour, salt and gold, and taking them away again.

Queen Louhi gazed proudly at her riches and said, 'What do you think of that?'

'There are no words to describe our thoughts,' Vainamoinen sighed. 'But perhaps a little music would help.'

He picked up his kantele, and played so hauntingly, so wondrously, that everyone present stood still and listened, forgetting about everything. Soon they were all lulled into deep sleep by the sound—including Halli and Lukki the dogs, who were always on guard and never fell asleep.

The brothers then took possession of the golden sampo and hastened to their boat. With the red sail flapping in the wind, they were soon skimming the surface on their way home back to native Kalevala.

They were nearing their own shores when Queen Louhi awoke back in the distant, desolate Pohjola. As soon as she opened her eyes, she noticed that the thousand armed men were fast asleep, and Halli and Lukki too — the dogs who were always on guard and never fell asleep. She realized immediately that Vainamoinen must have put everyone to sleep with his music. Her eyes fell on the silver table and she saw it was empty. She knew full well who had taken the golden mill.

'Alas, three times alas!' she cried in a fit of temper. 'This time you have won, Vainamoinen. But who knows, perhaps the sampo has not yet reached your native shores!'

Louhi then turned for help to God Ukko, and cried,

'God of air, sky and fire
make the waves rise higher and higher!
Mighty Ukko, let your will be
to sink Vainamoinen's boat in the sea
taking the sampo to eternal sleep
among the pike and eels in the ocean deep.
Master of the world
let your voice be heard!'

Powerful Ukko heard Louhi's plea, and with all his might he blew into the sea. Waves rose and crashed, lightning flashed, thunder struck and Vainamoinen's little boat broke up and sank right by the shore. The brothers only just managed to escape with their bare lives. They were not able to save the sampo, the magic golden mill. It fell to the bottom of the sea, where it caught on a rock and where it remained for ever. And it only grinds with the second set — always salt. This is why the seas of the world have been so terribly salty ever since.

Beowulf the Dragon Fighter

King Hrothgar of Denmark was a sovereign who was brave in war and merciful in peace. He ruled from his magnificent palace Heorot, where he frequently entertained travellers who came from near and far to pay homage to the wise and generous ruler. They marvelled at his stately home and enjoyed feasting on good wine and excellent foods and listening to the beautiful songs of the minstrels. But this was not to continue.

One night, when the harps had stopped playing and the voices of the famous minstrels had died down and in the banqueting hall only the regular breathing of the sleeping men broke the silence. Then the monstrous dragon Grendel rose from a nearby lake. Up till then he had avoided men, but now he broke into Hrothgar's palace and discovered the thirty tired, sleeping men. He sank his teeth into the first and enjoyed the taste of human blood so much, that he slaughtered them all. He then picked up the thirty corpses and carried them, like a huge, horrific bouquet of flowers to his lair in the lake. Only the scarlet trail of blood was left as proof of his attack.

The inhabitants of the castle and of all Denmark were gripped by terror, and wailed with dread for the following night. Their fears were justified. The monstrous Grendel came again, the ghastly slaughter was repeated. After that

he never missed a night, choosing his victims as and when he pleased. Nobody escaped, not even the bravest of the warriors.

The magnificent Heorot became neglected and deserted. Guests avoided it and minstrels sang sorrowful songs about the castle of death throughout the country. Twelve long years passed before the mournful tidings of the reign of terror reached the ears of Beowulf, nephew of Hygelak, and king of the Goths. Beowulf was young, brave and had the strength of thirty men. When he heard the minstrel's song, his noble heart was moved to action. He selected fourteen strong, valiant warriors, had a fast vessel built, and before long they were on their way to Denmark.

'Who are you and why have you come in full armour?' King Hrothgar enquired, when they came to him in the beautiful, but now desolate castle.

'We are Goths from the kingdom of Hygelak,' Beowulf replied. 'These are my men, who will face any foe bravely and I am Beowulf, the son of a chieftain, whose life was full of heroic deeds. We have come to slay the monstrous Grendel.'

'Welcome, Beowulf, and welcome to your friends,' Hrothgar said. 'You have set yourselves no easy task. Many daring warriors have spent the night at Heorot, yet not one of them survived to see the dawn. Fearful Grendel broke their swords and lances, as if they were blades of grass.'

'If death waits for us here, then that is our destiny,' Beowulf replied. 'But we shall not give up our lives easily.'

It was as in days of old: the hall glittered with lovely robes of beautiful ladies. Beer and wine flowed and entertainment was laid on. The queen graced the hall with her presence and took a cup of wine with the Danes. When the banquet was over, the king and queen retired to safety with their companions. Only the fifteen Danish warriors remained. Before long they heard a strange whistling sound, followed by

the rattle of the iron bolts, and the hideous Grendel tore into the hall. Slippery and slimy, with protruding, fiery eyes, terrible fangs and daggerlike claws. He was about to pounce on one of the sleeping warriors, when a terrible pain shot trough his body. For by then Beowulf held the dragon by the throat with one bare arm whilst with the other he broke his talons. Grendel writhed and wriggled and screeched, till the whole castle shook, but Beowulf held on. The dragon made one last desperate attempt to break free and managed to tear away from Beowulf's grasp. But one hideous arm fell severed to the floor. Howling in agony, the monster limped back to the lake, there to die. Beowulf did not pursue him. But in the morning, after Hrothgar's men rushed to the banqueting hall to see the monstrous arm for themselves, they followed the bloody trail to the lake. The scarlet surface of the water proved that the monster was buried for ever.

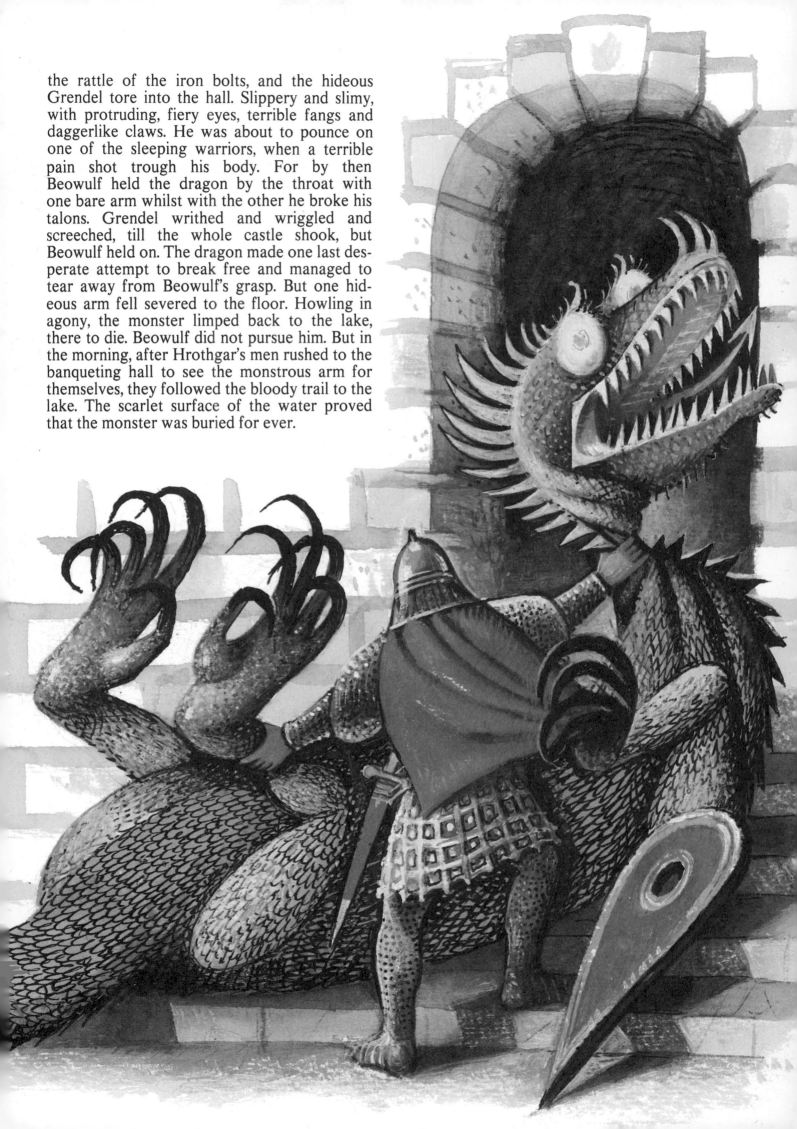

King Hrothgar, tears of gratitude in his eyes, embraced the hero. Once again the banqueting hall came to life, and once again the queen and all her attendants were present. That night, when all was quiet and the merrymakers retired to bed, the Danes stood guard, according to the old custom.

Whilst there was only joy and laughter in Heorot, there was sadness and sorrow at the bottom of the lake. This was the grief of Grendel's mother, and old, ugly witch, in whose arms her son breathed his last dragon breath. Though the witch lacked his strength and had never ventured from her lake abode, the thirst for revenge drove her to Heorot castle. She stormed into the banqueting hall, but the Danish guards were after her at once. The sorceress realized she was too weak for them, so she made a hasty retreat. But she managed to seize a precious prize — Grendel's severed arm and also Aescher, one of the Danes, who was king Hrothgar's most loyal advisor. The King was

grieved at the tragic news. He summoned Beowulf and said, 'I must ask one more favour, but it will be the very last. God knows what a great loss Aescher's death is for me.'

'I shall gladly help,' Beowulf replied. 'I guessed that the deep waters of the lake hid yet another enemy.'

Hrothgar and Beowulf immediately mounted their horses and rode like the wind towards the lake. There, on a boulder, they found Aescher's severed, blood-stained head.

The king grew scarlet with anger and grief. Without the slightest hesitation, Beowulf dived into the lake. It took a long time to sink to the bottom, but at last he felt firm ground under his feet. He found himself in front of the dragon's lair. Strangely enough water did not penetrate into it, and in the glow of the fire which was burning inside, Beowulf could see the witch squalling by a pile of human bones. She turned and pounced on him, taking him unaware, but Beowulf threw her aside, and with his sword

dealt her a vicious blow. Yet the sword bounced off her body as if it were of steel, and the witch lunged at him again. Beowulf then spotted an enormous sword hanging on the wall. He seized it swiftly, and with one blow severed the ugly hag's head. Something else lay by the fire—Grendel's monstrous body. Beowulf severed his head too and swam to the surface with both fearsome trophies. Now that the land of the Danes had been freed from the terrible reign of the awful lake monsters, Beowulf grew homesick and so decided to return with his companions back home. His uncle, King Hygelak, died just then, and as he had no sons, Beowulf was crowned the king of the Goths. He reigned wisely and justly for fifty years.

When the fiftieth year of his reign was nearing its end, an unwelcomed guest flew into the land of the Goths—a gigantic dragon, who with his fiery breath burned everything which stood in his path.

As in his younger days, Beowulf assembled his warriors and they rode to the dragon's lair. The monster was waiting for them. Poisonous flames were shooting from his mouth and green smoke hid everything round him. Beowulf's knights took fright at the sight of such a fearful monster and took to their heels. Only Beowulf remained, and a loyal, brave youth named Wiglaf.

With his sword Beowulf struck the dragon hard and viciously, as if old age had not robbed him of the strength of thirty men. The sound of the death rattle was coming from the monster's throat, and blood was streaming from the mortal wound in his chest. Beowulf was about to strike a second blow when to his horror he realized that his sword had broken in two. But out of the green mist a voice cried, 'I am coming to help, my king!'

Young Wiglaf then attacked the dragon and ended his life, but by then the monster's poisonous talons had pierced the king's unprotected throat.

'My life is ebbing away,' whispered Beowulf, feeling the poison seep through his body. 'I name you my successor to the throne. Take my steel shield as proof of my words.'

These were the last words spoken by Beowulf, the famous dragon fighter. He was happy with his fate, for he knew that Wiglaf, the bravest of the brave, the most loyal of the loyal, the best of all good men would succeed him to reign over the Goths.

The Battle at the Palace of Mountain Ash Trees

The land of the Danes, which used to be called Lochlann, was once ruled by King Colga. He was a powerful king and it angered him greatly that an island in the far west refused to accept him as their king. It was called the isle of green hills, or Ireland, and King Cormac was its sovereign.

King Colga decided that time was ripe for a decisive battle. His forces boarded swift crafts, which sped towards the Irish shores. Cormac, however, was warned that the Danes were approaching and sent for Finn, the leader of a group of brave young heroes, the Fenns, to give them an unexpected welcome. Finn's followers included his son Ossian and grandson Oscar. No sooner had the Danes anchored and come ashore, than they were attacked by the Fenns, who were hiding among rocks.

A vicious battle followed. The Danes, taken by surprise, soon regained their composure and fought back valiantly. It occurred suddenly to Oscar, that whichever side lost its leader would be the loser. He therefore gradually fought his way towards king Colga's banner, till they stood face to face. The king accepted Oscar's challenge to a duel. At first they hovered over one another like a couple of hawks, then their shields clashed, as their swords met with a deafening crack. Both of them were bleeding badly, but neither would accept defeat. Not until Oscar's sword struck Colga's head so viciously, that his helmet cracked and so did his head.

But the Danes refused to retreat, but fought on, preferring to die rather than to admit defeat whilst their hands were capable of holding their swords. They fell to the last man in that vicious

battle. There was only one soldier left alive, a mere boy. This was Midac, King Colga's youngest son.

In those days it was not customary to punish a defeated foe, and Midac was placed among the greatest Irish warriors, the Fenns, where he lived as their equal. Midac, however, recalled vividly the cruel battle in which his father and the whole Danish army had perished, and hatred towards the Irish grew in his heart. He hid his feelings well. Sly Conan, a podgy, bloated man with eyes like a falcon and tongue like a viper was the only man to sense how Midac felt. He said to Finn, 'I think we are rearing a snake in our bosom. Midac sits with us, hears all our secrets, but never speaks, never gives

a word of advice. Oscar slew his father in battle. I am sure he thinks of nothing but revenge.'

Finn believed what he heard and decided to get rid of Midac. He called the youth to him and said, 'It is the custom here when a boy reaches manhood that he lives on his own feudal territory. As you are of noble birth, choose the place where you wish to build your house and your children to be born.'

Midac chose the land surrounding the River Shannon, with good reasons. Firstly it was one of the most fertile places in Ireland; and secondly, in the wide river mouth there were many tiny isles and inlets, where war ships could land unobserved. Finn favoured the choice, and presented Midac with a herd of cattle and many servants. But Midac never invited any of the Fenns to his new territory, and never returned to Allen, the home of Finn. Fourteen years went by.

Finn and the Fenns were out hunting one day and without realizing they came to the River Shannon. There they saw a handsome warrior riding towards them. His heavy armour, the sword, the lance, the wide shield and satin cloak pointed to Lochlann origin.

'Who are you?' Finn asked in greeting.

'Why, it is Midac!' Conan cried, adding bitingly, 'In all these fourteen years you have never invited us here, nor have you visited Allen.'

'You did not remember me either,' Midac snapped. 'But now you are here, I invite you all to my Palace of Mountain Ash Trees. You are probably weary and hungry.'

Finn and his party did not have to be asked twice, and gladly accepted. But Finn, recalling Conan's warning, left five warriors outside the palace, including his two sons, Ossian and Ficna.

The Palace of Mountain Ash Trees rose above an impassable, rocky precipice, with only a narrow path leading to it from the river. A welcoming fire was burning in the dining hall, giving a delicious, strange scent. The walls were inlaid with expensive wood and had seven entrances. The floor was strewn with soft mats and furs.

The guests sat down, but Midac remained standing. He measured everyone present with a glance showing a glint of hate, and then left. The Fenns were embarrassed, but their embarrassment turned slowly to horror when they noticed that the fire was no longer giving aroma, but smoke and soot, which poured forth at an alarming rate. The mats and furs had disappeared too and the Fenns were sitting on the bare floor. And instead of the seven doorways, there was only a single closed door.

'Let us get out of here,' Conan cried, leaning on his lance to raise himself to his feet. But he could not get up. He seemed to be glued to the spot.

'I shall ask my wisdom tooth what all this means,' Finn said, placing his thumb in his mouth. A moment later he groaned. 'For the past fourteen years Midac has been plotting our destruction to avenge the death of his father and countrymen. His moment has now come. In his second abode, the Island Palace, the Danish army is waiting. Sinsar, the king of the world, is in charge, and with him are three kings from the Isle of Torrent. Their knowledge of magic is responsible for all these unnatural happenings.

Only a drop of their own blood can break the terrible spell!'

The terrified Irishmen began to panic and cry. Finn said in reproach, 'You are behaving like cowardly women. If we cannot avoid our fate, let us meet it proudly, singing the war song, as is the custom of heroic men.'

Ossian had been waiting by the palace for some time. When he heard the singing, he said to the others, 'I fear something evil has happened to my father and his men, for they are singing the war song.' And he sent his brother Ficna and Innsa, the son of Swen Selga, to the Palace of Mountain Ash Trees to investigate. At the palace doors they heard Finn call from inside, 'Who is out there?'

'It is I, Ficna, and I have Innsa with me!'

'Don't come in,' Finn warned them, 'but hurry to the ford, for the enemy is approaching.'

Innsa ran swiftly down the mountain path, and saw that the Danish soldiers were already wading through the water from the opposite bank. As the ford was very narrow, only one man at a time could get across. Innsa was the first to arrive and he fought valiantly, slaying his enemies one by one until the river turned scarlet with blood. But his young strength began to ebb, and when the last, strongest warrior towered above him, he did not have the strength to battle on, and fell.

By then Ficna was on the scene, ready to avenge the death of his friend. The vicious fight went on and this time it was Finn's son who came out of it the victor. But as he sat breathless on the Bank, Midac appeared at the ford, leading his warriors.

'Clear my path, Ficna!' he cried.

'Clear it yourself,' Ficna laughed, but by then the furious Midac pounced upon him.

It was a vicious duel, with the clatter of their clashing swords echoing near and far. Ossian heard it too and so sent the last two warriors, Dermat and Fatha, to go and see what was happening.

'It's Ficna!' Dermat shouted. 'I hear his war cry.' The two men rushed to the ford and saw the wounded Ficna protecting himself against Midac's blows with his shield. Dermat realized they could not reach the ford in time to help, so he threw his lance at Midac and it passed right through his body. But as Midac collapsed dying into the river, he stabbed Ficna with his sword, killing him too. Midac's soldiers retreated in panic.

Heavy-hearted, Dermat returned to the Palace of Mountain Ashes, leaving Fatha on guard.

'Whoever you are, do not enter,' he heard Finn say from within. 'How did the fighting go at the ford?'

'I am Dermat and I have just avenged the death of Ficna.'

There was silence, then Finn spoke sadly, 'I bless your victory. But yet another fight awaits you. Three kings from Torrent are approaching the ford, and only their blood can set us free.'

The gluttonous Conan then said, 'There will be nothing left but our corpses to set free, because we shall die of hunger. I shall be the first. Before anything else, bring us some food. Our enemies are assembled in the Island Palace. I am sure they are not without food and drink.'

Dermat feared Conan's sharp tongue more than the enemy, so he went to the Island Palace, and hid until a servant passed him carrying a cask of wine and a dish of roast. Dermat knocked him down with one hard blow, picked up the meat and drink and hurried back to the Palace of Mountain Ash Trees. Conan was waiting impatiently.

'How am I to pass you the food, if I am not allowed in?' Dermat asked helplessly.

The artful Conan had an answer. 'Push the food through the little window in the wall. It will fall right at my feet. Then climb up on the roof, cut a hole through with your lance and pour the wine straight into my mouth.'

Dermat did as he was told, and when at last he heard contented burping from the now satisfied glutton, he breathed a sigh of relief and went back to the ford.

Fatha was fast asleep. He had no idea that the three kings from Torrent were amassing their soldiers on the other shore. So Dermat stood alone in defence of the ford and faced the enemy with great strength and courage. Time after time he warded off their attack and eventually slew the three kings. He cut off their heads and hurried with them to the Palace of Mountain Ash Trees, so that Finn and his men could at last be free.

The moment he smeared the banqueting hall floor with a few drops of blood of the kings of Torrent, the spell was broken and the Fenns jumped joyfully to their feet. 'You have saved us, Dermat,' Finn said, 'We are still too weak to help you hold the ford. You, Fatha and Ossian must face the enemy alone till dawn.'

The night passed slowly. Soldier after soldier tried vainly to cross the river, but the three brave Fenns did not let anyone through. Sinsar, the king of the world, sent his own son, Borba, to fight, but he too was no match for the Irish, and ended dead in the river.

Deadly silence followed, the silence before the last battle. All around, there was nothing but death. And the few left alive did not stop fighting, did not ask for truce, for here their destiny was to be decided. The king of the world himself now appeared heading his soldiers. Ossian and his comrades were anxiously waiting for dawn. They knew that alone they could not hold out against him.

The last battle began. The Danes came surging down to the river, but now it was dawn and the Fenns, fit once more, rushed from the Palace of Mountain Ash Trees to help their three lone warriors. With the river as the battle field, there was a desperate fight, with heroes dying on both sides, with lances flying, bloody swords flashing. Oscar fought his way through to the king of the world, who greeted him with angry laughter.

He motioned to the others to stop their fighting and in the hush that followed, all eyes were on the two leaders, engaged in a terrible duel. Sinsar, enraged by the death of his son, fought like a lion, and as slyly as a fox. His blows came down heavily on his adversary's shield. Oscar lost his balance, and turned, as if to flee. But just as Sinsar's sword was poised, ready to deal the mortal blow, Oscar whirled round and severed Sinsar's head.

The battle was over. The remaining Danes fled in chaos and panic to their ships. The Irish, weary, but victorious, marched back to Allen, their banners flying high, their heads held proud and with a song in their hearts.

The Beautiful Deirdre

During the reign of King Conchobor, a renowned musician named Fedlimid lived in the kingdom of Ulster. The king respected him more than many a gallant knight, so when Fedlimid held a banquet in the king's honour, he attended, bringing his most important men.

When the entertainment was at its height, Fedlimid received news that his wife had given birth to a baby girl.

Everyone rejoiced and congratulated the happy father, except the aged sage Cathbad, who could tell the future from the stars and the clouds. He sat in silence and frowned. When asked why he had not joined in the celebrations, he replied,

'The baby girl is called Deirdre, which means threat. Her loveliness and beauty, through no fault of her own, will cause many terrible battles and loss of blood.'

Now there was a hush in the hall, broken at last by the king. 'I shall make sure that your prophecy will not come true. Deirdre will be

cared for in a secret place, and when she grows up, I myself shall marry her.'

Deirdre therefore spent her childhood in seclusion. An aged, loyal nurse called Levarcham was her only companion. The child grew into a lovely maiden.

One wintry day, when the frost was biting hard, Deirdre sat staring at the snow-covered yard, where a calf had just been slain. A black crow flew down and began to peck at the bloodstained snow. The girl laughed, and said to her nurse, 'Imagine, Levarcham, a man with a skin as white as snow, cheeks as ruddy as fresh blood and hair as black as the crow's feathers...'

'I know such a man,' the nurse admitted, and having started the tale, she had to continue. 'His name is Naisi, and he is one of Usna's sons. He and his brothers Ainli and Ardan are some of the ablest knights in the Red Wing of the royal palace.'

'I must meet him,' Deirdre whispered.

The nurse knew, of course, of Cathbad's prophecy, and as she feared King Conchobor, she refused to give in to the maiden's pleas. But eventually she relented, and brought Naisi to Deirdre. When she saw that they fell in love at first glance, she warned them, 'Run away from Ireland, if you wish to stay alive. Otherwise Conchobor will kill you.'

The young lovers did not hesitate. That same night Naisi told his brothers of his intentions, and they insisted on coming too. Soon they had left the Irish shore behind them, and were sailing towards Scotland.

Once there, they built themselves simple huts at the edge of the sea, and they often gazed into the far distance, where they thought their home must be.

After some time, King Conchobor held a banquet at his country seat. When the entertainment was in full swing, he said to his faithful knights,

'You all know that in the whole world there is not a palace to match mine, and that no one holds such lavish feasts as I. And yet the three sons of Usna choose to reject my hospitality.'

'They do not reject it,' the knights protested. 'They would gladly return to Ulster, and we would welcome them back, for they were the pride of the Red Wing.'

'If that is the case, let them return!' Conchobor decided. 'I give my word that as long as they bend to my will, I will give them back their estates and will not harm a single hair on their heads.'

When the feast was over, the king called his faithful, honest knight Fergus to him, and said, 'No one knows Usna's sons better than you. Go and ask them to return, but do not dawdle on the way. 'Tell them I am waiting with a royal welcome.'

Fergus left for Scotland, taking his two sons, Ilan and Buini.

The king now summoned Barach, a knight who lived near the sea, and said,

'Naisi will come ashore near your house. He and his companions will be in a hurry. You can let them go, but detain Fergus for three days at least.'

When Fergus found Naisi and passed on the king's message, everyone rejoiced, and prepared to return to their homeland.

Only Deirdre was sad. 'Let us not leave!' she pleaded. 'I had the strangest dream. I saw three birds flying to King Conchobor's palace. In their beaks they carried three drops of honey. But on

their return flight, their beaks were full of blood.'

Honest Fergus assured them, 'I vouch for the king's word. And if all Ireland stood against you, I would defend your lives whilst capable of holding a sword.'

When they all reached the Irish shore, Barach hastened to meet them. Turning to Fergus, he cried, 'Welcome, friend! It is a long time since we last met! I hope you will not refuse my invitation to come to my house. The dinner is ready and waiting.'

Fergus was embarassed. He did not like to refuse Barach, but neither did he wish to let the others go on alone. Naisi settled the matter. 'Stay here, Fergus,' he said. 'We know the way. We shall continue on our own.'

Fergus therefore remained behind, whilst his sons travelled on with the three brothers and Deirdre. Then Deirdre had another bad dream. 'I dreamed that we had to fight King Conchobor. Buini betrayed us, but Ilan lost his life in the fight.'

'You must not believe dreams,' Naisi scolded her, and they marched on. As they neared the palace, Deirdre had a third dream.

'I dreamed that the king did not welcome us in his palace, as was promised, but sent us to the Red Wing, which is the home of his knights. Treason and death only were waiting for us there.'

'The Red Wing is a happy place, and our home! How can death and destruction await us there!' Naisi objected laughingly.

King Conchobor had prepared a feast for the returning knights in the Red Wing. This startled them, and they were even more uneasy when the king failed to join them. So they kept on their guard.

The king summoned the old nurse Levarcham and sent her to the Red Wing, to find out whether Deirdre was still so beautiful. When the nurse and Deirdre embraced each other, Levarcham whispered, 'Beware! This palace is filled with armed men.'

Then she hastened back to the king and told him that Deirdre had lost her lovely looks. But knight Trendorn, an old enemy of Usna's sons, shook his head and said, 'I have seen Deirdre. She is lovelier than ever.'

The king wanted to see her with his own eyes, so he accompanied Trendorn to the Red Wing. They climbed up to a small window under the roof, and gazed inside. Deirdre was playing chess with Naisi, but she felt someone's eyes upon her.

Naisi seized one of the chessmen, and threw him at the window. Trendorn cried out, clutching his eye, 'See how beautiful Deirdre is, my king! The moment I looked upon her, I lost an eye!'

The king was gripped by violent envy, and he exclaimed, 'To arms!'

And immediately a band of hired armed men attacked the Red Wing. But the strong oak walls resisted the onslaught, and the brothers guarded the windows well. Deirdre and Naisi carried on with their game of chess, as if nothing was happening.

'Set the building alight!' the king cried, when he saw the useless efforts of his men.

The soldiers quickly stacked dry wood round the walls, and lit it. Thick smoke soon cloaked the Red Wing.

'I am going to put that fire out,' Fergus's son Buini announced, and opened the door. He managed to put the fire out, but he did not return. The others feared he had perished, till they saw him at the head of the armed men, who were once again preparing to burn down the Red Wing.

Unfortunately all of Deirdre's dreams were coming true.

'I shall atone for Buini's treason,' Ilan cried, as, sword in hand, he pounced on the enemy. He fought valiantly and managed to extinguish the flames. But he received terrible wounds. There in the green grass, he fought and died like a true hero.

The day was ending, and the Red Wing seemed impregnable. But dusk brought Conchobor's reinforcements. Yet Naisi, Ardan and Ainli still somehow managed to keep the enemies at bay. The king's men vainly tried to break into the Red Wing.

The three brothers knew full well they could not keep up the defence for ever, so they decided to fight their way out, and lead Deirdre into safety under the cover of their shields. Their plan would have succeeded, if King Conchobor had not stepped onto the scene of battle and exclaimed, 'Let there be peace! Throw down your arms!'

Usna's sons were glad to let their weapons slip to the ground. As they turned to their king, he sneered evily, and said, 'Tie them up! Because you dared to resist me, you shall be shorter by the head!'

Not one man present was willing to raise his sword against Usna's sons. Then a stranger stepped forward, and severed their heads with one swift stroke.

Deirdre sank to the ground by the side of the lifeless bodies, and cried,

'Oh, Naisi, why have you left me? I chose you for my husband, and without you I cannot live. Conchobor, dig a grave for four people! My place is with Usna's sons. With them peaceful sleep awaits me.'

When she had spoken, the beautiful Deirdre breathed her last breath.

All four of them were buried as requested in the same grave, and their names were carved on a lily-white stone for eternity.

How King Arthur Came to the Throne

In bygone days there lived in England a wise old man named Merlin. They said he was the son of the devil, and that by being hurriedly baptised at birth, he lost his demonish strength; but he was left with magic powers and so could change his image, transport himself from place to place, know of people's past and of their future. He was wiser than all other men, and was therefore chosen to be King Uther Pendragon's right hand man and chief advisor. And Merlin made it possible for the king to marry the lovely Igerne, the duchess of Tintagel.

When the royal couple had a baby son, Merlin expressed his wish to educate the boy. The king gladly agreed, cheering up the queen, who was loathe to part with the infant, with the words, 'The wise Merlin plans a great future for our son. Let him have the child. It is for his own good.'

So Merlin took away the little prince, who was not seen again for quite some years.

Soon afterwards the king fell gravely ill and even the best physicians could not cure him. When enemies from the North heard this, they sailed to England and plundered the lands of the ailing king.

Merlin then said to Uther, 'You will have to lead your troops into battle, though you are so ill. Only your presence will bring victory.'

As always, the king heeded Merlin's wise advice and was carried to the field outside St. Albans where the decisive battle was to take place. And truly, the soldiers took heart to see their sick king with them, and attacked the enemy with great force and courage. The enemy, surprised at their sudden strength, fought back valiantly, but suffered heavy losses and were forced to flee back to their ships.

Finally there was much rejoicing in the camp of Uther Pendragon, but the poor king was not there to celebrate with his men. He died just as victory was at last in their grasp.

After his death chaos and unease spread throughout England. The whereabouts of the king's son were not known and several men of noble birth strove to take the crown and the throne. The country was rapidly going downhill, and the royal councillors' attempts to restore order and law were useless. The wisest one, Merlin, was the only one not to lose his optimism. And without doubt it was he who, by some magical means, put a large stone outside a door of a London church, in which a sword was firmly wedged up to the hilt. The following words were engraved on the stone,

'Whoever withdraws the heavy sword from

this stone, is both by birth and law the rightful king of England.'

Many famous men who hankered after the throne tried to extract the sword, but they all failed.

At that particular time, royal tournaments were being held in London. Among those who arrived to take part was Sir Hector and his sons Kay and Arthur. Kay was to take part in the tournament for the very first time, but unfortunately he broke his sword. Arthur rushed off to find him a new one, and came upon the sword in the stone. He seized it by the hilt and drew it out with ease, without having read the inscription. But others had read the message on the stone and the news that the magic sword had found its rightful owner, spread rapidly through the city. Arthur was astonished by what he heard, until Sir Hector explained, 'You are not my real son. When you were born, the wise Merlin brought you to me to bring up. The brave King Uther Pendragon and Queen Igerne were your parents. The crown should justly be yours!'

Merlin then appeared at Arthur's side and confirmed the truth of Sir Hector's words. And Arthur was taken to the Archbishop of Canterbury to be crowned the king of England.

It was not easy at first for the young king to enforce his will in his kingdom. When he and his retinue came to the royal castle Camelot, there were six kings and numerous noblemen waiting for him, not to pay him homage, but to oppose him with force. Arthur took Merlin's wise advice and hid with his men in the strong castle tower. His enemies vainly besieged it.

A fortnight later, when the attention of the attackers had slackened Arthur and his knights, though greatly outnumbered, struck the enemy's camp. The rebels, caught unawares, were forced to flee. King Arthur and Sir Kay distinguished themselves as excellent swordsmen and valiant warriors. Though the foes were forced to flee, they refused to accept defeat. The six kings persuaded five more kings to join them in their fight against King Arthur. They came, bringing fifty thousand men.

King Arthur, however, had also been busy. Acting on Merlin's advice, he sent messengers to Brittany to ask aid from King Ban and King Bors, who were very powerful rulers. They gladly promised to help and soon were crossing the sea with ten thousand soldiers.

The opposing armies pitched camp in the woods, and waited for daybreak and the decisive battle. But at midnight Arthur's knights

came charging forward, riding like the wind, joined by King Ban's and King Bors' cavalry. There was great confusion in the enemy camp. Tents were pulled down, horses broke loose, and the soldiers ran about unable to form ranks. They suffered heavy losses: in that fight alone, the eleven rebel kings lost ten thousand men. But by dawn the tables were turned. Eleven kings were still a force to be reckoned with and it now seemed they would win after all. The foresighted Merlin then stepped in and led King Ban and King Bors with their ten thousand men away from the battlefield to hide in the forest.

King Arthur and his knights fought on like

lions. The eleven rebel kings could not take him, corner him, nor force him to lay down arms, though he was greatly outnumbered. And then King Ban and King Bors rode like the wind out of the forest, at the head of their men. The eleven rebel kings could not withstand such a force. They retreated to their ships and hurriedly sailed away.

When Arthur returned to Camelot Castle, he heard that King Ryence of Ireland was about to attack King Laodegan of Carmalide. 'Will these wars never end?' Arthur sighed and prepared for battle. King Laodegan happened to have been his father's loyal friend whereas the Irish king had always been a staunch enemy. So once again Ban and Bors set out at Arthur's side.

As they were riding past a lake, King Arthur suddenly realized that he was without his sword.

'No matter, sir,' Merlin said with a smile. 'Hop into this little boat and row across for the one over there!' King Arthur followed the direction in which Merlin pointed, and, to his astonishment, saw a slim arm emerge from the water, holding a sword. He dismounted and jumped into the boat which lay in the reeds. As soon as he had rowed across and taken the sword which it held the arm disappeared.

'The Lady of the Lake gave you this sword,'

Merlin explained. 'It is called Escalibor, and it will bring you many a victory. And when you fight with this sword, not one drop of your blood will be shed. But you must never lose the sword. If you do, you will lose your life!'

Merlin's prediction proved true, for when King Arthur arrived at King Laodegan's castle, which was besieged by the Irish army, his new sword dealt so many fierce, fateful blows, that he could have almost wiped out all the enemies single handed. Wherever the royal banner with the scarlet dragon was seen, the adversaries took to their heels.

Guenevere, the lovely daughter of King Laodegan, who watched the fighting from her window, admired the bravery of the hero. She had the chance to meet him at the great banquet which was held in honour of King Arthur, after the victorious battle was over. Arthur and Guenevere grew fonder of each other minute by minute and before long she gladly promised to be Arthur's wife. Merlin was not too keen on his king's choice, but he would not tell why, so King Arthur went ahead with the magnificent wedding which was held at Camelot.

King Laodegan sent a hundred brave knights to serve his daughter and her new husband. He gave them countless other treasures, among them the most precious gift of all — the Round Table. On seeing it, Merlin remarked, 'Your power, my king, depends entirely on this table! One hundred and fifty chairs go round it, and on these one hundred and fifty knights will sit, with you at their head. They will all be equals, they will all be brothers. King Laodegan has already sent a hundred knights; I shall find the rest in your kingdom.'

This was the beginning of the glory of King Arthur's Round Table, about which so many wondrous tales are told today.

Sir Gawain and the Green Knight

'This is the Perilous Seat,' Merlin remarked, pointing to one of these. 'It is intended for the most pious knight of the Round Table. If anyone who is not dares to sit down in it, he will meet death. Now eat, drink and be merry, for great adventures await you, more exciting than everything you have ever seen even in your wildest dreams.'

All of a sudden, the door flew open and a giant knight in green armour burst into the hall astride a green mount, on his head a green helmet, in his hand not a sword but a heavy axe. The giant stranger did not reply to their friendly greeting, but mumbled,

'So this is the famous Round Table? I can see only scared children sitting here, playing at being knights.'

King Arthur rose and cried, 'Let us convince you, sir, that we are true knights! I myself will fight you.'

His nephew Gawain jumped up at the same time. 'This is not a matter of your honour, my king, but of the honour of all the knights at the Round Table. Please allow me to fight this duel. What are the conditions?'

The Green Knight smiled. 'They are quite simple. Your sword must strike my bare neck now, and mine will do likewise in exactly one year's time.'

Now the hall was abuzz with surprised whispers; nobody had ever heard of such a strange duel.

Sir Gawain solemnly gripped King Arthur's sword, Escalibor, and sliced off the Green Knight's head.

The Green Knight calmly picked his own head up from the floor and tucked it under his arm. The severed head then said, 'Do not forget!

After the wedding, King Arthur knighted the most valiant youths, as was the custom. Sir Gawain, Arthur's nephew, was one of them. The knights then all sat down at the Round Table. Suddenly the name of each knight appeared in gold letters on the back of each seat. Two chairs, however, remained empty.

96

I shall expect you in the Green Chapel in a year from this day.'

With that the mysterious stranger disappeared as quickly as he had come.

Time flew by, filled with many exciting adventures of King Arthur's knights. But Sir Gawain did not forget his promise. When six months had gone by, he set off in search of the Green Chapel, where he was to meet the Green Knight. No one had heard of the place and he was beginning to doubt that he would find it.

Month after month Sir Gawain journeyed through the kingdom, crossing countless rivers and countless mountains, but he did not find the Green Chapel. His steps eventually led him to North Wales. It was winter, snow was falling and frost seeped in to his very bones. He was hopelessly lost and wondered whether he would freeze to death before finding shelter. Suddenly he noticed imprints of a boot in the snow before him. They led to a clearing, from which he could see a majestic castle on a crest of a hill.

The lord of the castle welcomed Sir Gawain most kindly, and was courtesy itself when he learned that he belonged to the knights of the Round Table. His beautiful wife gave their guest more attention than to anyone else, and so did all the lords and ladies who were staying in the friendly castle just then.

The days passed happily enough, but Sir Gawain was restless. He was due to meet the Green Knight in the Green Chapel in exactly two weeks' time. 'I must leave,' he said at last to his host. 'I have to find the Green Chapel before the end of next fortnight, and I still have no idea where it can be.'

'The Green Chapel?' laughed his host. 'It is nearby. Barely two miles from this castle. What do you want there? Or is it a secret?'

'It is no secret,' Sir Gawain replied and told the lord of the castle of his encounter with the Green Knight. His host nodded and said, 'Now that you know where the Green Chapel stands, you do not have to rush off.'

Sir Gawain remained in the castle till the last evening but one before the year was up. It was then the lord of the castle said to him in the course of a friendly conversation, 'Tomorrow I am holding a great hunt, but I do not wish to tire you before you meet up with the Green Knight. Stay here and rest. I promise that whatever game we kill will be yours. You must promise in return, that you will give me everything you receive during the day.'

Sir Gawain readily agreed, though he was somewhat surprised at such a strange request.

The hunters left for the forest before dawn, leaving Sir Gawain fast asleep. He would have probably slept till the evening, if he had not been awakened by a kiss. Startled, he opened his eyes and saw to his astonishment that the lady of the castle was sitting next to the bed.

'You would sleep through your Judgment Day,' she said. 'But now that everyone has gone hunting, you must rise and look after me.' And she kissed the knight a second time.

Sir Gawain was so taken aback, he could not think of a thing to say. He got up quickly, dressed, and went to see his hostess. He spent the whole day amusing her as best as he could, and she enjoyed all the attention paid to her. That evening, she said, 'Thank you, gallant knight, for a lovely day. You were a lovely companion. Please take this lace sash as a token of my appreciation. You will be glad of it tomorrow, for it will keep you safe from any blow. But you must not breathe a word of this to my husband.' So saying, she kissed Sir Gawain again.

The clatter of hooves and the blare of horns, accompanied by the barking of hounds, announced the return of the hunters.

The lord of the castle greeted his guest by pointing to a handsome stag he had shot and saying, 'This is yours.' 'And this is yours,' Sir Gawain promptly replied, and gave his host a kiss. The lord of the castle did not seem at all embarrassed and had an enormous boar brought in. 'I also killed this boar for you,' he said to Sir Gawain, who then kissed him again. And when he was given a beautiful fox he kissed him for the third time. But he did not mention the lace sash.

Next morning Sir Gawain, the lace sash firmly tied round his waist, went to the Green Chapel. He found the chapel in a snow-covered copse. The Green Knight was standing in front of it. 'I see you have kept your promise,' he mumbled from behind his closed visor. 'The knights of the Round Table always keep their word,' Sir Gawain replied, baring his neck.

The Green Knight raised his huge axe and with all his might struck at Sir Gawain's bare throat. But the axe bounced off, as if the neck was of steel, and not a single drop of blood appeared. The Green Knight raised his axe once more.

'Oh no, you don't,' Sir Gawain cried. 'We

agreed that each of us would strike only one blow.'

'That was a year ago,' the Green Knight said with a sneer. 'Since then you have broken your word which you gave to your host only two days ago!'

The Green Knight opened the visor of his helmet and, to his astonishment, Sir Gawain found himself looking into the face of his recent host. He blushed with shame, fully aware what the Green Knight was referring to. He untied the sash and handing it over to the lord of the castle, he said.

'I am aware why you broke the promise you gave me. My wife asked you to keep her gift a secret and you were too gallant to refuse. But what passed between you, happened with my knowledge and was meant as a lesson against the wishes of women. They have brought ruin to many a fine knight.'

'I shall not be taken in by them in the future,' Sir Gawain promised, looking somewhat uncomfortable. 'But tell me, sir, where did you learn your magic?'

'The Lady of the Lake taught me,' the Green Knight replied. 'She in turn was taught by Merlin. Come, return with me to my castle and we shall celebrate today's events!'

Sir Launcelot and the Knights of the Holy Grail

There were fine knights who sat at the Round Table, but one outshone them all in strength, valour, horsemanship and courtesy. His name was Sir Launcelot. He was the son of King Ban of Berwick, King Arthur's faithful friend and ally. Soon after Launcelot was born, King Claudas attacked Ban's kingdom with devastating results. King Ban was forced to retreat to Trebes Castle, from where he vainly sought help. His brother Bors was mentally ill, and King Arthur was involved in a fierce war with the Saxons. King Ban was therefore forced to flee from the castle with his wife and baby Launcelot, to seek help of other allies. When they paused to rest by a beautiful lake, the king turned to look for the last time at his castle. To his horror he saw that it was aflame. The treacherous steward he left in charge had surrendered to the enemy, who burnt Trebes to the ground.

Grief broke the king's anguished heart and he slowly died. His unhappy wife vainly tried to revive him. Whilst her attention was on her dying husband, a young beautiful nymph rose out of the lake and took the infant Launcelot from the grass. Still unseen, she carried him in her arms away from his mother. She was the Lady of the Lake.

She cared for the boy for eighteen years, and this is why he became known as Launcelot of the Lake. When he reached his eighteenth year, the Lady of the Lake took him to the court of King Arthur, where he soon became the favourite knight of the lonely Queen Guenevere. She named him her own champion and protector. It was in her honour that Launcelot undertook all his battles and conquests.

Messengers from King Pelles arrived at Camelot Castle one day. They told frightening tales of a fearful dragon, who had suddenly appeared in the vicinity of their castle and now terrorized the whole country. Each day he demanded a maiden, whom he then devoured. King Pelles begged the knights of the Round Table to slay the murderous monster.

'Let me go!' Launcelot offered and set out straight away. King Pelles was glad to see him, but he had his doubts whether such a youthful knight could defeat such a dragon. But there were no doubts at all in the mind of the king's daughter Elaine, who liked Launcelot at first sight.

At dawn the next day Launcelot accompanied the unfortunate maiden who was to be sacrificed to the dragon's cave. When the fearsome monster appeared, Launcelot pounced on him with the strength of a lion. The dragon, taken by surprise, suffered several nasty wounds before he started to fight back. Then, shaking with fury, the monster retaliated, and attacked, roaring wildly and frothing at the mouth. It seemed the brave knight would be torn to shreds. Yet somehow he managed to escape from the dragon's huge talons, and to strike the fatal blow. Finally the monster lay dead at his feet.

The king and his subjects were overjoyed when Launcelot brought the dragon's severed head, and they hung it proudly above the castle gates. Launcelot was in no hurry to leave. He had fallen in love with the beautiful Elaine, and as she returned his love, King Pelles decided that Launcelot would make an ideal husband for his daughter. Everyone was soon celebrating their wedding. After a year, an infant boy was born, and they called him Galahad. Though Launcelot missed the Round Table and King Arthur's court, he did not leave King Pelles' castle till something very strange happened.

One day, as he sat talking to King Pelles, a lovely maiden appeared, bearing a goblet covered with white lace. The hall was immediately flooded with the sweetest, headiest odour on earth, and the tables became laden with the choicest dishes and wines. The atmosphere filled Launcelot with a wonderful, mysterious sense of well being. King Pelles and all the courtiers fell to their knees in wonder.

'Is this some miracle?' Sir Launcelot cried.

'You are looking at the most precious object on earth — the Holy Grail. Our Lord drank from this goblet at the Last Supper, and Joseph of Arimathea caught a few drops of blood from our Lord's wounds in it. It was he who brought the goblet to this land. But it is prophesied that the Holy Grail will disappear because we are sinners and will not reappear until it is found by three knights of the Round Table. But even then it will not return to our kingdom.' Launcelot gasped on hearing this prophecy. How he wished that he would be one of the three knights destined to find it! So he left his family, to search for the Holy Grail.

Launcelot searched in vain. The wise Merlin could, perhaps, have helped, but he had disappeared without a trace. Even to King Arthur his disappearance was a mystery.

Merlin was with the Lady of the Lake. He had taken such a liking to her, that he deserted Camelot, King Arthur and the knights of the Round Table. Unfortunately for him, the Lady of the Lake only wanted to learn Merlin's magical secrets. Once she had mastered all he knew, she led him deep into a forest, sat down with him under a hawthorn bush and waited for Merlin to fall asleep. Then she marked with her veil nine magic circles round him. Merlin was now unable to leave the spot, unless she herself broke the spell. The wise Merlin had to pay a high price for falling for her charms.

Sir Launcelot, of course, knew nothing of this, otherwise he would have done his best to persuade the Lady of the Lake to release Merlin. Instead he vainly searched for him and for the secrecy of the Holy Grail for many long years. One day at last Sir Gawain came to the fateful forest. When he hit against the powerful, invisible wall of the magic circles, he heard a familiar voice, 'Hurry back to Camelot! The Holy

Grail is about to leave us and the time has come for the knights of the Round Table to go in search of it. Those destined to recover the Holy Grail have been selected already.'

Sir Gawain was astonished to hear all this, but he hastened back at once to Camelot. It was not until he was well on the way, did he realize that the voice he heard was the voice of Merlin.

Several of Sir Gawain's friends were assembled in Camelot castle. His brother Sir Gareth was there, and Sir Kay, Sir Hector, Sir Launcelot and his brother Sir Bors; Sir Perceval was also present, sitting next to the Perilous Seat, still covered with a veil. Suddenly a hermit entered the hall, holding the hand of a young knight in red armour. To everyone's amazement he sat him upon the Perilous Seat. There was a complete silence in the hall, as King Arthur rose and removed the cover from the chair. Straight away a golden inscription appeared on the back of it which said 'This is the seat of Sir Galahad, the good knight.'

In all the excitement that followed, Sir Launcelot warmly welcomed his son to the Round Table. A sudden clash of thunder shook the castle; the hall grew unbearingly bright and the Holy Grail was seen floating in the air. Once again the hall was filled with a heady scent and the tables became laden with delicious foods and wines. Sir Gawain then rose and said, 'When I was passing through a forest, I heard Merlin's voice, which said "The Holy Grail is about to leave us and the time has come for the knights of the Round Table to go in search of it."'

One by one the knights rode off in search of the Holy Grail, each in a different direction. For most of the hundred and fifty knights the search was fruitless, and they eventually returned to Camelot. As in the case of Sir Gawain and Sir Hector, who met a hermit who said, 'Go back, for you are not destined to find the Holy Grail.' Yet that same hermit said to Sir Bors, who was with them, 'Put on a scarlet cloak as a mark of your quest and remain without food till your appetite is satisfied by the Holy Grail.'

One night during his search Sir Launcelot came to a huge castle, which appeared to be deserted. As he walked through the empty rooms and passages, he noticed a dazzling glow pouring from one chamber. He was about to enter when he heard a voice, which said in warning, 'Return, Launcelot! You are not destined to find the Holy Grail.' Instead of retreating Sir Launcelot went further. Suddenly he felt as if his face was lashed by fire, and he faint-

ed. When at last he regained consciousness he found himself in King Pelles' castle. His father-in-law was sitting at his bedside, but there was no sight of Launcelot's lovely Elaine. Sir Launcelot asked in vain. She had died but a few days earlier.

Some time later, three other knights came to the deserted castle. They were Sir Galahad, Sir Perceval and Sir Bors, who was so famished he could hardly keep up on his horse, for he had obeyed the order to fast.

The three knights met by chance in front of the castle and were now beginning to believe that they were nearing their destination. They made their way through, and entered the chamber which shone with the dazzling light, without hearing a warning voice, and without being lashed by fire.

The Holy Grail lay on a silver table, it was scenting the air and making rare foods and wines appear on tables before them. The three knights sank to their knees and prayed, then sat down and ate a hearty meal for they were all extremely hungry, particularly Sir Bors.

That night, they all dreamed the strangest dream. An angel appeared and said, 'You must hasten to the coast, where you will find a white ship with the Holy Grail on board. The ship will take you to the city of Sarras, the holy goblet's rightful home.'

Next morning the knights discovered that the Holy Grail had disappeared, so they followed the angel's instructions and hastened to the coast. The ship was there, waiting for them. The moment they boarded, it sailed away, though there was no crew. The bewildered knights searched the ship and near the mast found a silver table with the Holy Grail on top. The ship sailed on calm seas for fourteen days, until it reached the city of Sarras in the country of Babylon. The knights placed the silver table with the golden goblet in a local chapel, and kept vigil.

They soon discovered what miracles the Holy Grail was capable of. Not only did it feed the

hungry, but it had all the power to cure the sick and the lame, even those who were dying. The legend of the Holy Grail spread and thousands of pilgrims flocked to the city, not one of them to leave disappointed for all gazed in wonderment at the Grail.

The greatest sages of Babylon came to the three knights and said, 'Honourable guards of the Holy Grail, we have come to ask if one of you would become the ruler of our kingdom. We know the Holy Grail is the most sacred and precious object in this world. We feel that those who were destined to find and guard it, must be the very best men and therefore worthy of being kings. You yourselves must decide which one of you should be our sovereign. We shall abide by your decision.'

'Sir Galahad should be made king,' Sir Perceval said. Sir Bors agreed, happy to vote for his nephew.

So Sir Galahad became the king of Sarras, but his reign was short. Sir Launcelot's son was not destined for long life on this earth. The Lord called the young king to him, when he was barely a man.

His death brought sorrow to the kingdom of Babylon. The people asked for another knight to take the crown, but Sir Bors and Sir Perceval both refused, for the angel had returned to them in their dreams, and said, 'Your duty to the Holy Grail is now completed. You may now do whatever you wish.'

Sir Perceval decided to enter the monastery, where he led a godly life for a year, helping others and tending the sick. But at the end of the year his strength ebbed away and he too parted from this life.

Sir Bors was the only survivor of the three knights of the Holy Grail. He had no wish to remain alone in that distant land, so he crossed the sea and returned home.

There was much rejoicing at the Camelot Castle when Sir Bors appeared. And, after a royal welcome, there was much to tell about his adventures in the quest for the Holy Grail.

The Death of King Arthur

The knights of the Round Table who returned from the expedition in search of the Holy Grail rejoiced it had been found and placed in the holy city. They were happy to be all together again at Camelot. King Arthur and Queen Guenevere were the happiest of all. This happiness was not destined to last long. The friendliness which had reigned in the past among the knights of the Round Table was suddenly gone, and was replaced by envy and slander. Many a knight would have liked to see his comrade dead and buried, Sir Pinel, for instance, who hated Sir Gawain.

During a banquet given by the queen, Sir Patrice ate a poisoned apple, which Sir Pinel had intended for Sir Gawain. Sir Patrice ate it and died. His cousin, Sir Mador of Port, turned on the queen, accusing her of treachery and demanding an eye for an eye. Sir Bors of Ganis came forward and offered to defend Guenevere's honour by fighting a duel with Sir Mador. 'I shall gladly take up my lance on the queen's behalf, but only if no better knight that I is found,' he added.

He was, of course, referring to Sir Launcelot of the Lake, the queen's champion. Sir Launcelot was absent from the court just then, but Sir Bors knew his whereabouts and intended to inform him of the impending duel. On the day of the duel, when Sir Mador and Sir Bors were already mounted and ready to charge, their visors lowered, a rider on a white horse suddenly burst out of a nearby wood. He attacked Sir Mador with such brutal strength, that he soon had him pinned on his back, begging for mercy. The victor was Sir Launcelot, of course.

Shortly afterwards he was called upon again to defend the queen's honour. Guenevere had been taken a prisoner by Sir Meliagrance, during the May festivities and carried off by force to his castle. On this occasion Sir Launcelot himself set out in pursuit and caught up with Sir Meliagrance before he even reached the castle. He killed all his men and ran his sword through

Sir Meliagrance's treacherous heart. Then he returned with Guenevere back to Camelot. Sir Agravain and Sir Mordred, king's nephews, were two of several knights who hated Sir Launcelot, for they were jealous of the favours the queen granted him. So one night the gang of the envious knights broke in on Sir Launcelot, taking him by surprise. Even then he managed to kill them one by one, with the exception of Sir Mordred, who managed to escape.

Sir Mordred now hated Sir Launcelot all the more, and purposely gave an unjust, slanderous report to the king stating that Launcelot was the attacker and that he slew his companions. He even said that Sir Launcelot and Queen Guenevere were secretly scheming to assassinate Arthur. The king, believing Mordred's accusations, decided that Sir Launcelot and the queen would have to be severely punished. The knights of the Round Table urged their sovereign to forgive them. Even Sir Gawain implored him, 'Do not be carried away by wrath, my king! I too have good reasons to hate Sir Launcelot, for he has killed my dear brother. But, nevertheless, I want to be just and I cannot help but remember Sir Launcelot's past services and his loyalty. Oh king, you must think of this too and not punish them severely.'

But King Arthur stood steadfast in his resolve.

Sir Launcelot, angered at such an injustice, prepared for battle against the king. His wrath gave him the strength and speed of a tiger and he slew many of his king's men, even some of his old friends, from the Round Table. Sir Kay and Sir Gawain's brothers, Gareth and Gaheris, were amongst them. When his victory was complete, Launcelot lifted Guenevere on to his horse and rode off to his castle. King Arthur, infuriated by his daringness, sent a large army to besiege Sir Launcelot's castle. Fierce fighting continued. The Christian world was greatly disturbed at what was happening, and in the end the Pope decided to intervene. He knew full well that this war was benefiting no one, and therefore he ordered King Arthur and Sir Launcelot to restore peace and to forget their differences.

This was done.

Sir Launcelot left England and sailed to his kingdom of Benwick, accompanied by several knights of the Round Table. Sir Gawain, however, having lost three brothers by Sir Launcelot's hand, was so full of malice and hatred that he persuaded Arthur to take his army across the sea so the treacherous knight could be humiliated and punished in his own country.

When the royal ships crammed with troops were on their way to Benwick, the king had a very strange dream: he saw an enormous bear fighting a dragon in the air. The dragon kept on attacking, till he brought the bear to the ground. As King Arthur had a dragon on his coat of arms, he took the dream to be a good omen for victory.

When they landed at the port of Barfleur, the king heard that a terrible giant was ravaging the country, and that he had just carried off Duke Hoel's young niece.

'I shall go after the giant,' the ageing king said to himself. 'I shall see at least whether I am strong enough for the battle.'

So he set off for the mountains where the giant lived. He wandered through rocky passes, climbed high hills, easing himself down into bottomless chasms, till at last he found the giant sitting by the fire in front of a huge cave. His protruding eyes, rolling wildly, he was licking his thick lips moist with the blood of a calf he had just devoured. The moment the giant saw the king, he picked up a gigantic cudgel and pounced on him. But Arthur drew his sword Escalibore and slew the giant with one smite. But he was too late to save the duke's niece.

Reassured that he had ample strength, King Arthur commanded the siege of Benwick to begin. The city, however, was strongly fortified and well defended. Sir Launcelot at the head of his knights surprised the attackers many times outside the city walls, causing them heavy losses. Sir Gawain almost died from the wounds he received in three combats with the knight. Yet Sir Launcelot, recalling their old friendship, three times held back his own hand from striking the mortal blow.

Who knows how this war would have ended, if one day a messenger had not rushed into Arthur's tent and cried. 'I bring bad tidings, my lord! Whilst you have been fighting here, back in England, your nephew Mordred has usurped your crown, announcing to everyone that you have been slain. Only a few of your most faithful subjects are doing their best to defend the queen in the Tower of London. Hasten home, and let us pray you will be in time.'

Too late, King Arthur realized how wrong he was to allow the treacherous Mordred to talk him into war against Launcelot. And with his troops be returned hastily back to England. Mordred was waiting for the king in Richborough at the head of a great army, for he had called in the pagan Saxons to help him. But Arthur was an experienced, clever warrior and eventually Mordred was forced to flee to the Camblam river.

In spite of retreating, Mordred's troops caused heavy losses among King Arthur's ranks. Many knights of the Round Table were slain, including Sir Gawain. When Arthur knelt by his side to look for the last time into his glazed eyes, Sir Gawain whispered, 'I am dying, my lord, and I deserve to die. It was I who set you against Sir Launcelot. If only he would forgive me.'

The decisive battle between the two armies took place on the banks of the Camblam river. It was a cruel, merciless slaughter with streams of blood flowing on both sides. From the knights of the Round Table only the loyal Sir Bedivere still stood by King Arthur's side. And it was he who witnessed his king's death.

As the battle was almost over and Sir Mordred stood alone amid the piles of the dead and the dying, King Arthur caught sight of him and, consumed with fury and hate, rushed to attack. It may have been his terrible anger which made him forget to draw his magic sword Escalibore and to use it instead a lance to run through the treacherous Mordred's body. This gave Mordred time to raise his own weapon and mortally wound the king, before he himself died. The faithful Sir Bedivere carried Arthur from the battlefield to a lake nearby, where he bathed his wound and heard the king whisper, 'I beg you to do me a last favour. Unfasten my sword Escalibor and throw it in the water. Return it to the Lady of the Lake, who gave it to me once.'

Sir Bedivere was loathe to discard such a splendid weapon in the lake. But as the king insisted, he obeyed. Soon a slender white arm appeared above the surface, holding the sword. The arm waved it thrice, then vanished below. Soon afterwards a boat sailed to the shore carrying three beautiful sad queens dressed in black. The Lady of the Lake was one of them. They put King Arthur's body in the boat and drew away from the shore.

Sir Bedivere heard the king's voice for the last time. 'I leave for the happy isle of Avalon. There my wounds shall be healed for ever.'

Siegfried
and Beautiful
Kriemhild

King Siegmund reigned in the city of Xanten on the lower Rhine. He was rather old and looked forward to handing his crown to his son Siegfried. But Siegfried wanted to prove himself worthy of it first by finding glory and riches by his own efforts. He bade his father farewell and set out into the world.

During his travels he came upon a forest, which was inhabited by dwarfs who were guarding the immense treasure of their late King Nibelung. Soon after entering the forest Siegfried met two of the dwarfs, Schilburg and young Nibelung, who were the sons of the deceased king. They eyed Siegfried's tall figure with curiosity. Young Nibelung then said, 'Is it true that you people are the strongest creatures on earth?'

Siegfried smiled and replied, 'I think I can beat anybody.'

'Even the terrible dragon who lives here in this cave?' Schilburg asked, pointing to a nearby rock.

Siegfried nodded.

'If that is so, please slay the dragon,' the dwarfs pleaded. 'We will make it worth your while.'

He had no sooner spoken than an enormous, ferocious dragon dragged himself out of the cave. His eyes gleamed like fiery torches, flames leapt from his huge mouth and his roar was so fierce it bent over the forest trees. The dwarfs swiftly hid behind rocks, but Siegfried stayed put, his lance at the ready, poised for action. The dragon pounced on him but Siegfried plunged the lance through the monster's throat.

Before the dragon knew what was going on, he was shorter by the head.

The two brothers then reappeared followed by their comrades, who brought an enormous tub to catch the black dragon blood which was oozing from the mortal wound.

'This blood has magic powers,' young Nibelung explained. 'If you bathe in it, your body will be invulnerable.'

Siegfried quickly discarded his clothing and climbed into the tub filled with dragon's blood. And truly, as he bathed, his skin became tougher than the strongest armour, so that no blow from a sword, lance or hammer could harm him. There was but one tiny spot where he was still vulnerable, right under his left shoulder blade, for as he undressed, a falling leaf had stuck to it.

Siegfried thanked the dwarfs, but Schilburg dismissed his thanks with a wave of the hand, remarking, 'It is we who owe you our thanks. The great treasure left by our late father, the king, lies in the cave where the dragon lived. Now at last we can reach it. This treasure belongs to us two, for we are his sons. But we cannot agree how to share it out. If you are as wise as you are brave, then decide for us. In return we shall give you this sword called Balmung, which strikes only fatal blows.' And he pointed to the heavy sword on the ground nearby.

'Why didn't you kill the dragon yourselves, when you own such a remarkable sword?' Siegfried asked.

'We may have the sword,' the brothers said sadly, 'but we haven't the strength to lift it.'

Siegfried gripped the sword and swung it high above his head. 'Balmung has found its master,' young Nibelung cried.

The dwarfs then brought the treasure out of the cave. There were a hundred crates piled with silver, gold and precious stones. No mortal being had ever seen such an immense wealth. 'If I only owned just one of those crates, I'd be the richest man in my kingdom,' Siegfried said to himself, as he divided the treasure in two piles. But the two greedy sons of the king did nothing but argue. No matter how hard he tried, they were never satisfied. One accused Siegfried that he favoured the other, whilst the second suspected his brother of bribing Siegfried. The dwarfs grew so angry, that they attacked Siegfried with their swords, whilst he, not wishing to harm them, tapped them gently on the shoulder with the sword Balmung. He had forgotten how mortal the weapon was, and at the touch both the brothers dropped dead.

As he gazed sadly at the two small corpses, he felt a sudden blow to his head, chest, arm and leg. The blows were not hard, and anyway, his skin was invulnerable. Yet he was frightened, for his attacker was invisible. Flinging his arms about, Siegfried's hand suddenly caught a corner of some invisible material. He gave a sharp tug and a dwarf appeared before him.

'I am Alberich, the guardian of the Nibelung treasure,' he said. 'Spare my life and I shall go on guarding it. Now it is yours. I shall also give you the cloak you pulled off me for whoever wears it becomes invisible.'

Siegfried accepted Alberich's oath of loyalty and the gift of the cloak, and turned homeward. His fame went ahead of him. Everyone was talking of his victory against the fearsome dragon and of the wonderful treasure he had acquired.

He did not linger at home for long. He heard rumours about the most beautiful girl on earth — Kriemhild, the princess of Burgundy, so he decided to court her at once.

'Do not be hasty, my son,' the queen warned him. 'The Burgundians are a powerful and proud people. Kriemhild has three brothers, Gunther, Gernot and Giselher, who are all great heroes. With their friend Hagen, a giant of a man, they guard Kriemhild at Worms court. She refuses every suitor.'

Such words made Siegfried all the more determined, and he soon left for Worms with a bare dozen men. 'I am Siegfried, son of the king of Xanten,' he said to Gunther, the Burgundian king. 'Does His Majesty wish to fight me, or is peace his desire?'

'If you are Siegfried, the hero, and the owner of the Nibelung treasure, the sword Balmung and Alberich's magic cloak, then let there be peace between us,' Gunther replied.

But Hagen found Siegfried's daring words insulting and he cried, 'If it is a duel you want, I accept your challenge!'

Giselher however, stepped forward to greet the newcomer in a friendly manner, and Gernot followed. Hagen therefore fell silent, but envy towards Siegfried set deep in his heart.

Siegfried enjoyed life at Worms court. There was a constant round of tournaments, hunts, banquets and festivals, which gave him ample opportunity to prove his strength and agility. Though greatly liked and admired, our hero was not content. For he had not even glimpsed the Princess Kriemhild.

Then Danish King Lüdegast and Saxon King Lüdeger declared war against Burgundy. They were mighty kings indeed. Their armies numbered forty thousand men, whereas Gunther had only one thousand warriors.

Siegfried offered to help his friends and fought at their side so valiantly, that he was largely responsible for the Burgundian victory. During the great feast which was held in honour of their victory, Siegfried's desire was fulfilled at last and he met Kriemhild. The lovely princess admired the brave handsome hero, who by then was famous, and Siegfried was dazzled by Kriemhild's beauty. They fell in love at first sight.

On this occasion, King Gunther turned to Siegfried with a plea, 'There is an island called Iceland, ruled by Queen Brunhild. She is incredibly lovely and also incredibly strong. Anyone wishing to court her must first compete with her in throwing the javelin, hurling a stone, and in the long jump. If he fails to win, he loses his head. Many suitors have come to such a sorry end, yet I should still like to try. I'd be glad of your company and help.'

'I shall come with pleasure, King Gunther, if in return you promise me the hand of your sister Kriemhild.'

Gunther gave his promise, and straight away

Gunther, Siegfried and Hagen set off. They sailed down the Rhine, each with a dozen men.

Queen Brunhild recognized Siegfried immediately and assumed it was he who had come to fight for her hand. So she said, 'Hero Siegfried, you are the only man who may perhaps defeat me. I welcome you, but I also warn you: go back from where you came, for if you fail to win, you will lose your head and your life will be wasted.'

Siegfried replied, 'It is not I who come to compete with you, Queen. I am only accompanying my sovereign, King Gunther. It is he who will be your opponent.'

The queen grew pale and said, 'Your audacity will cost you your life, King Gunther, and the lives of all your men.' Siegfried, in the meantime, slipped out of sight and put on the magic cloak and so became invisible. The contest began. Brunhild lifted a gigantic javelin above her head, and hurled it at King Gunther with such force that his metal shield cracked. Yet the king remained standing, for it was Siegfried who caught the full impact of the blow. Everyone

gasped in astonishment, but by then Gunther, aided by his invisible friend, had flung the javelin back, blunt end first. Brunhild's shield split in two and she sank to her knees.

Next a gigantic boulder was rolled by twelve men to the queen. She lifted it with ease and threw it to a distance of sixty-six feet. Then, in one tremendous leap, there she was perched on top of it. But Gunther threw the boulder still further and reached it easily in one long leap. He was, of course, helped again by the invisible Siegfried. There was a hush — no one could utter a single word. The defeated queen stammered, 'You have won, King Gunther! From this moment I am your wife and Iceland is our kingdom.'

In all the excitement no one noticed Siegfried's absence and no one was aware of the secret of Gunther's victory.

So Brunhild returned with the king to Burgundy, where a great wedding was held, and Siegfried married Gunther's sister Kriemhild at the same time.

Brunhild, however, could not bring herself to believe that it was Gunther who had defeated her. When, after the wedding feast, they retired to their bedroom, she insisted on another test of strength which she won easily, of course. Disgusted with her bridegroom, she tied him up with her belt and hung him on a hook on the door.

The unhappy king confided in Siegfried the next day, and his friend promised to help him once more.

That night, when Gunther entered the bedroom with his bride and put out the light, Siegfried, wrapped in the magic cloak, slipped in behind them.

When Brunhild attacked her husband, Siegfried overpowered her and left, taking her belt and her ring. Brunhild at last was convinced that it must have been Gunther who defeated her, and she was happy and content.

Kriemhild was happy too. Siegfried took her to live in his native Xanten. She remained proud of her husband, especially when he told her how he had defeated Brunhild, and showed her the queen's ring and belt.

The years went by, and when ten in all had passed, Kriemhild grew very homesick.

Siegfried, eager to please, left for Worms with her, accompanied by their little son, his old father Siegmund and a lavishly equipped retinue.

Their arrival was greeted with much glory and rejoicing. Once again there was a constant round of tournaments, hunts and feasts and once again Siegfried distinguished himself with his strength and agility each and every time.

Brunhild envied her sister-in-law for having such a strong talented husband. She was slightly comforted by the thought that he was Gunter's vassal and therefore his inferior, as he explained ten years ago in Iceland.

One day Brunhild and Kriemhild were on their way to church. When Kriemhild was about to enter first, as was the right of a guest, Brunhild pushed her aside and said, 'It is my right to go ahead of you. Your husband is, after all, only Gunther's vassal.'

Hearing this, Kriemhild burst out laughing and told Brunhild how she had been deceived in Iceland. Kriemhild did not forget to add that Siegfried too was a powerful king like Gunther and that it was he who had defeated her in her bridal chamber. As proof she produced Brunhild's belt and ring.

The shattered Brunhild demanded that Gunther question Siegfried in her presence. Bitterly regretting that he had not held his tongue, Siegfried denied all the accusations. In fact he swore on oath that there was not a grain of truth in what Kriemhild had said.

But the damage was done and Brunhild was far from convinced. She threatened Siegfried with terrible revenge and confided in Hagen who still hated Siegfried and had been patiently waiting for his opportunity to come.

'The traitor and deceiver must die!' he pronounced. 'The queen must be avenged.'

Sensing that Siegfried was in danger, Kriemhild also turned to Hagen for help.

'I shall guard your husband well and I will never let him out of my sight,' the sly Hagen promised. 'But please mark the spot where he is vulnerable on his shirt, so I can protect him better.' The unsuspecting Kriemhild embroided in yellow silk a cross on Siegfried's shirt, just bellow his left shoulder blade, where the fallen leaf had stuck, when he had bathed in dragon blood. Hagen needed nothing more.

Soon afterwards Gunther held a great bear hunt in Odenwald. Siegfried was naturally present, attended with Hagen at his side. The day was stifling and when the hunters saw a well, everyone stopped to quench their thirst.

'Have a drink,' Hagen said to Siegfried.

The moment Siegfried discarded his sword Balmung and leaned above the water, Hagen, who was close behind him, gripped his spear and with all his might thrust it into the very spot so clearly marked by the yellow cross on Siegfried's shirt. The spear pierced Siegfried's heart.

All the hunters were horrified, and Gunther cried in anguish,

'In God's name, Hagen, what have you done?'

'I killed Siegfried, for he was a traitor and a deceiver, who had greatly offended our queen,' Hagen replied, adding, 'I stand firm behind my act.'

The crestfallen king realized that Hagen had acted on Brunhild's instructions. The unhappy Siegfried had paid with his life for having helped Gunther. There was nothing the king could do.

That night when the hunters returned to Worms, Hagen placed Siegfried's corpse on the doorstep of Kriemhild's chamber. She found her dead husband at dawn, and wept so bitterly that her cries woke the whole town. Everyone was aghast to hear what had happened. But no one was told the name of the murderer; this remained the secret of those who participated in the hunt.

Siegfried was laid out in state in Worms cathedral and crowds of people came to pay homage to the dead hero. Kriemhild stayed kneeling at his side day and night, carefully watching everyone who entered.

When Gunther and Hagen arrived to the cathedral, and walked round the coffin with downcast eyes, Siegfried's wound suddenly started to bleed again. This was a sure sign that his murderer was nearby.

Straight away Kriemhild hastened to Siegfried's old father and told him what had happened in the cathedral.

King Siegmund seized his sword and swore he would ride at the head of his men to avenge the murder of his beloved son. But Kriemhild stopped him.

'There are too few of you against the Burgundians.'

King Siegmund listened to reason and said, 'You are right, Kriemhild! We cannot help the unfortunate Siegfried now. Come, let us return home. There is nothing else for us here.'

'I shall not return to Xanten, father,' Kriemhild said. 'Go without me and bring up our son to be like his father. I will remain here to avenge Siegfried's death.'

Siegmund did not try to change her mind. Soon afterwards he left for Xanten with his grandson and his men. Kriemhild stayed behind in Worms to plot her revenge.

Kriemhild's Revenge

Time was passing by, and the unhappy Kriemhild was still in Worms, a sad and lonely woman. All she lived for was to avenge the death of Siegfried. But what could a mere widow achieve against Hagen, next to the King the most powerful man. Then she had a clever idea. 'Riches bring power,' she said to herself. 'And I, after all, own the Nibelung treasure.' She sent messengers to the dwarf Alberich, who was guarding the treasure, asking him to hand it over to her. He allowed the men to take it away, for upon Siegfried's death, it was hers by right.

When the messengers arrived with the treasure in Worms, everyone gasped at such enormous wealth. So much gold, silver, pearls and precious stones. Kriemhild was immediately treated with greatest respect, any many sought her favours.

'I can achieve anything with such riches,' she said joyfully, giving generously to all whom she thought she might need. The suspicious Hagen viewed all these happenings with distaste. One day he said to Gunther, 'Can you not see, my king, what is going on at your own court? Kriemhild is giving away parts of the Nibelung treasure to anyone she fancies, so gaining more and more supporters. Mark my words, she will soon destroy you. If you do not wish to lose your throne and your life, you must take the treasure from her.'

Gunther was frightened by such talk and agreed that Hagen should steal the treasure from Kriemhild. So one night Hagen and his men crept into Kriemhild's chambers, stole the Nibelung treasure and sailed away with it up the Rhine to his estate. There he hid the treasure. No one but he and Kriemhild's brothers knew of its exact whereabouts.

When Kriemhild realized that Hagen had robbed her not only of a husband, but also of her inheritance, she fell into deep despair and her thirst for revenge flamed like fire.

One day an imposing delegation arrived in Worms, sent by Attila, the king of the Huns. Count Rüdeger of Bechlarn, a Christian knight, who was in charge, said to King Gunther. 'King Attila, the mighty sovereign of the Huns and ruler of many Christian lands, sends the renowned King Gunther wishes for good health and peace and begs for his sister Kriemhild's hand in marriage. Our king has recently been widowed and only your sister can disperse his sorrow.'

Gunther was delighted, for he dearly wanted to be rid of his sister, but Hagen warned him, 'All Kriemhild thinks of is revenge and Attila is extremely powerful. She might persuade him to destroy us. Do not say a word to her, and give the messengers a negative answer.'

This time, however, Gunther did not listen to Hagen and passed on to Kriemhild the message he had been given, leaving her to make her own decision. She made up her mind at once, though she told Gunther to give her a day to think it over. But she could see quite clearly, that as the wife of the mighty Attila she would at last be able to have her revenge.

When next day she informed Rüdeger she would marry the king, he was delighted. 'You have chosen wisely, your Highness. Attila is a just man and his love for you is genuine. Though he is not a Christian himself, his Christian knights and I will always stand by you. I swear I shall always be ready to avenge any wrong done to you.'

'Don't ever forget the oath you have taken!' Kriemhild said gravely.

When Kriemhild was ready to leave, she asked her brother to let her take the Nibelung treasure. But Hagen refused to give it up, saying, 'I shall never let Kriemhild have the

keep their weapons at their side for the first three days,' Hagen lied in explanation.

The following day Attila organized a great tournament. The Burgundians fought with such courage, strength and agility that they gained admiration not only from the Huns, but also from Dietrich of Bern. Then something unexpected happened. Volker, one of the Burgundian knights who apart from being a notable musician was also a valiant fighter, was engaged in a contest against a young Hun nobleman whom he killed by an unfortunate error. This made the Huns very angry, particularly Blödel, one of their leading nobles. Kriemhild saw her chance.

'Though I am of Burgundy blood,' she said to Blödel, 'your wrath is mine. Let the Burgundians pay for the murder. If you and your men kill them, I shall give you a rich estate of your own choice, and the most beautiful maiden for your wife.' Blödel promised to see to the Burgundians.

That evening, as they were all feasting, Blödel and his men unexpectedly burst into one of the halls where some of the Burgundians were dining. The Burgundians defended themselves bravely, particularly Count Dankwart, who slew Blödel and many of his men. But in the end he

was left standing alone and with the greatest difficulty he fought his way to the main hall to his king. Attila was seated at the head of the guests, Kriemhild sat at his side, with her brothers, Dietrich of Bern, Rüdeger and Hagen. The queen was just playing with her baby son Ortlieb who sat on her lap, when the blood-stained Dankwart appeared.

'Stay by the door and don't let anyone in!' Hagen cried, guessing straight away what had happened. 'Who wants blood shall have blood!' he added in a terrible voice and, raising his sword, he cut off little Ortlieb's head.

A vicious battle began. Dietrich managed to lead Attila and Kriemhild from the hall, other-

wise they too would have perished in the furious fight.

The Burgundians fought like true heroes. They slew many Huns, including Rüdeger, who stayed true to his oath and fought against his future son-in-law and his brothers; they murdered his men too, and did not spare the lives of Dietrich's Goths, when they came to ask for Rüdeger's corpse. Count Hildebrand, Dietrich's loyal friend, was the only man to remain alive but when reinforcements came, the Burgundians were greatly outnumbered. Eventually — King Gunther and his faithful Hagen were overpowered and taken prisoners.

Kriemhild at last had her revenge, but at what a price! Raging like a maddened lioness, she asked for Hagen to be brought to her and said, her voice filled with hatred, 'At last you are in my power. But if you give me the Nibelung treasure, which is mine by right, and which you stole from me, I shall show mercy.'

Hagen laughed. 'I swore I would never reveal where the treasure is hidden, while even one of my royal masters is alive.'

Without hesitation, Kriemhild then ordered Gunther's execution. She herself brought her brother's bloodstained head to Hagen.

'You are dead, my king, and that is good!' Hagen cried. 'Now there is no one who knows the whereabouts of the Nibelung treasure but God and I, and neither of us will tell!'

These were the very last words Hagen ever spoke. The infuriated Kriemhild raised a sword and sliced off his head. Everyone gasped in horror. Count Hildebrand raised his lance and plunged it into Kriemhild's heart, solemnly saying,

'I do this, queen, because you dared to raise your hand against an unarmed prisoner. You have dishonoured Hagen, who was cruel and uncompromising, but also heroic and totally loyal to his king right to the bitter end.'

Old Man Tanzagan

Long ago the old man Tanzagan was riding in the great Altai mountains. He was very old indeed. His skin was wrinkled, his hair thin, his beard snow-white. The remains of his teeth were yellow, like barley seeds. But his hand was still steady, and his copper-pointed arrows never missed their target. He had the strength of two men, and the agility of a squirrel. His narrow little eyes could see as well at night as by day. His ears could pick up the sound of a badger up in the mountains and of a mole under the ground. His nose could smell a duck in the sky and a pike in the stream.

One day, as Tanzagan rode through the forest, he came to a big lake. As he approached, he could see two big men fighting on the shore. But they were no ordinary men, but giant toads, one black, the other white.

'Why are you fighting?' he asked.

The black toad threatened Tanzagan with his fist, but the white one croaked despairingly, 'Isn't there anybody in the whole Altai to help me?'

The black toad attacked again, most viciously, and his white opponent fell moaning to his knees. The old man Tanzagan raised his whip and struck the black toad's back.

'Leave that white toad alone,' he cried, and the black toad collapsed dead to the ground.

'Thank you, my hero!' the white toad cried. 'On my behalf and on behalf of my people I thank you! The black toad, and his horrible followers have taken over our beautiful lake. They killed everything living in it, and turned us out. Please help us to drive away the other black toads from the lake!'

'Very well,' Tanzagan agreed, and reached for his sword. 'You cannot kill the toads with a bronze sword, nor with a copper-pointed

arrow,' the white toad said. 'Only the blood of your horse will kill them.'

'How shall I go on living, if I slay my horse?' the old man frowned. 'I cannot travel on foot through the Altai.'

'You can get a new horse, but you cannot help my people any other way,' said the toad. 'We are a peace-loving race. We harm no one, and we wish everyone well. Why should we perish? I am not asking for myself, but for my people!'

Tanzagan took the toad's words to heart, and with his bronze knife he slit his horse's throat. The blood poured into the lake, and shortly dead bodies of black toads began to float to the surface.

White toads hopped to the lakeside from the forest. They pulled the black bodies to the bank and buried them in a deep hole.

'In the name of all my people, I thank you, our gallant hero,' the white toad then said, handing a yellow ribbon to Tanzagan. 'If before sunset you hold this ribbon high towards the sky, any wish of yours shall come true.'

Tanzagan thanked the toad for the gift. As the day was growing to its close, he raised the ribbon towards the heavens and wished for a good horse, so he would not have to travel the Altai on foot. Then he fell asleep.

When he woke up in the morning, he was astonished to see a huge herd of horses round him.

'Such is the power of the ribbon!' he cried joyfully, turning a grateful glance towards the lake. But the white toad did not appear again.

That same evening Tanzagan wished for a cow, and by morning he had a herd of them too.

Tanzagan built a house at the lakeside, and settled down happily. His large, healthy herds, the sweet grass and clean water attracted other folks to join him.

The new settlers built their own houses and brought wives and families, and they all lived peacefully together.

Tanzagan now longed to have a wife and children of his own.

'I have spent my whole life riding over Altai, shooting game, fishing and living from hand to mouth. And now, that I am rich, I am too old to marry and have children,' he sighed.

Then he remembered the yellow ribbon. He held it towards the sky and wished for a young, beautiful wife.

But when he awoke the next morning, he found a white goose at his side. 'The gods are

unjust!' he cried in exasperation. 'They have cheated me. Instead of a beautiful, young woman, they have given me a goose!'

He seized his whip and was about to strike the goose. The moment he touched her, she turned into a lovely maiden. Her hair was golden, like the evening sky, her eyes blue, like the water of the lake, her lips scarlet, like grouse's brows.

Tanzagan felt weak at the knees; his face began to twitch; his eyes were brimming with tears.

'Who are you, beautiful maiden?' he cried.

'I am the youngest daughter of Kurbustan, who reigns in the third heaven. I have come to your hearth from this third heaven. Now I have breathed in the smoke of your fire, I can never return home. The seven-headed giant Delbegen would laugh at me with his seven mouths; the

strong-man Kobon-odun would cover me with sparks from his steel pipe, and Teneri-kaan, the highest master of the heavens, would not permit me to enter. I shall stay and live with you.'

'We shall spend our lives together, and never part,' the old man Tanzagan solemnly said.

Tanzagan was very happy and content with Kurbustan's daughter. Soon they had children, two boys and a girl. They were lovely youngsters, but their mother was lovelier still. Whoever looked at her face, saw the golden sun on the right and the silver moon on the left. Whoever looked at her back, saw bright stars shining round her.

The men envied the aged Tanzagan his beautiful wife. They muttered, 'Why should such an old man have such a beauty? Why can't we have her, we, who are young, with hair that is thick and black? Why are our wives dark and grubby?'

No one dared to say such things to the old man's face. For Tanzagan still had the strength of two men and the agility of a squirrel, and his arrows never missed their target.

One day Tanzagan went hunting. He chose a mount from his herd of horses, secured a new string on his bow, and set out for the forest, armed with copper-pointed arrows and his bronze sword.

That same night, the men in the settlement sneaked to his house, surrounded it with dry leaves and twigs and set it alight.

'If we can't have the beautiful daughter of Kurbustan, then the aged Tanzagan shouldn't have her either,' they cried, waiting for the lovely woman to burn to death together with her beloved children.

But Tanzagan's wife did not perish. She appeared suddenly in the thick smoke, her children held in her arms. They rose into the sky and flew straight to heaven.

The men were terrified, and they scattered immediately in all directions.

When Tanzagan returned home from the hunt and found only a pile of ashes, he cried bitterly. He sank to the ground and did not eat, drink, nor sleep. Without saying a single word, he gazed sadly at the tragic remains of his happiness. So he sat for three days and nights.

But during the third night, when he suddenly looked into the sky, he noticed four new stars glittering there. The mother shone in front, with two sons at each side, and the little girl behind her.

'My beautiful wife has flown with the children into heaven!' Tanzagan cried out.

He named therefore the new constellation the White Goose. It is also known as the Crow constellation.

Tanzagan then took out the magic yellow ribbon, wound it into a ball and tossed it into the sky, as a present for his children. The yellow ball fell behind the last star and is shining there still.

When this was done, Tanzagan's grief turned to great anger. He seized his bow and fired his copper-tipped arrows at the cruel men, who robbed him of his beautiful wife and children. There was not an arrow that missed its target, and those who were struck, were instantly killed.

Many men were slain by Tanzagan's arrows. Those who were left fled with their wives and children far away from the Altai mountains. Only one dark, grubby young woman was left behind. She did not belong to anyone and no one offered to take her.

'Come and live with me,' Tanzagan offered. 'I can no longer live alone. I would rather be with you, though you are dark and grubby, than alone again.'

They spent many years together, and had lots of children, all dark-skinned and dark-haired. These children eventually settled all over the Altai, and their descendants are living there still.

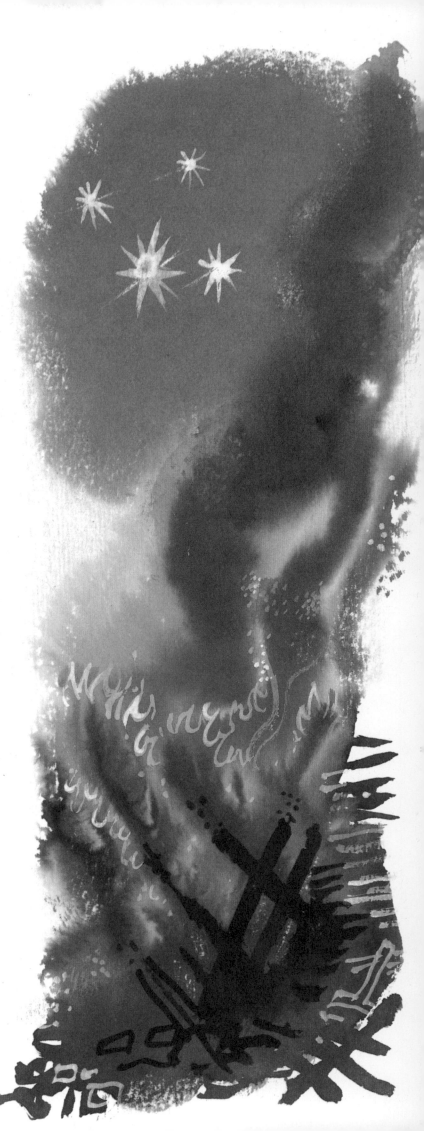

Renaud and the Faithful Bayard

The powerful king of France, Charles the Great, once invited many knights and noblemen, who had distinguished themselves in battle, to spend Easter with him at his court in Paris. Everyone came, including Roland, the king's brave nephew and Olivier, his wise loyal companion. The Danish knight Ogier was there too, and so was Bishop Turpin, who was as good a warrior as he was a servant of the Lord. Boves of Egremont was the only man missing.

King Charles, greatly displeased, was angry not only with the rebellious lord, but also with his four sons, Renaud, Alard, Guiscard and Richard. This was unjust, for they were not responsible for their father's absence, and had come to Paris to be presented with knight's golden spurs. But instead of that, they were driven out in shame, barely saving their lives by fleeing on Bayard, Renaud's stallion.

The four brothers hid in Arden Forest, where for seven long years they lived like wild beasts, tasting hunger and thirst, in bitter cold and rain. At the beginning of the eighth year, Renaud said, 'Now that so much time has elapsed, perhaps the king's anger has gone. Let us go to the south and build a strong castle far away from other people. Maybe the king will let us live there in peace.'

His brothers agreed, and all four mounted faithful Bayard and set off. On their journey southwards they were joined by their cousin Malgis, who was something of a magician. In a desolate part of the south they built their castle and named it Montauban, which means the Mountain of Foreigners. But Egremont's sons were not destined to live there in peace for long. When the king learned where they had settled, he led a huge army in order to seize the castle and punish the brothers.

Montauban, however, was well fortified and the brothers were excellent warriors. Furthermore, cousin Malgis used his magic to trick and trouble their attackers. He even managed to steal into the king's tent and drug him with magic wine, then carry him off to the castle.

When the king awoke and realized where he was, he went frantic. His anger was aimed mainly at Malgis, because he had dared to trick and shame him. 'I shall never make peace with you till you give me Malgis!' he stormed, when Renaud demanded pardon for all five in exchange for the king's freedom.

'What?' Richard, the youngest, cried indignantly. 'You, our prisoner, dare threaten us? We have never been disloyal to you, by word or deed. Why do you persecute us so?'

'Silence, brother!' Renaud cried and continued, turning to the king, 'We shall neither give you Malgis, nor harm you. You are free to leave. Let all France see how unjust you are, let her see that it is not us who seek quarrels and fights.' The king did not reply, but hastened back to his camp. And the siege of the castle continued.

The defenders faced great hardships. There was not a grain of corn left in Montauban and all the animals had been slain and eaten. Only Bayard remained, for no one could bring themselves to harm Renaud's faithful horse. Out of desperation, they bled him and drank his blood and so quenched the worst pangs of hunger.

It was then that an old man, who tended the castle gardens, came to Renaud, and said, 'My lord, forgive an old man's bad memory! Only today I remembered that when we were building this castle, we dug out a long underground passage leading from the cellar to a distant wood. Through this we can all escape!'

Renaud was delighted to hear this and hurriedly left with his brothers, loyal Bayard, Malgis and the other defenders. When the king at last broke into the castle, he found only deserted barricades and towers.

The brothers, in the meantime, travelled to distant Dortmund, where the lord of the castle made them most welcome and gladly agreed never to betray them to the king.

King Charles, however, soon discovered the whereabouts of Renaud and his party, and set out in pursuit. On this occasion, even his most faithful knights opposed him. 'Be just, my king! The whole of France condemns your conduct. Make peace with Renaud and his brothers. They have done you no wrong and if it were not for their goodness, you would be dead.'

Roland, the king's nephew and the bravest hero of all France, went as far as to say, 'If you do not end the fight, I shall leave your service and join Renaud.'

When Olivier, Ogier, even bishop Turpin spoke in the same manner, the king gave in. 'Very well, I shall seek reconciliation, but only on the condition that Renaud and Malgis leave France and give me the mount Bayard.'

Renaud agreed to his terms. Alard, Guiscard and Richard returned to Montauban, whilst he left France with Malgis, unhappy at having to part from Bayard.

The king was camped by the River Mosel when Bayard was delivered. Everyone admired the magnificent stallion, but Charles ordered his men to tie a mill wheel to the horse's neck and to throw him in the river. Yet the stallion did not drown. He broke the mill wheel with his hooves, swam to the opposite shore and galloped to Arden forest.

The story goes that there he lived for many years, free as a bird, and that when Renaud heard, he left the distant foreign land and joined Bayard. They lived together in the Arden Forest in joy and contentment, their hearts at peace.

Brave Roland

King Charles the Great reigned for many glorious years over France and won many battles against the Spanish Saracens. Much of Spain was already his, when he was halted by Marsil, the ruler of the town of Zaragoza. Marsil's forces repelled every attack, and eventually made Charles accept Marsil's request for truce and his promise of obedience. The French king sent his advisor Ganelon to negotiate, and agreed to withdraw from Zaragoza.

But Marsil was cunning and Ganelon thirsty for wealth. The two struck a bargain. For the price of seven hundred camels laden with gold and silver, the traitor Ganelon advised Charles to leave his best warriors to guard the Pyrenees gorge, whilst the rest of the French army began their retreat. He had arranged with Marsil that the Saracens would attack the rearguard and kill them to the last man. Without his ablest and most loyal knights, the king could hardly dare embark in further battles.

Charles took Ganelon's advice and left twenty thousand warriors headed by Roland, his friend Olivier and bishop Turpin, to protect the gorge. Everything went according to the treacherous plan: a large Saracen army approached, ready to attack. The Frenchmen were greatly outnumbered, for Emperor Baligant had come to Marsil's aid with forces from Jericho, Africa, Turkey, Persia and the lands of the Huns. Some of his men were covered in bristles like pigs, their neckless heads perched right between their shoulders; others had such thick skins that they had no need of a helmet or armour; some men were so strong that with bare hands they could break a lance, smash a shield and crush an enemy skull.

'Sound your horn Oliphant,' Olivier urged Roland. 'The king will hear its call and will hasten at once to our aid.'

But Roland replied, 'The king has left us here with twenty thousand men, and there is not a coward among us. We shall fight alone.'

Olivier implored Roland once more, 'There are too many of them. Blow your horn Oliphant!'

Yet Roland refused once more, then finally refused for a third time. A terrible battle broke out in Roncesvales Pass. The Frenchmen fought bravely. Roland, Olivier and Turpin struck thousands of blows, bringing down enemy after enemy. But what use was their bravery when they were so greatly outnumbered? For every adversary who fell, a dozen came forward, for every ten men who took to their heels, a hundred rushed in from the reserves. Only then Roland decided to blow the horn Oliphant.

'It is too late,' Olivier sighed. 'When I asked you to blow it, there was still time. The king could have been here by now and we would not have lost our lives so needlessly.'

Bishop Turpin cried, 'Sir Roland and you, Sir Olivier, stop your quarrel! Let Roland sound his horn! The king cannot help us now, but he will at least avenge our death and bury our bodies with due honours.' So in the end Roland did sound his horn.

King Charles heard Oliphant's voice in the distant mountains, and realized at once that his rearguard had been ambushed, and that all this was the doing of the treacherous Ganelon. Immediately he turned his forces round and hastened back through the Pyrenees. He rode at the head of his troops, his long flowing beard like a flying banner. The riders behind him were unable to stop the flow of their tears, as they mourned the loss of their friends and cursed the enemy.

When the king and his men reached Roncesvales, the battle was over. The green grass was strewn with the bodies of all the twenty thousand French warriors; they found Olivier, Turpin, then Roland, whose face was turned towards the enemy, so that everyone would know that he had not tried to escape. His sword Durandal and his horn Oliphant were hidden and protected by his body.

The Saracen army had suffered far heavier losses, and the soldiers who were left, were soon slaughtered by the enraged Charles and his men in a vicious, merciless battle. Marsil, the sly ruler of Zaragoza, was one of the first to fall. Emperor Baligant witnessed with horror the death of his son and watched his banner bearing the sign of the dragon gradually disappear. Vainly he tried to stop his warriors from fleeing and to make them face their raging enemies. King Charles pursued the Saracens all the way to Zaragoza, where he stormed the gates and took the city.

The French heroes of that bloody battle were buried with full honours and glory — Roland, Olivier, bishop Turpin and all the twenty thousand men. Their sacrifice had not been in vain after all, for the proud, impregnable city of Zaragoza had now fallen, and the power of the Saracens in Spain had been dealt a severe blow.

As for the traitor Ganelon, he did not escape just punishment. On a meadow beyond the city of Paris he was tied to four horses and torn to pieces as they pulled him apart.

Bertha with the Big Feet

When the French king Pipin decided to marry, his counsellors recommended several noble young ladies from various kingdoms. Yet the king just could not decide upon his bride. One day, a travelling minstrel told him of beautiful Bertha, daughter of the king of Hungary. She was said to be wise and kind, with only one minor defect to her perfection — a pair of very large feet.

'Feet are always hidden under skirts,' said the king. 'Let Bertha be brought to Paris!' Thirty horses laden with gold and silver and a dozen magnificently dressed messengers were sent to Hungary to entice the princess to come to France.

Beautiful Bertha consented to become the wife of the French king, but she was loathe to say goodbye to her home.

Her parents reassured her frankly, 'Why, you are going to sweet France and there is no other land as beautiful in the world. Go. We will not forget you!'

So Bertha left for France. During the journey, the procession visited the Duke of Mainz who was astonished at the sight of Bertha. He had

a daughter Aliste, who happened to be the image of Bertha, with the exception of her tiny feet.

The two young ladies soon became friends, and so Bertha suggested that Aliste should become her lady in waiting and should accompany her to France.

When at last they reached Paris, the Hungarian princess was so tired after the long journey, that she asked Aliste,

'Please, my dear friend, go in my place this evening to be presented to the king of France. It will not take long and no one will know. We are so alike.'

Aliste was glad to help and went to the royal reception dressed in Bertha's best gown. But she enjoyed being at the king's side so much, that she decided to take the place of her mistress permanently.

She then bribed two servants to tie Bertha up and to take her to a deep dark forest, where they were to kill her. But her beauty stirred pity in their hearts and they left her alive in a desolate, barren clearing.

The unfortunate girl wandered endlessly

through the dark forest, scratching her feet on the thorny undergrowth, sleeping on hard, bare ground, surviving on wild raspberries and strawberries.

Eventually she stumbled into a small clearing, where she saw a tiny cottage. It was the home of collier Simon, his wife and two daughters. Moved by her beauty and her plight, the kind collier took Bertha in.

She lived happily in the little cottage. The whole family was nice to her, and as Bertha was modest and good, she was loved and treated as one of the family.

Nine and a half years went by, without Bertha disclosing who she really was.

The queen of Hungary had not forgotten her daughter. She missed no opportunity to send messages to France, and grew most uneasy at the sparse news she had in return. Aliste, of course, was very cautious with her replies. When the queen invited Bertha home, Aliste made the excuse that she was ill and could not come.

Bertha's mother then said, 'I shall go to Paris myself to see Bertha.' The king warned her of the hardships of the journey, but she declared, 'Bertha endured it all, and so will I.'

As soon as Aliste heard the queen was coming, she took to her bed, pretending to be seriously ill. In this state the Hungarian queen found her, in her chamber with the heavy curtains drawn. The queen groped her way to the bed and embraced and caressed the young pretender. Suddenly she noticed that she had the feet of a child.

'You are not my daughter, you are not my Bertha!' she cried in horror, and ran to the king, to tell him the shattering news.

King Pipin was horrified. He summoned Aliste, who confessed everything. The two servants owned up too and offered to take the king to the clearing where years ago they had abandoned poor Bertha.

The king searched the whole forest, but there was no trace of Bertha. He was trying to come to terms with the thought that she must have perished, when he came upon the collier's cottage.

A lovely girl carrying a pail of water was passing by just then. On her feet she wore enormous clogs. Pipin called out, 'Tell me who you are! I am the king of France!'

The frightened Bertha replied, 'Don't harm me, please! I am Bertha, daughter of the king of Hungary, Pipin's bride.' 'I am Pipin!' the happy king cried, lifting Bertha into his saddle.

So everything had a happy ending. The king was merciful, and punished Aliste only by sending her in disgrace from Paris. The two servants were first given a sound hiding, then were handsomely rewarded for not killing Bertha, as they had been ordered to do.

Simon the collier, who still found it hard to believe that for ten long years he had sheltered the bride of the king of France, was knighted and received a coat of arms with a golden flower in a blue field.

The Hungarian queen laughed and cried in turn and rejoiced that she had not listened to her husband's warnings. Who knows how it would all have ended, if she had not gone to France.

'If you had not found my Bertha,' she said to Pipin, 'I swear I would have cut your head off with my own two hands.'

Soon another wedding was held — the wedding of King Pipin and the real Bertha. The royal pair lived for many long years in happiness and contentment, reigning justly and wisely over the French kingdom.

The Valiant Cid Campeador

Rodrigo of Vivar, son of the highly respected Diego Lainez, was raised at the court of the Spanish King Fernando. The king thought the world of the young knight and kept him constantly at his side. No wonder too, for Rodrigo had many virtues and was braver than any other man.

The Moors, who were always fighting the Spaniards in a bid to retake the land which Fernando had conquered, hated and cursed him.

On the rare occasions, when Rodrigo visited his father, he found it hard to leave and bid him goodbye, for he could see how his strength was ebbing away with age.

He always said in parting, 'If you ever need me, my dear father, just send for me and I shall return immediately. You can depend on me in any circumstance.'

The day came when the father needed his son's help. The proud, stubborn Count Lozano, a neighbour of Diego Lainez, had offended and humiliated the old man. It was easy to be daring when he knew that Diego was too frail to face him in combat.

The unhappy nobleman sent a message to his

son. 'You are the only one who can avenge me and who can wipe out the shame which has smeared our family,' he wrote. 'You must bring honour back to our house!'

Rodrigo immediately hastened to Count Lozano. 'Do you think it is brave to insult an old man?' he exclaimed. 'I have come to wash that insult away with your blood!'

Count Lozano was an experienced soldier and sneered at the young man's indignation. 'Go away, little boy!' he cried. 'Or I'll have you whipped like a naughty child!'

Rodrigo was unafraid and challenged Lozano to a duel. The count accepted, thinking his would be an easy victory and rode out proudly and daringly. But it was Rodrigo who dealt the mortal blow. The count fell and the young avenger left victorious.

After this Rodrigo remained with his father for some time and was a great comfort to the old man. All the knights in the neighbourhood greatly respected him, and all the noble maidens admired his handsomeness and bravery; Jimena, Count Lozano's lovely daughter liked him most of all.

It happened that King Fernando came to the nearby town of Burgos and the nobility from all around gathered to pay him homage. Jimena was there too. She stepped before the king and said,

'Our lord and king, my mother and I are living in great shame. Knight Rodrigo of Vivar, who slew my father, day after day rides past our castle, with his falcon and his hawk. He never fails to look into my eyes, and his eyes haunt me day and night. If you are a just king, put an end to my suffering. But if you are unjust, then you are not worthy of wearing gold spurs, in fact not worthy even of eating bread!'

The king, startled by such a daring speech, was at a loss how to answer the lovely daughter

of the deceased count. He had no wish or intention of punishing Rodrigo, for he had killed the count in an honourable duel and had distinguished himself in wars against the Moors. Yet he did not wish to refuse the lovely Jimena. So he explained his predicament to her.

'If things are so difficult,' the count's daughter suggested, 'then give me Rodrigo for a husband. He has killed my father and therefore brought me much unhappiness. Let him now, as a husband, make me happy.'

When Rodrigo presented himself to the king, he was greeted with a smile and friendly words. 'You are most welcome, Rodrigo of Vivar! I have some wonderful news for you. The noble Jimena has forgiven you for killing her father, since justice was on your side. But to make amends for the grief you caused her, I now ask you to marry her. As proof of my high esteem, I shall give you rich estates as a wedding gift.'

The king's words made Rodrigo very happy, for he had admired Jimena for quite some time, but had never dared to dream she would take for a husband a man who had killed her father, however justly.

'I shall abide by your wishes as always, my lord,' he replied. 'I shall be honoured to take Jimena for my wife.'

Before long the great wedding of gallant knight Rodrigo and Jimena, the beautiful daughter of Count Lozano took place. The king was there to lead her to the altar.

The reign of King Fernando was short, for destiny did not grant him long life. King Sancho was next to rule, but was soon succeeded by King Alfonso. Rodrigo served each one faithfully and gallantly, showing great courage in wars with the Moors. This earned him such respect that the Moors gave him the name of Cid, which means a lord, whilst among the Spaniards he was known as Campeador, which means a warrior.

Jimena loved her husband dearly and lovingly cared for their two daughters, Elvira and Sol who were born later.

Their happiness did not last long. Cid Campeador had been sent to collect taxes from the defeated Moorish kings and was accused by envious courtiers that he had kept part of the money for himself. It was wicked slander, yet the king believed the words of the jealous accusers, flew into terrible anger and expelled Cid from the land, giving him nine days only to leave the kingdom of Castile.

Cid did not argue, but obeyed. He called together his relatives and vassals, and said, 'I shall leave Castile as the king wishes. Those of you who want to come with me, the Lord will repay for their loyalty; those who decide to stay, will always remain my friends.'

His cousin Alvar Fanez then replied in the name of them all. 'We'll go with you, Cid, and as long as we live, we shall help you and never leave you.'

His heart full of gratitude, Cid thanked them all. They left without further delay, leaving behind in Vivar an empty house, with open doors and unlocked gates.

Heavy hearted, Cid and his companions travelled further and further from home. When they entered Burgos, people ran out of their houses and leaned out of windows to show their admiration and support. Yet there was not one person who would have dared to offer so much as

a slice of bread, or a glass of water to Cid and his men; so afraid they were of the king's anger.

Sad and hungry, Cid and his retinue pitched camp after crossing a bridge. Suddenly there was a clatter of wheels and a cart appeared, being driven from the direction of the city. They all wondered who it was that dared to come to them.

Their visitor was none other than Martin Antolinez, a noble knight from Burgos. Turning to Cid, he said, 'Campeador! I bring bread, meat and wine for you all. You will not suffer hunger and thirst. I shall, of course, be reported to the king for having helped you, and so I cannot remain in Burgos. I shall leave with you and follow wherever you go and other fair minded men of Burgos will come with me.'

Cid was touched by the words of the noble Martin Antolinez, who then continued, 'Campeador! Before you leave your homeland, you will have many followers and you will need a great deal of money to feed them. You have been accused of keeping Moorish money belonging to the king. Money-lenders will therefore believe you have gold, and will be only too pleased to lend you money. Take it and repay them with the rich booty you are sure to take during your battles with the Moors, and no one will have been cheated. I know two rich men in Burgos, Raquel and Vidas, who will be very happy to lend you what you need.'

'I shall do as you suggest!' Cid agreed. He took two chests covered in red leather and equipped with gilded locks, and filled them with sand to make them heavy. Then he waited for the money-lenders.

At midnight Martin Antolinez appeared with Raquel and Vidas, who, quite willingly, lent Cid six hundred marks for the period of one year. As a guarantee that the money would be returned, they took the chests, which they thought were full of gold.

When the sun appeared in the morning sky, a further hundred riders galloped into Cid's camp. They came from Burgos, to join him in his expedition to the land of the Moors. On their way they called at the San Pedro monastery, where Cid's wife Jimena was staying with their two daughters. The abbot welcomed his guests and assured Cid that his family could rely on the hospitality of the monastery for as long as it was necessary.

Jimena then said, her eyes welling with tears, 'Campeador, dear Campeador, we must bid each other farewell, but I trust not for too long. Fight bravely, as you have always done, and you will see that the king will forgive the crime you have not even committed.'

When all the goodbyes had been said, Cid rode out of Castile at the head of his men. Other warriors joined them along the way, and so, though only he had been sent into exile, when he finally left his homeland, he was accompanied by three hundred men. His campaign against the Moors lasted a whole year. He gained large territories for King Alfonso and Spain, going from victory to victory. Then came his most famous conquest of the proud city of Valencia.

That had been a particularly hard battle, for Valencia was well fortified and the Moors had no intention of surrendering such an important city. Cid was aware that he could not take it by direct attack, so he concentrated first on nearby villages and towns, till Valencia was completely surrounded. Though its walls were strong and its defenders prepared to fight till death, Valencia, alone in the middle of Spanish territory, could not survive.

After the fall of Valencia, Cid Campeador called his cousin Alvar Fanez and said, 'I think the time is ripe for you to return to Castile. Stop in Burgos and repay Raquel and Vidas the six hundred marks, and add a further hundred as interest. But your main task is to present yourself to the king, kiss his hand in my name and beg him to permit my wife Jimena and my daughters to come and join me here in Valencia. If he gives his consent, as surely he will, ride to the San Pedro monastery. Give the abbot five hundred marks for looking after my family, and bring Jimena and my little daughters to me. Take from my booty two thousand marks to cover your journey and my debts. And select one hundred best mounts. These horses will be my gift to the king.'

Alvar Fanez left for Castile without delay. The magnificent procession stirred interest everywhere, so the king heard about it long before it arrived in Carrion, where he happened to be. King Alfonso, curious what tidings Alvar Fanez was bringing, was delighted when Cid's cousin fell to his knees, kissed his hands and cried, 'Have mercy, our lord and king! Cid Campeador kisses your hands, for he is a loyal vassal of yours. He sends you a hundred horses as a gift, begging you to accept these and to allow his wife Jimena and his two daughters to leave the San Pedro monastery and to join him in Valencia.'

The king beckoned Alvar Fanez to rise and said 'My heart rejoices from Campeador's victo-

ries. I accept his gift and thank him. Dona Jimena can leave with her daughters any time. I shall personally ensure they have all they need and will give them protection on their journey to Valencia.'

The king then turned to his courtiers and said, 'Hear me, all of you! I do not wish that Cid and his followers should suffer any losses for they have served our kingdom most loyally and gallantly. Let all their properties be returned to them and let them know that they have nothing to fear from me. Moreover, if any of you wish to leave this country to serve Cid, you have my permission.'

Diego and Fernando, two young counts of Carrion, volunteered to go. They were not thinking of serving Cid, but of laying their hands on some of his immense wealth. They decided they would court his two daughters, so that the riches would come to them by inheritance. They had no desire to take part in dangerous battles with the Moors, and preferred to remain at the king's court for the time being, promising they would join Cid at a later date.

Alvar Fanez, pleased with his reception at the king's court, rode on to Burgos, to repay the money-lenders, Raquel and Vilas. They thanked him for the generous interest Cid paid, and when Alvar Fanez opened the chests filled with sand, they laughed and said, 'What better guarantee could anyone have than Cid's word! We would have lent him the money on the strength of it alone.'

Cid's messenger rode on to the San Pedro monastery. When Dona Jimena learned that the

king had agreed to let her follow her husband, her joy had no bounds.

Alvar Fanez then gave the five hundred marks to the abbot and left with Dona Jimena and her daughters for Valencia. Their party was constantly growing. New riders kept on appearing, their banners tied to their lances, eager to join Cid's band of men.

When Cid heard that Alvar Fanez and his family were approaching Valencia, he mounted his magnificent horse Babiec, whom he had recently gained from the king of Seville, and rode out to meet them. He was overwhelmed at seeing such a large, imposing party of supporters and overjoyed to greet his beloved wife and daughters.

'Some time ago I fled from my country, as a penniless refugee,' Cid remarked. 'Now we are united again, I am rich and I have my king's pardon. So much has changed in just one year!' After their reunion, life went on happily, though Dona Jimena's joy was marred by the constant battles with the Moors. They repeatedly attempted to retake the wealthy city of Valencia, but their efforts were futile. Cid managed to ward off all the attacks, his most famous victory being the battle against King Yusuf and his army of fifty thousand men.

After this triumph, Cid sent a new deputation to his king, led by Alvar Fanez as before. This time the king was given two hundred magnificent mounts, and was asked to receive Cid personally.

'I shall be happy to meet Cid,' the king replied. 'I have a double reason for wishing to see

him. Diego and Fernando, two young counts of Carrion, who during your last visit expressed their wish to be Cid's warriors, are eager to wed his daughters. Give Cid this message, and tell him to come three weeks from now to the bank of the river Tajo, which will be our meeting place.'

Cid Campeador arrived at the river Tajo with fifteen fine knights, exactly three weeks later. The king was already there. Cid dismounted and threw himself at his sovereign's feet. But the king made him rise, kissed him on his lips and said, 'Let us forget, Campeador, all the bad things which were between us. You have proved yourself a loyal vassal and have proved that the slanderous accusations against you were unjust.'

The counts of Carrion stepped forward then, and the king continued, 'I ask you, Cid Campeador, to give your daughters in marriage to these two counts. This is their wish and mine too, for I would consider such unions honourable and suitable. I shall give three hundred marks in silver as my contribution for the wedding. So I beg you to accept Diego and Fernando as your own sons.'

To this Cid replied, 'I did not intend my daughters to marry just yet, for they are still very young. But the counts of Carrion are of noble birth and are imposing suitors even for daughters of nobler families than mine. So, my lord and king, marry them to whomever you wish. I shall not object to your choice.'

So it came to pass that Diego and Fernando became the husbands of Elvira and Sol, and the sons in-law of Cid Campeador and Dona Jimena.

After two whole years of living in Valencia, the counts of Carrion had still never fought in any battles with the Moors. They always had some plausible excuse to avoid the fight. Cid was unhappy about his sons-in-law aloofness, but he kept silent, not wishing for them to be suspected of cowardice.

Then one day, after many years, the Moors marched in great strength against Valencia, led by King Bucar, who sent a messenger to Cid demanding that he abandon the city. Cid ignored the demand and prepared for battle. This time Diego and Fernando could not stand aside and had to take part.

When Cid and his warriors rode out of the city gates, Fernando turned on a valiant Moor Aladraph, but the moment Aladraph raised his sword, the terrified young count took to his heels. Pedro Bermudez rushed to the scene and killed Aladraph.

Then he said, 'Say it was you who killed Aladraph. I shall confirm it.'

A vicious battle followed, in which Cid's enemies were completely crushed, with Cid personally killing King Bucar in a duel. They returned to Valencia carrying rich spoils.

Cid, happy with the victory, was happier still because his sons-in-law had taken part in the battle and that Fernando in fact had killed the gallant Aladraph.

The counts of Carrion could see, however, that no one else believed in their bravery. Though Pedro Bermudez never breathed a word that it was he who had slain Aladraph, they could feel everyone looking with doubt and suspicion on Fernando's heroic act.

One day at noon, when Cid and his sons-in-law were taking a nap on a seat in the park, a lion escaped from its cage and crept towards them. The counts of Carrion were scared to death.

Fernando crawled under the seat and Diego pelted away like a scared rabbit, and climbed into the crown of a high apple tree. But Cid stayed calm and gripped the lion by its mane and led it unresisting back to its cage. By then a crowd of people had gathered, and they roared with laughter when Fernando was dragged from under the garden seat and Diego was helped down the apple tree.

The humiliated counts of Carrion now could see that life in Valencia would not be easy and that fortune would not fall into their lap, so they waited for the chance to return home.

Soon afterwards Diego and Fernando came to Cid and Jimena and said, 'Give us your permission to take our wives for a short visit to Carrion. We should like to show them our estates and make them a gift of a village or two.'

'If this is your wish, dear sons-in-law, go by all means,' Cid replied.

Cid then assembled a magnificent retinue for his daughters and their husbands, led by Felix Munoz, the son of his loyal cousin Alvar Fanez. They took with them many valuable gifts, also

horses and mules and three thousand marks in silver.

'Let all Spain see the riches Cid sends with his children,' he said in parting.

That first night they camped in an ancient oak forest, and in the morning, when everyone was ready to continue, Diego and Fernando sent the rest ahead, and stayed behind with their wives.

The minute the others had disappeared from sight, they pounced on Elvira and Sol, stripping them to their underclothes and tying them to massive oak trees. Then they whipped their unfortunate wives with reins, until they lost consciousness.

'No villages shall be yours!' they cried. 'Here you will remain, to be torn apart by wild beasts!'

With that Diego and Fernando leapt into their saddles and rode like the wind to catch up with their companions.

Felix Munoz was surprised to see that his cousins were not with their husbands. He kept his silence, but slipped away and turned back towards the oak forest.

Felix Munoz searched and searched, till he found Elvira and Sol, unconscious and bleeding, tied to the trees. Aghast at the sight, he hurriedly untied them and carried them to safety on his strong horse.

When Cid learned of the terrible way the counts of Carrion had dealt with his daughters, he was filled with sorrow and anger. At once he sent messengers to King Alfonso to inform him of what had happened, and to deliver his personal message. 'You yourself, my king, had married my daughters to the counts of Carrion. Therefore it is not only I, but you also who has been dishonoured and shamed.'

The king, who had welcomed the messengers warmly, was enraged at such tidings, and said, 'Yes, it was I who favoured the marriage and my heart now is full of sadness and anger. Tell Cid to bring his knights to Toledo three weeks from today. There we shall hold court and sit in judgement over the two treacherous counts of Carrion.'

Crowds of onlookers gathered in Toledo for the trial of Diego and Fernando. Cid was there with his knights, and then the counts of Carrion were brought in, pale with fear, yet arrogant and proud. Cid accused his sons-in-law of two crimes. He demanded that they return the three thousand marks and all the gifts which he had given to his daughters. And he demanded just punishment for the dishonour brought on Elvira and Sol.

The spokesman for the counts refused to accept Cid's charges. The money had been spent and the sons-in-law were loathe to return the valuable gifts. As for the shame brought on Cid's daughters the spokesman argued that the counts of Carrion were of nobler birth than they. 'These fine gentlemen acted within their rights, when they got rid of their wives, for they were not worthy of husbands of such noble birth and blood,' he concluded.

Everyone, including the king, was astonished at such an arrogant speech.

Pedro Bermudez jumped to his feet and cried, 'I know your nobility and grandeur, Count Fernando and Count Diego! It is the nobility of cowards and the grandeur of liars. Do you remember how bravely you conducted yourselves in the battle with King Bucar? You, Fernando, fled before the Moor Aladraph like a frightened dog, and then boasted that you had killed him in

combat. And when a lion escaped from its cage, you hid under the seat, whilst your terrified brother climbed up the apple tree.'

These just words roared like thunder and the counts trembled with rage and shame.

Then something unexpected happened. Two knights stepped before King Alfonso and said, 'We are the messengers of the king of Navarre and the king of Aragon. Our sovereigns beg you to permit them to marry Cid Campeador's daughters. They wish Dona Sol and Dona Elvira to be their wives and queens of their kingdoms.'

Everyone gasped, but Cid rose and cried, 'Justice has won over the wrong which had been committed. I ask you, my lord, to let my daughters marry the two kings. Then what has happened, but should not have happened, will be rectified.'

The king gladly agreed and the messengers departed, well satisfied.

Alfonso then said. 'Cid Campeador's accusations are just. I order the counts of Carrion to return immediately everything that Cid demands. As for the dishonour they brought on his beautiful daughters, Sol and Elvira, for that they must answer in a duel.'

The counts did not want to fight, but they had no choice. Pedro Bermudez and Martin Antolinez were their opponents. The duel was soon over. Cid's knights, who had distinguished themselves in so many battles with the Moors, made short work of the two counts, who soon were pleading for mercy, anxious to save their skins.

Cid Campeador lived for a long time. He was highly respected and much loved by all the Spaniards, and highly respected but much feared by all the Moors. His fame still lives on today.

The Mighty Maui

Four Gods lived in Hawaiki, the land of plenty, which lies hidden beneath the human world. They were Ra, the god of the sun, Hine, the goddess of darkness and death, Mahuika, the goddess of fire and Ru, the god of water.

Ru often wandered about the human world, but it was very low, and people had to bend right over to avoid banging their heads against the heavens. Ru therefore cut down trunks of trees and with their support raised the heavens, by placing the trunks at each end of the world and in the centre. Now men could stand erect, hunt birds and fishes and build dwellings.

Makea Tutara and Taranga were husband and wife living in Hawaiki. They had four sons, but they dwelt in the human world above. By the time Maui, their fifth son, was born, the others were grown men. Maui was tiny and frail, more dead than alive. His mother wept and in her grief she cut off a plait of her hair. In this she wrapped her son and put him down on the sea shore, whilst she counted the waves to find out whether he was destined to live, or to die. Before she had finished counting, she turned round to look at the baby and saw that he was no longer there. The sea had carried him away.

Yet Maui did not drown. Seen by mighty Ru, the god of water, he was taken in his arms to his home and laid in the net hanging over the fireplace. Maui grew in body and strength, and the god of water taught him everything a man needed to know, and much of what only gods know.

When Maui grew older, he decided to venture into the human world, to seek out his parents and brothers. 'Go!' said Ru, 'you belong among people.'

Maui entered the human world, and soon found his native village. It seemed all the inhabitants were preparing to dance. Maui recognized his brothers and mother, who was about to lead her sons in the dance. Maui attached himself to his brothers and waited.

Taranga looked them over and said, 'You are all present, Maui-taha, Maui-roto, Maui-pae, Maui-waha. But who is the fifth one?' and she pointed at the small Maui.

'I too am your son, Maui.'

Taranga grew angry. 'Don't try to teach a mother to know her own children!'

'Then I must have only dreamed that I was your son, Taranga,' Maui replied. 'Then I must have only dreamed that you wrapped me in your hair and laid me on the sea shore, that the waves carried me away and that I was then rescued by mighty Ru, the god of water.'

'You are my son, you are Maui!' Taranga exclaimed, embracing him. 'You are Maui from the holy plait of Taranga's hair, Maui-tiki-tiki-a-Taranga! From now on you will live with us and share my bed.'

The brothers were upset that Maui the youngest was so favoured, but they dared not oppose their mother.

As Maui was raised by the god Ru, he knew far more than normal people. He was particularly good at turning himself into various birds. But two things worried him. Firstly, he had still not met his father, and secondly, the food eaten by people was no good. For fire was unknown to the world, but Maui knew it was fire which gave food good taste and smell. He questioned his brothers about these matters, but they merely shrugged their shoulders.

Maui noticed that early each day, before the break of dawn, his mother went away, to return in the evening carrying a woven basket, from which she ate, sitting apart from everyone else. Maui secretly tasted some of the food in the basket, and realized straight away that it had been cooked on a fire. 'Mother meets my father somewhere, and together they cook good food,' Maui concluded, and watched her carefully from then on.

One morning he managed to wake before his mother and watched her rise silently, then hurry to the nearby thicket, where she disappeared. Maui hastily followed and in the bushes found a deep hole in the ground. He turned quickly into a red-chested pigeon and dived down the gap till he came into Hawaiki.

In this guise Maui flew about, till he found his mother sitting under a tree with a stranger. 'That must be my father,' Maui decided. He settled on a branch and chirped loudly.

The man looked round and remarked, seeing the bird, 'That pigeon has red feathers and red eyes. It does not come from here, for we, the people of Hawaiki, do not know red colour!'

The pigeon jumped to the ground, changed back into Maui, and cried, 'I am Maui-tiki-tiki-a-Taranga! I am your son.' 'I am your father Makea-Tutara,' said the man, embracing Maui. 'You will be the pride of our clan! You will spread into two countries: the land of people above, and the land of Hawaiki below. You alone will be able to bring fire to men, you alone will be able to prolong day for men, you alone will be able to give men a new land, you alone will be

able to destroy Hine, the goddess of night, so that she no longer can threaten men with death.'

He led his son to a running brook, where he bathed him from head to foot, pronouncing important magic formulae to make him capable of such deeds. But he left out one magic word, which rolled away like a pebble. Without it, the magic formula was useless.

Sometimes Maui lived with his parents, sometimes with his brothers on earth. He prospered. He ate boiled and roasted food, but he wondered how to bring such good food to people.

'That can easily be done,' Taranga said. 'Take a burning log to the world above. The fire must, of course, be well tended, so it does not die out. If it did die, no one could rekindle it except mighty Mahuika, the goddess of fire.'

'I don't want the fire which must be looked after,' Maui objected. 'I want to teach men to light a fire, like Mahuika does.'

Once, when everyone was asleep, Maui poured water on the fires and stamped out the cinders. The next morning everyone was in tears.

'Why doesn't someone go to Mahuika for more fire?' Maui asked.

No one felt like going, so Maui set out. After a long journey, he came to a high mountain, from which constant smoke escaped. Mahuika lived here in a hut. The brave Maui stepped inside and saw Mahuika, sitting amid her fires, cooking various dishes.

'Old woman,' he said, 'give me fire.' Mahuika asked, 'Who are you?'

'I am Maui, Maui-tiki-tiki-a-Taranga, the son of Makea-Tutara and Taranga. The fires in Hawaiki have all gone out and I have come to ask you for new fire.'

Mahuika nodded and raised her finger. A flame leapt out from under her nail and jumped on to Maui's hand and sat there. Maui then left. But when he came to a brook, he threw the flame into the water and returned to Mahuika for more fire.

Mahuika gave him the flame from under the nail of her second finger, then the third, and the fourth, till there were no flames left under her finger nails, nor her toe nails. They had all died in the brook.

'What will the old woman do now, when there is no more fire left?' Maui asked.

Mahuika frowned, realizing that Maui had tricked her and made her look foolish.

'I shall give you nothing else,' she said.

'Then teach me, old woman, to kindle fire,' Maui begged.

'That is a great secret and you have to fight me for it,' Mahuika said. She was full of strength and sure she would overpower him.

'Very well, we shall fight,' the boy agreed.

Mahuika wrapped a belt round her waist, which she always wore in battle. She seized Maui and threw him ever so high, as far as where coconut palms have their crowns. Maui flew upwards like a pebble, but when he began to fall to the ground, he turned into a pigeon and landed slowly and gently. Mahuika threw him higher still, above the crowns of the coconut palms, but Maui came down as a cormorant. The third time she tried, Mahuika could not throw the boy. She was scarlet in the face, breathing heavily, her strength gone.

Then Maui tossed Mahuika far above the crowns of the palms, but instead of letting her fall to the ground, he caught her and threw her upwards again. When he had done this the third time, Mahuika begged him not to do it again. 'I shall keep on throwing you, until you tell me the secret of how to light a fire,' Maui insisted.

'Very well, I shall reveal this secret,' the goddess agreed and he let ler down. Mahuika then led him to a corner with two piles: one of tinders, made from coconut beards, one of wood splinters from the bark of a banana tree. Mahuika took one of the splinters, passed another to Maui to hold, then placed one upon the other, adding the tinders, chanting at the same time, 'Give me fire, make the flames leap higher and higher, banana tree! Fire right now I want to see! How I will thank you, banana tree!'

Once these magic words were spoken, a spark flew on to the tinder and lit the fire.

Maui thanked the goddess and turned for home, happy that he was bringing the secret of fire from gods to men.

With fire, the world prospered. The people were able to cook good food, make tools and pans, use fire to burn down bracken so new fields could be ploughed, and their harvest could be increased many times.

But the days were too short. Ra, the god of the sun, always sped across the sky, then disappeared in his cave down in Hawaiki.

'It is impossible to do a good day's work in such a short time,' Maui would sigh, wondering how he could force the god of the sun to shine longer in the sky.

Maui went to see his brothers and said, 'Come, let us make a strong rope! When Ra, the god of the sun, climbs out of his cave, we shall bind him and force him to walk more slowly across the sky. Then we shall have a longer day.'

The brothers' mouths gaped in astonishment, and as their heads were as hollow as coconuts, they said, 'That would be foolish. Ra is all fire, he would burn through the rope.'

'I shall make the rope from green flax, which cannot be destroyed by fire,' Maui explained, and set to work.

The brothers looked on suspiciously. They did not wish to anger the god of the sun, but they feared Maui, and in the end they accompanied him to Ra's cave.

It was still dark when they got there. Maui made a loop with the rope, and waited by the mouth of the cave for Ra to come out. At last he emerged, shaking his golden locks till sparks and fiery flashes of lightning flew around him. Maui threw the loop over his head and shouted, 'Now!' His brothers pulled the rope tight and

god Ra was caught. He fought hard, trying to tear the rope, to burn it with his heat, but it was no use. In the end he begged, 'Let me go! Why are you doing this?' Maui replied, 'We have a good reason for trapping you, mighty god! We want to stop you from running so fast across the sky and hiding for so long in your cave. You don't shine long enough. The day is short and the night is long. We need a long day and a short night.'

'I'll stay out longer,' Ra agreed, somewhat unwillingly. 'Now let me go!' But Maui was clever. He let him go of the rope, but left the legs of the god of the sun bound together. Ever since then, Ra has to walk slowly across the sky and the day has lengthened.

'Thank you, Maui, for our long day,' people cried and his fame spread to heaven itself.

The more people prospered on earth, the more they grew in numbers till there was not enough space for them all. 'I shall have to provide another land,' Maui decided and wondered how to set about it.

He spent all days sitting in the shade of the palms, doing nothing but chewing leaves and talking with his own head. As he had as many ideas as there are potatoes in a potato field, he soon had the answer. He called on his brothers and said, 'Take me fishing!' The brothers did not feel like going, but they agreed to take him.

When they had rowed their boat out to sea, the brothers prepared to cast their lines. 'Row further out,' Maui advised. 'You'll find bigger fish there.' This proved true. When the brothers rowed further still and cast their lines, they caught so many fishes, that the boat could hardly hold them. 'Now it is my turn,' Maui said and pulled out an enormous rod with a line as thick as an arm. A coconut wrapped in laurel leaves was used for bait. This he threw into the deep.

Down fell the coconut to the bottom of the sea, where it was swallowed by a huge whale. When Maui felt that he had a bite, he tugged hard, and held on with all his might. The boat was tipping over dangerously, the brothers were moaning they would all be drowned, but Maui pulled and pulled, till a huge whale rose to the surface. It was so big, in fact, that human eyes were too short to see all of it.

When the whale lay lifeless on the sea, the brothers stepped on to it, greedily eyeing the enormous body. 'Don't touch it yet!' Maui warned them. 'First we must make a sacrifice to Ru, the god of water, and ask him to bless this fish.'

Maui walked along the whale's back out of sight, to give the offering to the god. But his impatient brothers, whose eyes only led to their mouths, did not wait till this was done, but started cutting the flesh of the fish. Suddenly the giant head rose, the tail beating the water, the fins whipping the surface. The huge mouth opened as if to complain that the brothers dared to touch it before the sacrifice was made. With one jerk the fish arched its back, which wrinkled deeply, and so it remained. This is why this fish today is all mountains and valleys, without any plains, as it had been to begin with.

So a new island had been created for men to live on. White people call it New Zealand.

Nguranguran, the Son of a Crocodile

Long ago the Fangs lived by a great river. It was so big and wide that no one could see from one bank to the other.

A gigantic crocodile lived in this river. He was the chief of all crocodiles. Ombur was his name. His head was as big as a Fang hut, his eyes as large as a pair of goats, and his teeth could squash a couple of men at once as if they were soft bananas. His skin was awfully hard, like iron, and every spear just bounced off it. He was indeed a fearsome beast.

In those days Ngan Esa was the chieftain of the Fangs. One day, when he strolled from the village to the river bank, the gigantic crocodile appeared and said, 'Listen carefully!'

'I am listening,' Ngan Esa replied.

'I am aware that men are much tastier than fish. I want you therefore to bring a man to this spot every single day, so I can have him for my dinner. In addition, I want a woman once a week, and a maiden once a month. If you don't obey, I'll eat every person in the village. That is all.' With that the crocodile proudly swam away.

All the folk in the village were terribly upset to hear what the crocodile had said.

'Don't be afraid,' Ngan Esa told them. 'We still have some enemy prisoners here. We'll feed those to the crocodile.'

'And when he has eaten all the prisoners, what then?' the Fangs asked.

'That I don't know,' their chief sadly replied.

So each day the Fangs led an enemy prisoner to the bank of the great river, adding a woman

prisoner each week, and one young enemy maiden each month. And the fearsome Ombur, whose head was like a hut and eyes like a pair of goats, munched the prisoners to a pulp, as if they were ripe bananas.

The day came when there were no prisoners left. Ngan Esa then said, 'We must go away from here. We'll travel far into the mountains. Ombur won't find us there and we'll be happy and safe.'

The dry season had not yet ended, so it was a good time to travel, for all the paths were dry and the rivers low. The Fangs loaded up all their possessions, drove their animals together, and set out on their journey. They walked in silence, downcast and sad. Only their children were crying.

'Don't cry,' their mothers said. 'If we had remained, all of us would have been devoured by the crocodile.'

Ombur waited in vain for his next victim. He waited the whole day, then the second and the third. After this his patience ran out and he grew very cross. 'I'll go and eat up the whole Fang tribe,' he vowed, and turned towards the village.

He found it empty. There was not a living soul about and nothing to eat.

'What's happened here? Where is everyone?' the crocodile wondered, and then summoned the forest spirits to help,

'Forest spirits, you must appear,
the one who calls, you must hear,
the mighty chief of all crocodiles!
Answer my question now,
now I say! Don't dilly dally,
or I'll send lightning to slice the sky
and winds to tear trees from the ground.
Do you hear? Answer at once
in fear of my anger. Where are the ones
who lived here, but live here no longer?
Where have they ran to?
Where do they hide?
Forest spirits, answer me now!'

But the forest spirits were on the Fangs' side. So they did not appear, and they did not answer Ombur's questions. Ombur then turned to the water spirits, and cried,

'Water spirits, you must appear,
the one who calls, you must hear,
the mighty chief of all crocodiles!
Answer my question now,
now I say! Don't dilly dally,
or I'll send storms to wash everything away
and rain to drown all living things.
Do you hear? Answer at once
in fear of my anger. Where are the ones

who lived here, but live here no longer?
Where have they ran to?
Where do they hide?
Water spirits, answer me now!'

The water spirits favoured the crocodile, because he was a water creature. So they told him the Fangs had ran away far into the mountains. Ombur decided to go after them.

The Fangs, in the meantime, walked on and on.
Every evening, when they camped for the night, their chief summoned the forest spirits and asked,

Forest spirits, please appear,
the one who calls, you must hear,
the humble chief of the Fangs!
Answer my question, please,
and don't send lightning to slice the sky
or winds to tear trees from the ground!
Don't be angry with us, forest spirits,
but say if we, the unfortunate Fangs
should go on, or stay,
for we don't want to see the day
when we are slain by the fearsome crocodile.
Forest spirits, please answer me now!'

As the forest spirits were on the Fangs' side, they advised them to travel further and further.

So the weary Fangs plodded on and on. Their children grew into men, men grew old and old men died, yet the Fangs still walked on and on.
Till one day they began to complain. 'The forest spirits cannot like us. They are not honest with us. Ngan Esa, why don't you ask the water spirits what they think? They are more likely to know what Ombur is up to.'
Ngan Esa therefore summoned the water spirits.

'Water spirits, please appear,
the one who calls, you must hear,
the humble chief of the Fangs!
Answer my question, please
and don't send the storm
to wash everything away
don't send the rain, to drown all living things!
Don't be angry with us, water spirits,
but say if we, the unfortunate Fangs
should go on, or stay,
for we don't want to see the day
when we are slain by the fearsome crocodile.
Water spirits, please answer me now!'

As the water spirits were against the Fangs, and on Omur's side, they advised Ngan Esa to stay put.
The Fangs were overjoyed to hear their journey was at an end, and they began to build huts,

hoping that at last they could live in peace and safety.

Their joy did not last. Three days later the fearsome crocodile suddenly appeared and turned on Ngan Esa, 'How stupid you are, and how stupid are your people! Now, listen carefully!'

'I am listening,' replied the terrified chief.

'As you failed to keep our agreement, from now on you must provide two men a day for my diet. In addition, I want two women each week and also two maidens each month. And before this day is gone, you must give me your only daughter!'

Ngan Esa was heartbroken, for his daughter Alena Kiri was very beautiful and he loved her dearly. But he did not dare oppose the will of the fearsome crocodile.

But when Ombur met the chief's daughter, he was spellbound by her beauty and he fell in love with her at once. Instead of devouring Alena Kiri, he sat her astride his back, and swam away up the great river.

Some time later Alena Kiri gave birth to a baby boy—the son of Ombur, the crocodile. She named him Nguranguran.

He was a bright, strong lad, and grew with amazing speed. While others of his age were still toddling, he was walking as firmly as a youth; while they were uttering their first few words, he was speaking and behaving like a grown man.

Though he was the son of a crocodile, Nguranguran longed to see his grandparents and the other members of the Fang tribe. Though he was Ombur's son, he wished to avenge the wrong his father had committed. Nguranguran had never met the Fangs, yet he loved them. His mother Alena Kiri taught him to do so.

He said to her one day, 'Come mother! Let us run away from here to your parents and the other Fangs!'

Alena Kiri only smiled sadly. 'That is not possible. The fearsome Ombur would be sure to find us. We would fare badly, and the Fangs would fare even worse. First you must slay Ombur.'

'How can I kill him, when he is so strong, with a skin like iron?'

'Call the forest spirits, and ask for their help,' Alena Kiri said.

Nguranguran therefore summoned the forest spirits.

'Forest spirits, please appear,
the one who calls, you must hear,
the humble grandson of the Fang chief!
Answer my question, please,
and don't send lightning to slice the sky,
or winds to tear trees from the ground!
Don't be angry with me, forest spirits,
but say how I, poor Nguranguran,
can slay Ombur, the terrible crocodile,
who is immensely strong
with an iron-like skin
and whose whim is to devour
all the Fang tribe.
Forest spirits, answer my question now!'

The forest spirits hated Ombur and liked the Fangs, so they led Nguranguran deep into the forest and showed him the palm tree palmyra.

They told him to cut into the bark and catch the sap in a large pot. Nguranguran took their advice, and soon had a large jug filled to the brim. When it had fermented, it turned into a heady, sweet liquid, known to please and lighten the heart of every man.

Crocodile Ombur, who was hungry and very greedy, took a sip and immediately turned very merry. And he began to sing,

'I drink the drink which pleases my heart,
I drink!
I drink the drink which lightens my heart,
I drink!
I, the great crocodile chief
whom everyone fears,
even the forest spirits and the water spirits.
I, great chief Ombur!
I drink the drink which pleases my heart,
I drink!
I drink the drink which lightens my heart,
I drink!'

He drank and he sang, till the whole jug was empty. Then he fell soundly asleep.

Nguranguran seized a strong stick and placed one end in the fire. When it turned red hot, he thrust it with all his might into the crocodile's throat.

Ombur let out a terrible cry of anguish, and

treasure. In her hands, it would bring about our destruction.'

So Kriemhild rode away without her riches, though Gunther presented her with precious gifts and an imposing company of knights, as was proper for the sister of the Burgundian king.

Attila was waiting for his bride in Vienna. The moment he saw Kriemhild he was dazzled by her beauty. A great wedding was held and the celebrations went on for fourteen days. The Goth king Dietrich of Bern, who was Attila's friend and a frequent guest at his court, was the centre of attraction. Kriemhild had heard many stories of this notable hero and it pleased her greatly to have him near.

After the wedding the newlyweds sailed on the Danube to Etzelburg, the capital of the Hun kingdom, where Kriemhild became aware of the great wealth and power that Attila held.

She lived at the side of her husband for a year, and appeared to be happy, particularly when their son Ortlieb was born. But in reality she was not at peace. The great yearning for revenge was still very much alive in her heart. So one day she said to Attila, 'I have now spent a whole year in Etzelburg, I miss my brothers and should like to see them again. Please ask them to visit us!'

Attila gladly agreed and at once sent messengers to Worms. Kriemhild ordered the messengers to include Hagen in the invitation and to make sure he came back with them. All she lived for was to see the day when she could pay him back in full.

When Attila's men arrived at the court in Worms, Gunther, Gernot and Giselher were delighted with the invitation they had been sent. 'It is obvious our sister no longer bears a grudge against us. We shall gladly come.' But Hagen frowned. 'You do not know your own sister,' he said. 'This is a trap. You will ride to your death.' 'You are mistaken,' Gunther protested. 'But stay at home, if you fear some calamity is waiting for us in Etzelburg.' 'I have never abandoned my king!' Hagen cried, and prepared for the journey.

Brunhild also felt that the visit to Etzelburg would have an unhappy ending, but nobody paid her any attention, for they all knew how she hated her sister-in-law.

The three royal brothers and Hagen, accompanied by a large party of men, were soon on their way to Etzelburg. Apart from Hagen, they were all in excellent spirits. A few days later the expedition came to castle Bechlarn. Count

Rüdeger welcomed the travellers like old friends. Though the stop at the castle was only brief, it was long enough for young Giselher to fall in love with Rüdeger's daughter and request her hand in marriage. Their engagement was announced at once, and it was arranged that the wedding would be held on the return journey and that afterwards Giselher would take his bride to Worms. Rüdeger then attached himself to the visiting party and accompanied them to Etzelburg.

When the Burgundians entered the capital, they were amazed by the wealth and magnificence, which surrounded them everywhere. Proudly they rode through the throngs of onlookers, who were particularly eyeing the huge Hagen with interest. When the heavy gates of the castle closed behind them, they felt strangely depressed. 'We are in a trap,' Hagen whispered. 'We shall not escape alive.'

Just then Kriemhild appeared before them, beautiful and proud, and as cold as ice. Without a word, without a smile, she nodded to Gunther and Gernot, but Giselher she kissed. Hagen she measured with a look of hate.

Attila welcomed the guests with warmth and held a ceremonious feast in their honour. He noted with surprise that none of the Burgundians discarded their arms, not even for a moment.

'In our countries it is customary for guests to

leapt up, trying to spit out the burning stick. But he was helpless, for the stick was firmly wedged deep in his throat. So the mighty crocodile chief choked to death.

Nguranguran was very happy when he realized the crocodile was dead, and his mother Alena Kiri burst into tears of joy. They left immediately for the distant mountains, the home of the Fangs.

Their journey was long and hard, so they were terribly tired and weary when at last they reached the Fang village. Ngan Esa could hardly believe his eyes when he saw his daughter, and he was all the more surprised to learn that the handsome youth at her side was his own grandson.

But when Nguranguran told how he slew the fearsome crocodile Ombur, the Fangs only smiled sadly, and Ngan Esa remarked, 'I have a handsome, strong grandson. What a shame he is a liar!'

Though Alena Kiri swore that Nguranguran was telling the truth, and the young hero showed the crocodile tooth, which he had torn from Ombur's mouth and now used as a dagger, the old chief would not be convinced. But when Nguranguran led the Fangs deep into the forest to the palm tree palmyra and taught them to make the heady, sweet liquid which pleases and lightens every man's heart, they at last began to believe him.

The Fangs loved the new drink so much, that in the end they did not know whether to be more grateful to Nguranguran for slaying the fearsome Ombur, or for giving them the heady liquid.

The Fangs then moved deeper into the forest, where many palmyra trees were growing. They built a village and called it Akurengan, which means freed from the crocodile.

When Ngan Esa grew old, his brave grandson Nguranguran was elected their new chief.

They worship him still as the great forefather of all their people.

Heroic Ilya Muromets

a hero. I am so happy, that if I could grip mother earth, I would turn her upside down!'

The pilgrims smiled and said, 'Don't turn mother earth upside down, Ilya, but go and serve Holy Russia, conquer her enemies, and help the poor and needy. But do not try to match your strength against giant Svatogor, for mother earth can barely support him, such a giant is he.' With that the pilgrims left.

Ilya Muromets hastened after his parents, who were felling old oaks and digging out roots.

Ilya noticed that only a small patch of their field had been cleared and that the couple, exhausted by the hard work, had fallen asleep under a bush. Ilya walked along the field, using one hand to knock down the massive oaks, and the other to tear out the strong roots, till there was nothing left to do but to burn the wood and clear the stubble.

When his parents woke up, they were amazed and delighted to find their son cured and filled with such divine strength.

Ilya was born in the village of Karachov near the town of Murom in Russia. The son of a peasant, he was a sickly child and too weak to walk and use his hands. All he could do was to sit helplessly on top of the oven, letting his parents look after him. Thus he spent thirty long years.

One day, when his mother and father had left to work in the fields, three holy pilgrims entered the cottage and said, 'Rise, Ilya, and go down to the cellar to fetch us a jug of beer. We are very thirsty after our long journey.'

'I cannot get up,' Ilya sadly replied. 'I cannot use my legs, not my arms.'

'Go on, try,' the pilgrims urged, 'you will see that you can.'

Lo and behold! Ilya stood up, jumped off the stove, ran down to the cellar and brought the pilgrims a jug filled with beer. They drank thirstily, then handed the jug back to Ilya. 'Drink the rest and you will have the strength of a hero!'

Ilya did as he was told and felt great strength seep into his body. 'Thank you, holy men!' he cried joyfully. 'With all my heart I thank you! For curing me, for giving me the strength of

'Who has ever heard of some Ilya Muromets?' Svatogor sneered, then picked Ilya up, horse and all, and stuffed them both into his saddle bag. He rode on.

All at once Svatogor's horse stumbled. 'What is the matter, little horse?' Svatogor wondered. 'How can you expect me not to stumble, master, when I am carrying two heroes. That is a heavy load indeed.'

Svatogor pulled Ilya and his mount out of the saddle bag, put them both down on the ground and said, 'You surely must be a very strong hero when my horse cannot carry you. Come, let us be brothers and ride on the Holy Mountain together.'

So Ilya Muromets and giant Svatogor became firm friends and spent a whole year riding on the Holy Mountain. They experienced many adventures and performed many heroic deeds. Together they suffered and together they enjoyed life.

One day they came to a high pine and found a coffin under it, bearing a strange inscription: 'Let the one whom this coffin fits lie in it,' it said.

When Ilya returned home, he chose from the stable a weak, puny foal which was hardly worth anything at all. Day after day he fed it with maize, gave it water from the spring to drink, led it to graze in the green pasture. Soon the sickly foal grew into a strong steed fit for a hero.

Ilya then saddled his mount with the finest saddle, placed the silkiest bridle over his head, then equipped himself with a strong bow and fast arrows, a steel mace and a sharp sword. So armed, he rode into the world.

His first stop was the Holy Mountain, the home of giant Svatogor, who lived there because he was so big and heavy that ordinary plains could not support him. Svatogor was the strongest of all warriors and Ilya wished to get to know him.

He soon came upon the giant figure astride his huge mount; Svatogor was so tall, his head disappeared in the clouds and when he waved his hand, it almost touched the sun.

'Who are you?' Svatogor cried.

'I am Ilya Muromets,' Ilya replied. 'I am here because I wanted to meet you.'

Ilya tried the coffin first, but it was far too big. When Svatogor stretched out in it, it fitted as if made to measure. Making himself comfortable, Svatogor closed the lid, but when he tried lifting it, the lid would not move. 'Take my sword, Ilya,' he cried, 'and slash the lid open, or I shall have to stay here for ever!'

'I can't lift your sword, Svatogor,' Ilya replied, 'it is too heavy.'

'Then lean over the coffin and I shall breathe some of my hero's strength into you,' Svatogor called.

Ilya Muromets leaned over the coffin and soon felt the breath of Svatogor upon him. Then he raised the giant sword with ease and bore it down upon the coffin.

But alas, wherever the sword struck, an iron band appeared.

'I am doomed,' Svatogor cried. 'This coffin was meant for me and in it I must die. Lean down once more, brother, so I can breathe my remaining strength into you.'

Ilya declined. 'Thank you, Svatogor, but I am strong enough. If I had more strength, mother earth would not be able to support me and I would be forced to stay for ever on the Holy Mountain, as you had done.'

'You have chosen wisely,' Svatogor replied. 'My breath would have brought you death and you too would have perished.'

Ilya Muromets bade his unfortunate friend a sad farewell, and rode on to the town of Chernigov.

On the outskirts, his horse suddenly stopped. With his sharp eyes, Ilya saw the famous Chernigov was surrounded by a terrible heathen army, poised to attack, like a dark cloud of ravenous vultures. Three Tartar czarevitches were leading it, each with forty thousand men. So tightly was the town encircled, that no-one could escape, even on the finest mount; nobody could slip past the guards, not even a swift hare, or a little mouse.

The only thing which escaped from Chernigov was the sound of the weeping peasants trapped and waiting to die sooner or later behind the town walls.

Anger flamed in Ilya's heroic heart. Tearing a green oak out of the ground, he swept upon the Tartars.

With the first swing of the oak, he cut a path through their ranks, with the second swipe he wiped out a whole platoon. In no time he slew the whole army to the last man.

Once he had killed them all, Ilya Muromets

entered the white tents of the three czarevitches, dragged them out by the roots of their yellow hair, and said,

'Now, young Tartar czarevitches! Go and spread the word that Holy Russia is no longer defenceless and destitute, and that anyone with evil intentions will fare the same as your army has done!'

With that Ilya remounted, and leapt like an arrow over the town walls, landing in front of a stone temple, where all the citizens were weeping and lamenting.

'Why do you weep?' he cried. 'Look down from the walls and you will see the paths are clear and the Tartar army destroyed.'

The peasants praised and thanked the heroic Ilya, rewarding him with silver, gold and precious stones, and begged him to stay, to be their duke and to rule over them.

But Ilya turned them down with the words, 'I shall not remain with you, but shall travel to the city of Kiev to see Prince Vladimir. Mother Russia is still seeped in blood, I must rid her of her enemies. I shall take the fastest route.'

His last words frightened the peasants, who tried to persuade Ilya to take the slower path, for the direct road to Kiev was terribly dangerous and had not been used for thirty years.

'In the black marshes by the Levanidov crossroads, near the River Smorodina, Nightingale the robber sits in the crowns of seven oaks. He robs and kills anyone who tries to pass,' they warned.

'Nevertheless I'll take the direct route to Kiev,' Ilya insisted and bade a heartly goodbye to the citizens.

When Ilya Muromets was nearing the seven oaks, where Nightingale the robber had his nest, he heard the most piercing whistling, which made the earth tremble, the grass burn, the trees bend their crowns. Ilya's horse sunk to his knees and Ilya himself went dizzy. Such terrible power had the whistle of Nightingale the robber.

But Ilya was not afraid. He reached for his bow and fired an arrow straight into Nightingale the robber's eye.

'Alas, alas!' Nightingale the robber cried. 'Who is this hero, who has not been knocked out by my fearful whistle? Who is this hero, who is not afraid and who almost killed me with his arrow? Could he be Ilya Muromets, who is destined to humble me and rob me of life?'

'Yes, I am Ilya Muromets!' the hero cried, knocking the robber from his nest. He tied a rope round Nightingale's neck and led him to Kiev to Prince Vladimir.

When they reached the palace, all the courtiers and guards crowded round them. Prince Vladimir and Princess Apraxia looked down into the courtyard to see what all the excitement was about.

Ilya looked up and cried, 'I have brought you the notorious highwayman, Nightingale the robber, who thieved in the deep forest by the River Smorodina. Go on, Nightingale, show them how you whistle, but not too loud, mind you!'

The robber replied. 'I'll have my last whistle, as death is waiting for me.' And for the last time he whistled with all his might, till the courtiers and guards clutched their heads in fear and agony: Prince Vladimir almost fell out of the window and princess Apraxia fainted. Ilya Muromets then unleashed his sword and severed Nightingale the robber's cheeky head.

Ilya remained at the prince's court. He clashed many times with the fearsome Tartars, but he always ended up the victor, slaying them, forcing them to flee. The Tartars eventually gave up attacking Holy Russia, and Ilya had nothing much to do. He lounged about at the prince's banqueting table, while the years flew by and he grew old.

'I am not going to die sitting at the prince's table, facing a plate of roast and a goblet of green wine,' Ilya suddenly decided.

He mounted his horse, and rode out into vast Russia once again.

Climbing down, Ilya took off his cap and swung it round, belting the scoundrels. With one swipe ten were dead, with the second twenty were turning up their toes, with the third, forty were pushing up the daisies.

The rest of the thieves sank to their knees and implored, 'Don't slaughter us all, Ilya. You can have all our gold, silver and jewels, but please spare our lives!'

'Keep your worthless lives, but give the gold, silver and jewels to the poor,' Ilya replied. 'Now scatter, the lot of you, and give up your highwayman's trade. Or I'll return and cut the throat of every man here.'

The robbers ran in all directions and Ilya returned to the crossroad, where he added to the inscription,

'I went to the right, but I did not die.'

Then he turned to the left.

When he had gone a little way, he came upon

After travelling for quite some time, he came to a crossroad where three paths met.

On a large boulder an inscription was engraved, which said,

'Who goes to the right will die,
who goes to the left will marry,
who goes straight on will be rich.'

Ilya shook his grey head. 'What would an old man like me do with riches? What use would be a marriage? I shall die in battle, like a true hero.' And he turned to the right.

He had not travelled very far when he came upon a camp of robbers. There must have been five hundred of them at least. They surrounded Ilya, swearing and shouting, and tried to pull him off his horse. Ilya laughed and said, 'So you want to rob an old man, you thieves? Then wait, I'll dismount.'

a magnificent palace. A woman of uncommon beauty was waiting by the gates.

'Come with me, Ilya,' she cried, beckoning him to follow. 'I have yearned for you for so long and I so want to be your wife.'

'An old man like me?' Ilya smirked.

He was led to a beautiful chamber where there was a bed piled high with soft feather mattresses. Instead of climbing into the bed, Ilya gripped the white hands of his enchantress and threw her onto it. The bed turned upside down and the beauty fell into the cellar.

'So that was the wedding you had in mind!', Ilya roared, whilst he helped his enchantress out of the cellar.

Then he pulled out forty kings and princes, forty czars and czarevitches and forty strong Russian heroes. He left the lot to look after themselves and returned to the crossroads and added to the inscription,

'I went to the left and I did not marry.'

Then he took the centre path.

After riding for some time, he noticed a huge boulder by the roadside, on which was written, 'Who moves this boulder will be rich.'

Ilya gripped the boulder with both his hands, but it did not move. But when with all his strength he pushed against it with his shoulder, the boulder rolled away and where it stood was a chest filled with gold. Ilya loaded the chest on his mount and returned to the crossroads, where he added to the inscription,

'I went straight on, but I did not become rich.'

For Ilya used some of the gold in the chest to build a large temple and gave the rest away to the poor.

The Faithful Love of Popocatepetl and Ishtla

Ishtla was the daughter of the Aztec king. She was incredibly beautiful and many noblemen longed to win her love. But Ishtla's heart belonged to young Popocatepetl, the bravest warrior of the royal army. He was not only courageous, but wise and just, and the king therefore favoured his daughter's choice, happy to know that the Aztecs would have a valiant and a prudent sovereign. Preparations were being made for a great wedding.

Suddenly enemies attacked the Aztec kingdom. Showing no mercy, they burned and plundered palaces and villages, devastating fields and orchards, slaughtering or enslaving the inhabitants. The king hastily assembled his army and entrusted Popocatepetl to take command. The young hero bade Ishtla farewell and went into battle.

This was the beginning of a terrible war, which lasted several years. At times good fortune favoured the king's soldiers, at times the invaders, but neither seemed able to clinch a victory. On both sides many men perished without an end to the war in sight.

The unhappy Ishtla kept thinking of her Popocatepetl and saying, 'If my beloved does not return, I shall die of grief.' But Popocatepetl was alive and well, facing his enemies with great courage. He was always in the centre of the fiercest tussles, fighting like a ferocious jaguar, giving a fine example to his men. At last the king's army was slowly gaining ground. When the decisive battle took place, Popocatepetl came out the victor. His heroism was boundless and luck was with him. Though always in the centre of the most vicious skirmishes he managed to escape without a scratch.

The defeated enemies fled in all directions. They could see they would never defeat the Aztecs in battle with Popocatepetl at the head, but they were loathe to accept their crushing defeat.

Thirst for revenge inspired their leader with a treacherous idea.

The cunning commander called together some of his most loyal men and said, 'Though we have lost the battle, we can avenge our defeat. Popocatepetl's beautiful bride to be happens to be Ishtla, daughter of the king. She loves Popocatepetl with all her heart, and she is his life. We shall creep into the city in disguise and spread the word that Popocatepetl fell in battle. We shall see whether Ishtla will survive.'

The plan was put into action. Several enemy men sneaked into the city, telling everyone, that although the king's army had won the war, brave Popocatepetl had been slain in the struggle. These rumours spread through the city and soon reached the ears of lovely Ishtla in her palace. At first she refused to believe such evil tidings, but when she heard it from several sides, she was forced to accept it as the truth. 'Alas, alas,' she cried. 'Without Popocatepetl I do not wish to live ...'

Stricken with grief, she fell gravely ill. Even the finest physicians could not cure her, nor avert her death. Just as Popocatepetl was marching back to the city at the head of his victorious army, Ishtla's life ebbed away.

There are no words to describe Popocatepetl's profound grief, for no words of comfort could ease his sorrow. 'What use is my good fortune in battle? What use is the glory and the gratitude of the whole nation, when I have lost the most precious thing I ever had, my own beloved Ishtla?' he moaned.

He locked himself in with the lifeless body of his bride, refusing to take part in any celebrations of their victory. He did not eat, he did not drink, he did not sleep, but sat gazing at the lovely face of the dead princess. During that night, when everyone else was asleep, he lit two torches, gathered his Ishtla in his arms and left the city. No one ever saw either of them again.

The next morning, however, the inhabitants noticed with astonishment two high mountains which, as if by magic, had grown overnight near the city. They were no ordinary mountains, but volcanoes, out of which flames shot into the sky.

When the king rode out to view the mountains, he remained deep in thought, then turned to his Aztecs: 'These are no ordinary volcanoes, but Ishtla and Popocatepetl. They died with grief, for they could not bear life without each other. Their love turned them into these wondrous mountains. Their hearts will burn for ever with the bright flame, and for ever they will light up our kingdom.'

Robin Hood

In the green glades of Sherwood Forest, near Nottingham in England, there once lived a famous outlaw about whom remarkable tales are told.

His name was Robin Hood and there was no archer living who could match his skill. With his band of one hundred and forty men, all clad alike in Lincoln green, he dwelt wherever he pleased within the forest, living on the king's venison, robbing monks and lords on Watling Street highway.

'There is too much injustice in this world,' he would say, as he distributed the money he took off the rich lords and the fat monks among the poor and needy.

The sheriff of Nottingham swore he would seize and punish Robin, but what use were his threats, when the outlaw always managed to give him the slip!

Aided by his merry, gallant band, particularly the long-legged Little John, his right hand man, Robin had no trouble in outsmarting the frustrated sheriff.

One day, just before noon, Robin said to his men, 'We'll enjoy our lunch much better if we can share it with some noble knight or abbot, who happens to be travelling along Watling Street. Off with you, men, and find me one!'

Three of the outlaws went to the highway, but met no one, except a sad-looking knight riding a skinny filly. They jumped to his side and invited him most politely to lunch. The Sorrowful Knight was glad to accept and rode back with them to their camp.

'Welcome, knight!' Robin Hood cried out, and asked him to sit at the table. It was quite a feast. Apart from bread and wine there was roast pheasant, duck, venison and boar. The Sorrowful Knight thanked them sincerely, saying that he had not eaten so well for good three weeks.

'I am glad you enjoyed it,' Robin Hood remarked, 'but you'll have to pay for such a fine lunch.'

'I would do so glady,' the knight replied, 'but all I have is ten shillings.'

Robin Hood ordered the Sorrowful Knight

be searched, and was quite surprised to find he had been telling the truth.

'I have been stricken by misfortune, through no fault of my own,' their guest explained. 'I had to mortgage my estate for the sum of four hundred pounds to the York monastery of Virgin Mary. Tomorrow my repayment is due, but I have no money. I shall ask the abbot to wait another year. Perhaps Virgin Mary will put in a good word for me. Otherwise I shall lose the estate.'

Feeling sorry for the knight, Robin Hood said, 'My good sir, it is nice to have faith in our Holy Mother, but take my word for it, that abbot will refuse to wait. However, I shall lend you the sum you owe. You can repay me in one year from today, right here, under this green oak.'

With tears of gratitude in his eyes, the Sorrowful Knight thanked Robin, took the money and rode off to York. Once in the monastery, he fell to his knees before the abbot, pleading for an extension of time.

The abbot only laughed and said, 'I am glad you can't repay the loan! Your castle and fields are worth far more. At least our monastery will get them cheap.'

The Sorrowful Knight then rose and proudly handed the purse with Robin Hood's money to the abbot, who turned scarlet with anger. There was nothing he could do, but give the agreement to the knight, who returned home a happy man.

Back in Sherwood Forest, Robin heard that the sheriff of Nottingham had decided to hold an archery contest. Robin of course wanted to take part, but Little John warned him, 'Don't go to Nottingham, it is sure to be a trap. I'll go in your place. But, somehow or other, I'll bring the sheriff back, right to this very oak.'

Robin Hood agreed and Little John set off for Nottingham.

It was a great contest. The very best archers had gathered from far and wide, but Little John excelled among them all. Three consecutive times his arrows split the thin little stick which served as the target.

'Glory be,' the sheriff whispered, 'isn't that

Robin Hood himself?' But those who knew Robin, shook their heads. 'Though Robin Hood is big and strong, he's not such a tall, strapping fellow as this man here.'

The sheriff summoned the worthy competitor and asked, 'Who are you and where are you from?'

'They call me Reynold Greenleaf and I was born in Holderness,' Little John replied.

'Very well, Greenleaf. How would you like to work for twenty pounds a year?' the sheriff went on.

Little John agreed, thinking secretly that he would be the very worst servant the sheriff had ever employed. And he had no intention of remaining in his service for long. In fact he decided it was time to leave the moment the sheriff went hunting. But first he went into the kitchen to feed up for the journey. Just as he was biting into a succulent roast chicken, the sheriff's fat cook appeared in the doorway, waving a giant wooden spoon. 'You greedy, thieving rascal,' he cried, pouncing on Little John.

'Wait a second,' Little John protested, doing his best to defend himself. 'You're quite a fighter! Good enough, in fact, to be one of Robin Hood's men!'

'I'd join them this minute,' laughed the cook, 'if only I knew where to find them!'

One word led to another, and Little John admitted who he was. With very little persuasion the cook agreed to accompany him to Sherwood Forest.

First they had their fill of the very best the sheriff's kitchen had to offer, then they stole into the treasury and took three hundred pounds, helping themselves also to silver cutlery. And merrily they were on their way.

Robin Hood was delighted to see them and wanted to hear all that had happened. But Little John said, 'First I must keep my old promise to you. Wait here!'

With that the long-legged Little John disappeared in the forest. Before long he found the huntsmen and the sheriff, who was complaining he had lost sight of the magnificent stag he was chasing. 'I know where he is hiding! Follow me!' Little John cried.

'Goodness me!' exclaimed the sheriff, 'you really are the most invaluable servant, Greenleaf.'

And the furious sheriff hurried after him. Before he knew what was what, there he was, right under the green oak, face to face with Robin. Much too late, the sheriff realized that he had fallen blindly into Little John's trap.

Robin proved the perfect host, treating the sheriff with respect, lavishing the best food upon him and allowing him to leave in peace. 'All I want from you is your promise that from now on you will not harm my men or me, and that you will always use your strength and influence to help us. This you must swear on this sword.'

The sheriff was vexed, but he was in no position to protest, so he gave his promise.

Twelve months had now gone by, and here was the day when the Sorrowful Knight's repayment to Robin was due.

Robin was waiting from early morning for his debtor to turn up and kept sending his men to the highway, to take a look if he was coming. 'Lord knows I shall not sit down to eat until he arrives,' he declared. 'Surely Virgin Mary will not cheat me.'

But the outlaws waited by the roadside in vain, and eventually brought Robin a plump monk, who was travelling from York.

'Are you, by chance, from the York Virgin Mary monastery?' Robin Hood enquired.

'That I am,' was the monk's reply.

'Our Holy Mother has not let me down after all,' Robin said with delight. 'She is sending me four hundred pounds with this worthy monk.'

'What four hundred pounds?' wondered the monk. 'I swear that in all I only have twenty shillings on me.'

By then two of Robin Hood's men were already opening the monk's pouch and pulling out eight hundred pounds.

'A miracle!' laughed the leader of the outlaws. 'Look how those twenty shillings have multiplied! The kind Virgin Mary has paid me double what the knight owed.'

Robin then dined and wined the monk most handsomely. As he toasted their parting with a goblet of red wine, he asked the monk to tell the abbot that he would appreciate such worthy messengers to be sent every day.

As soon as the unfortunate monk departed, the Sorrowful Knight appeared with the four hundred pounds.

'You don't owe me a single penny now,' Robin stated, refusing the money. 'A monk from the York monastery has just paid me a call and he gave me money from the Virgin Mary. Thank the Holy Mother, she has paid on your behalf! But that absent-minded monk made a mistake and left me eight hundred pounds instead of the four hundred. I only want what I lent you. Buy a good horse and new armour with the rest.'

So the knight returned to his castle with eight hundred pounds to the good.

Before long the sheriff of Nottingham held another archery contest.

'This time all of us will go,' Robin Hood declared. 'We will test the sheriff, and see if he can keep his word.'

'I would not rely on that,' muttered one of the men with a frown.

'So what!' said another. 'If we are all there, we'll make sure nothing goes wrong.'

On the day of the contest Robin Hood rode into Nottingham with all his friends. But it was decided that only Robin and his six best archers would participate in the competition. The others were to stand by.

Once again many excellent archers had gathered in Nottingham, and crowds of spectators, of course. The prize was a silver arrow tipped with gold. Robin Hood won it easily. Nine times in all his arrow slit the little stick that was the target. He was the best shot anyone had ever seen.

The sheriff, of course, recognized Robin at once, but he did not make this obvious. However, as he was handing Robin the prize, the sheriff signalled to the guards and they rushed to seize him.

But the leader of the outlaws was well prepared. Leaping down from the pavilion, he ran to his men, whose accurate arrows kept the sheriff's guards at bay. Then all the others jumped

on their horses and rode away like the wind. Robin was the last to leave, for Little John had been hit in the knee and was unable to climb in his saddle.

'Sever my head, Robin,' the long-legged Little John cried, 'rather than leave me here in sheriff's merciless claws!'

'Not for all the gold in merry old England!' Robin vowed, scooping Little John up and putting him down in front of him astride his own horse. Fearing the sheriff might pursue them to Sherwood Forest, the outlaws rode instead to the castle of the Sorrowful Knight.

On hearing their story, he opened the gates to let them in.

'In the name of St Quentin,' he vowed, 'I swear that you and your men can stay here as my guests as long as you like.'

The sheriff of Nottingham soon found out where Robin was hiding, and wasted no time in bringing his men to the castle. He did not have a friendly reception.

'I shall not allow you to take Robin or his companions,' the Sorrowful Knight declared. 'They are my guests, and as such, you cannot touch them. That is the English custom. If you are of different opinion, ride to London to see the king. Let him decide!'

The sheriff, almost frothing at the mouth with anger, truly went to London to complain to the king himself.

'Quite unbelievable!' snapped the sovereign, on hearing the sheriff's version of what had happened. He promised he would personally come to Nottingham to see justice done and agreed to Robin Hood's and the Sorrowful Knight's arrest.

The sheriff thanked the king and hurried back to Nottingham to assemble a thousand soldiers for the siege.

In the meantime, however, Robin Hood and his courageous men had returned to the safety of Sherwood Forest, where they were the masters and where no one could outsmart them. The sheriff had to be content with catching only the Sorrowful Knight.

When rumours of the arrest reached Robin's ears, he hastened with his band of men to Not-

tingham, where they ambushed the sheriff's guards and forced them to set the knight free. It was then Robin Hood came face to face with the sheriff.

'You did not keep your word, as you vowed, sheriff!' Robin Hood cried. 'You shall pay for this with your life!'

And with one swift swipe of his sword, he severed the sheriff's head.

Then Robin calmly rode off with his men and the freed knight to the green glades of Sherwood.

The king's arrival in Nottingham was filled with surprises. There was the sheriff in his grave, whilst Robin Hood and the Sorrowful Knight were in Sherwood Forest as free as birds.

In his wrath, the king confiscated the knight's estate and placed a high price on his head, and a higher price still on the head of Robin. The angry king combed the whole region. There were plenty of signs of Robin and his men helping themselves to his game, but no sign of the outlaws themselves.

'What would I give to lay my hands on that rebel,' the frustrated king muttered. The sheriff's old servant eventually gave him some sound advice.

'Your Royal Highness, nobody is likely to bring you the head of Robin Hood, nor the head of someone who is under his protection. You are wasting your time, and people are laughing at you. I'll tell you though, if you really want to meet Robin Hood, disguise yourself as a monk and travel along Watling Street!'

The king took the advice. In a nearby monastery, he put on the robes of the abbot, whilst his five knights dressed up as monks. So disguised, they rode along the highway, waiting what would happen next. They found they were surrounded by outlaws before they had gone a mile.

Robin's men greeted them politely and led them straight to the green oak tree. Robin gave the distinguished guests the most cordial welcome. No wonder too, for by then monks and abbots, afraid of being robbed avoided Watling Street, and so were rare visitors indeed. Robin asked the abbot in a most friendly manner to leave him some of his money.

'Forty pounds is all I have,' the disguised king said. 'I spent an awful lot at the court in Nottingham. But I'll share them gladly.'

Thanking him for the twenty pounds, Robin Hood gave his guests a splendid meal of game, bread and red wine. After dinner they held

a shooting match. Any outlaw who failed to hit the target, had to give Robin his arrow and collect a clip round the ear. Robin, of course, proved the best shot of all, but in the end even he slipped.

'Give up your arrow and come and get your clip round the ear!' one of the men cried.

Robin then obediently handed the arrow to the abbot, who rolled up his sleeve and gave Robin such a smack, that it knocked him to the ground.

'I swear to God you're a strong abbot with arms of steel! I bet you're also an excellent shot,' Robin said, with a laugh. It was then he had a closer look at the abbot's face and realized this man was no other but King Richard. Robin fell to his knees, with all the other outlaws and the Sorrowful Knight. They begged for mercy, assuring their sovereign that they loved and respected him, and knew that he was not responsible for the injustices committed in England.

'Rise,' King Richard bade them gently. 'I can see you are honest men and that you respect your king. Now let us proceed to Nottingham to put matters right.'

Great joy spread through Sherwood Forest. The king and his knights discarded the monk's robes and, like the outlaws, put on the Lincoln green.

On the journey to Nottingham they continued with the shooting match, and even the king collected a clip round the ear from Robin.

Passers-by gasped when they saw the flood of men in green, thinking that Robin Hood was about to try to seize Nottingham and the king by force. Young and old, they fled in all directions.

The king roared with laughter and told them not to be so silly and to come back.

In Nottingham a great feast was held. The Sorrowful Knight was given back his estate, and Robin Hood and his outlaws were given full pardon.

Furthermore, they were given official permission to hunt to their hearts' and stomachs' content in the royal forests.

Kao Liang, the Saviour of Peking

This happened in bygone days, when emperors of the Ming Dynasty ruled China. At that time General Liou Po-jun was building high fortifications round Peking. Just as they were finished, a rider appeared, galloping like the wind, bringing the most staggering news: the water in every Peking well had suddenly dried up.

General Liou Po-jun was not only an able commander, but also a wise man, with a great wealth of knowledge and he knew immediately what brought on such a calamity. He assembled his soldiers and said, 'Loyal men! You must be aware that water has disappeared from every well in Peking and that death threatens our city. Yet the man, whose heart is good and brave, can avert the destruction of thousands of innocent people. No easy task awaits him, but if his mission proves a success, he will earn the respect and love of the whole city.'

The soldiers remained silent, till one youth, still only a boy, cried out, 'General, let me go!' Kao Liang was the boy's name.

The general took Kao Liang aside and said, 'As I told you, it will not be an easy task. And whatever happens, you must tell no one about it. Tomorrow at dawn you must saddle a swift mount, and fully armed, you must ride northwest. Before long you will meet an old woman pulling a cart with two vats of water, and an old man who will be helping her by pushing the cart. That old man is no other than the Dragon King, and the old hag the Dragon Queen. They are responsible for the disaster. You see, long ago there was a sea here instead of our city. But the Chinese dried the sea out and built Peking. Now the Dragon King has nowhere to live. He had to move far from here to the sea and now he has decided to seek his revenge. Those two vats contain all the water of Peking. You must stop the cart going further!'

'How can I take all the water of Peking from

the mighty Dragon King?' Kao Liang asked worriedly.

'You must ride up to the cart at full speed and pierce both vats with your lance.'

'That does not sound too difficult,' remarked the boy.

'That part is not difficult, but it will be difficult to save your own life afterwards. You must turn back at once and gallop back to the city. And come what may, you must not glance round till your horse has ridden a hundred paces. Only then you will stay among us.'

The next day Kao Liang chose the swiftest mount the army owned. Clad in his strong, heavy armour, he seized a powerful lance, strong enough to pierce the iron doors of the emperor's palace, and rode out northwest.

Soon, in the dust of the road, he saw an aged couple, pulling and pushing a cart with two vats. They were so shrunken and frail, that the boy almost felt sorry for them, but he was a soldier, and a soldier always obeys a command. With the lance at the ready, he shot forward with the speed of lightning and in a flash pierced both the vats. In one quick move he then turned and was on his way back.

He heard two terrific explosions. It seemed the earth was breaking up and the skies were hurtling down. These were followed by dreadful screams and wails, mocking laughter and screeching shrieks. Mindful of the general's words, Kao Liang fled towards the city, shutting his ears to the fearful noise. The ground trembled under the horse's hooves and beads of sweat ran down the boy's brow. He felt as if a whole troup of fearsome riders were hot in pursuit behind him, catching him up with each step. But he remembered to count his horse's paces and when he was up to one hundred, he looked round.

But alas! In all the excitement he made a mistake and had counted one step too few. He had only gone ninety nine paces in all. He saw a torrent of fast flowing water rushing towards him, foaming and rumbling, catching up with him with each second. A gigantic wave knocked the unfortunate Kao Liang to the ground and drowned him at once.

Immediately afterwards, the flood died down. Peaceful silence came in the wake of the horror, and the water seeped back into the wells of Peking. On the outskirts of Peking there is a nephrite spring, which is the source of Lake Kchung-ming-chu. They say that on that very spot water gushed forth from the pierced vats of the Dragon King. And the bridge, which bears Kao-Liang's name, reminds us of the youthful soldier who saved Peking from certain death.

The Pied Piper of Hamelin

In bygone days the German town of Hamelin was very prosperous. Thanks to its enormous port, local merchants were able to trade with many countries of the world, for Hamelin vessels and foreign ships sailed constantly to and fro. Hamelin citizens lived in fine style and were proud of their high standard of living.

But one thing upset them terribly — the town was plagued with rats. Not only did these creatures hide in sewers and drains, but they scurried about merrily in cellars and storerooms, enjoying corn from the Ukraine, dried fish from the North Sea, oranges from Spain, even rare herbs from India. The cloth from Flanders was a great favourite of theirs and they crunched jade from the Baltic shores with great relish.

The streets were swarming with rats, playing under the generous skirts of respectable matrons, biting the calves of dignified councillors. They ran about in taverns, lapping up beer of thirsty customers, pinching bits of smoked meat right off the plate of the hungry ones. But it was in the homes of the Hamelin citizens that the rats proved to be the biggest nuisances. There they crawled into cupboards and beds, not giving anyone a bit of peace, day and night.

All efforts to rid the town of the uninvited four-legged guests were useless. Local constables beat them with coshes, boys took shots at them with catapults, housewives set traps and the town physician lured them with poison. Yet the rats increased day by day.

Suddenly a mysterious stranger appeared in Hamelin. Tall and skinny, poorly dressed, he had the proud bearing of a count. He booked into the best inn, then went to the Town Hall.

'I am a rat catcher by trade. I can clear your town of the vermin,' he declared to the clerk, and asked to see the mayor. The mayor looked the lean visitor over somewhat suspiciously, not caring particularly for what he saw. But he listened with attention.

'I believe you are plagued with rats. I can clear the lot,' the spindly fellow offered.

'You could do that?' marvelled the mayor.

'Most certainly,' nodded the stranger. 'But it will cost you a thousand gold coins.'

'That's quite a tidy sum,' frowned the mayor.

'I know,' said the stranger. 'However, if you find just one rat in your town after I have finished, you won't owe me anything at all.'

'Sounds fair,' the mayor declared. 'But come back this afternoon, when the town council meets. Let the councillors have the final say.'

The town council accepted the offer. But the town clerk could not write down the minutes of the meeting, for the rats had drunk all the ink.

Early next morning, when the town was still asleep, the rat catcher came out into the streets. He had a long pipe, on which he played a piercing, haunting tune. And as he whistled, mice and rats came swarming from every direction, and followed him as obediently as sheep follow a shepherd.

The Pied Piper strode slowly through the town, not forgetting a single alley, leading the gigantic rat procession to the sea. There he stopped, but played on on his pipe, till every one of the rats jumped into the sea. Not one of them was left behind; they drowned to the last one.

Naturally enough, the town was delighted to see all the rats gone. Only the councillors frowned, loathe to pay the thousand gold coins.

'It is a sin to give him all that money for strolling about our town for an hour or so, playing his pipe,' they grumbled. 'Anyway, he has nothing in writing. He can consider himself lucky if we give him a hundred gold coins.' This they did. Summoning the rat catcher, they offered him one hundred gold coins.

'I want my thousand, as I was promised,' the Pied Piper said.

'Promises, promises,' sneered the mayor. 'Can you show me a written promise? Be glad to get your hundred.'

'Keep your money! I'll make you pay in a different way. You'll be sorry!' that rat catcher hissed, turned on his heel and went away.

The next night, the Pied Piper went out into the street once more. Merrily he skipped along, playing his haunting, piercing tune on the pipe. This time he was not followed by rats, but by the children of Hamelin, sleepy-eyed, still in their night shirts, lured from their beds by the rat catcher's whistle. He led them all to the sea, where he himself was the first to jump into the waves. Every child followed him. The sea closed over them and no one ever heard of them again.

But the story goes that the children of Hamelin did not drown. It is said that the Pied Piper led them along the sea bed all the way to Transylvania. It is true that many Germans reside in Transylvania today. Yet no one can be sure whether they truly are the descendants of the children of Hamelin.

Prince Marko

When Queen Yevrosima and King Vukashin had a baby son, all the people of Prizren rejoiced. For three days and nights wine flowed freely. For three days and nights the sound of rejoicing echoed from the castle walls. There was much to celebrate. Not only was the boy strong, big and handsome, but it was prophesied that he would become a famous hero of the Serbian people. They named him Marko and Czar Dushan himself consented to be his godfather.

The little prince grew amazingly fast. Soon, instead of toddling about the house, he roamed the hills with the shepherds, the woods with the huntsmen, the fields with the peasants.

One day he wandered high into the mountains and came to an ice cold spring, gushing forth from tall grass. Prince Marko drank greedily, then noticed a lovely maiden sleeping nearby. He realized straight away she must be a fairy. The sun was burning her delicate face and Marko therefore knelt down to carry her into the shade. As he gathered the fairy in his arms, she awoke and asked, 'Where are you taking me, Marko?'

'Into the shade, so that the sun cannot scorch you and spoil your beauty,' the prince replied.

'You are kind,' the smiling fairy murmured. 'I must reward you. What would you like? Great wealth or a sound steel sword? A beautiful maiden or a good horse?'

Marko replied, without hesitating, 'Give me the sword and the horse!'

The fairy clapped her white hands and immediately a dappled horse appeared, galloping like the wind, a damascene sword gleaming at the side of his saddle. 'His name is Sharets,' the fairy said. 'He will serve you well, and so will the sword.'

The prince thanked the fairy and swung into the saddle. The horse then spoke in a human voice,

'Let go of the reins and throw away your spurs, Marko. You will have no need of them.' The prince unfastened the spurs and dropped the reins. The horse shot forward like a bullet, his hooves hardly touching the ground.

Prince Marko soon became famous for his courageous deeds. Turks, thieves and arrogant lords throughout the kingdom trembled at the sound of his name, but he was loved by the people.

But all the glory kindled evil human envy. Yet it was not his enemies, nor his friends who envied him, but his own brother Andriya.

One day Prince Marko invited his young friends to his castle Prilep; his brother Andriya came too. After they had dined and downed a great deal of red wine, tongues loosened and Andriya said,

'Wine flows and things are said, often many stupid things. Such as the statement that my brother Marko is the greatest hero of our kingdom. Everyone knows this to be untrue. I am the greatest hero.'

They all gasped at such brazen words, but Marko laughed and said, 'Deeds, not words prove heroism. Everyone knows what I have done, and what you have done. Why argue about it?'

Andriya unleashed his sword and cried, 'Well said, why argue about it! We shall fight a duel and the one who remains alive will be the greatest hero.'

Marko shook his head sadly. 'Why should brother fight brother? Come with me to the mountains, where there are no brooks or wells. There we shall see which one of us will last longer without water. He will be the victor.'

Andriya was not enthusiastic about the idea, but he could not refuse. The very next day they set out for the mountains.

The hot sun beat upon them, but Marko was singing happily, whilst Andriya was so thirsty and his mouth so parched that he could not even speak.

When they had both settled to rest under a bushy tree and Marko had fallen into a peaceful sleep, Andriya could not bear his thirst any longer and so decided to go in search of water. After a while he found a path, which led him to a tavern.

Andriya went in, ordered a jug of beer and drank it in one go. When he had downed the second lot, he felt much better. 'Andriya, the son of King Vukashin, is the greatest, bravest hero!

Who could match his fearless courage, when he is not afraid of facing hundreds of terrible Turks?' he swaggered.

Thirty terrible Turks happened to be sitting in that very tavern and when they heard Andriya boasting, they laughed, rose, drew their swords and cut off the bragger's head. They stuck the head on a post by the fence and went on drinking.

When Prince Marko woke up, he wondered where his brother had gone. 'I expect he could not bear the thirst and went to find a drink,' he thought, and turned towards the tavern. As he approached, he saw Andriya's head on the post. 'Alas, brother!' Marko cried. 'Who has cut off your curly head?'

Drawing his damascene sword, he burst into the tavern. The terrible Turks pounced on him, but Prince Marko fought so fiercely, that soon he slew the lot. Then he downed some red wine, wrapped his brother's head in a silk scarf and returned to Prilep.

Prince Marko had a faithful friend called Ban Yanko. This gallant youth had chosen a noble bride from a distant Latin land, the daughter of King Michail of Kotsya. In vain he waited for the king's consent to the marriage. He waited one year, two, he waited nine long years in all.

At the start of the tenth year, when snow covered the paths leading to his castle, Yanko heard children's voices under his window, as they were having a snow-ball fight. 'Don't you dare!' one of them cried, 'I shan't let you bully me, like our Ban lets the Kotsyan king bully him!'

Yanko slammed his fist into the table, put on his best robe, fastened his damascene sword to his waist, saddled his bay and set forth towards the Latin land.

He galloped to Kotsya Castle like the wind; with one leap the horse jumped on top of the wall, with the next right to the royal tower. By then King Michail was coming out into the courtyard to welcome him. 'How nice to see you, dear son-in-law! Tie up your horse and come and drink a little wine with me!'

'There is no time to drink,' Yanko replied. 'Are you at last going to give me your daughter, or do I have to win her with my sword?'

'Why shouldn't I give her to you? Fetch the wedding guests! While you're gone, I will prepare everything for the marriage. Don't bring me any drunkards or ruffians, but wise old men, priests and sound citizens.'

Ban Yanko agreed and turned for home. As he was leaving the courtyard, a small window

guests. But there was no sign of Father Novak and his brigands.

'As old Father Novak has not turned up of his own accord, we'd better go and fetch him,' Prince Marko decided, and the whole party went to Mount Romanya. As soon as they arrived, Father Novak appeared to welcome them.

'Are you not coming to the wedding, brother?' Marko asked.

'How can I, when I haven't a single ducat? It is not fitting to attend a wedding without bringing a gift.'

Prince Marko did not speak, but handed a purse with a hundred ducats to Father Novak. Milosh, Relya and Yanko also gave a hundred each, and the rest of the guests collected a round thousand. Novak was more than content. He called his son Gruyitsa and his five hundred brigands, and they all set out for the Latin land.

King Michail could hardly wait for Ban Yanko and his guests to arrive. How he looked forward to chasing the priests and the feeble old men off his land, stealing their gifts and slaying Yanko! In such a manner he had already killed nine prospective husbands, and filled nine towers with their riches. The tenth was ready and waiting for Yanko's gold. When the king saw Ban Yanko approaching with the greatest Serbian heroes and huge army, he was so terrified he locked himself in his tower, and sent the terrible, unbeatable three-headed Moor to fight the bridegroom.

'Measure your strength against this monster,' King Michail cried. 'If you win, you will get my daughter, if not, your life is lost.'

Yanko jumped to his feet, but Relya got to the Moor first. Before the youth could raise his hand, the monster dealt him such a frightful blow that he collapsed to the ground. The Moor swiftly tied Relya up and threw him into a deep dungeon locked behind nine oak doors, secured with eighteen chains. By then Milosh Obilich faced the Moor, but he fared just as badly, and so did Prince Marko.

'I myself must fight!' Ban Yanko declared, but Father Novak held him back. 'Let me try first,' he said, and put on nine fur coats and three wolf heads instead of a helmet. Young Gruyitsa handed him his own sword. 'Your sword is too long,' he said. 'You would be knocked down before you had time to swing it. Take mine and don't wait for the first blow!'

The youth's sword was light and short. Before the Moor could swing his bludgeon, the old man

opened in the narrow tower above, and a letter from the king's daughter fell right into his lap. It read, 'My dear falcon, Yanko Ban, don't bring weaklings and old men, but choose only those who handle a sword well, those whose blood will be fired by a drink of wine. Otherwise you will not return home alive, never have me for your bride.'

Yanko therefore did not invite wise old men, priests and respected citizens to the wedding, but Prince Marko, Father Novak and his son Gruyitsa, Milosh Obilich and Relya Krylatich.

At last the chosen day came. Prince Marko rode into Yanko's castle, followed by five hundred fiery young men. Then Duke Milosh appeared with five hundred lads from Kosovo, followed by Relya, waving a banner, at the head of yet another five hundred selected wedding

jumped up to him and with one mighty blow cut off all his three heads. Using the bludgeon, he then broke down the nine doors and the eighteen chains and freed Marko, Relya and Milosh. By then Yanko found King Michail hiding in the royal tower. The terrified king ran to the window and crashed through the glass pane, falling to his death in the courtyard below. Now Ban Yanko could return home with his bride.

The wedding was celebrated at Yanko's castle. For three weeks the wine flowed freely. Then the gallant youths took their leave. Marko went to white Prilep, Milosh to Kosovo, Relya to Pazar and Father Novak to Mount Romanya.

Prince Marko was not only a valiant hero, but also a wise ruler. After the death of Czar Dushan, four noblemen met in Kosovo Field. They were King Vukashin, mighty Uglyesha, Duke Goyko and Czarevitch Urosh. They argued and argued which one of them was to be czar. Their dispute went on and on, with tempers rising, knives flashing. Only young Czarevitch Urosh stood aside, not daring to oppose his powerful relatives. Failing to agree, the magnates sent for priest Nedelyko, who was the czar's confessor and who should have therefore known which man the czar wished to succeed him.

But the priest brushed their questions aside. 'I have been the czar's confessor and I know his sins. But I know not of his last will and testament. Why not ask Prince Marko? He is the czar's godson and should know more about it.' The couriers remounted and rode to Prilep. Prince Marko heard them out, then saddled his faithful Sharats and rode off to Kosovo.

King Vukashin was delighted to learn his son was to decide who was to be czar. His uncles Uglyesha and Goyko were also full of hope. Marko had loved them dearly when they rocked him on their knees in days of old.

When Prince Marko arrived, he walked straight to the table and sat down. Then he said solemnly, 'The czardom does not belong to you, King Vukashin. Your own kingdom is more than large enough. And you, uncle Goyko, can surely be satisfied with your dukedom? Whilst you, uncle Uglyesha, would not even know how to manage a czardom! Just look at your own neglected estates! No, Czar Dushan has not named any of you as his successor. The czardom should only be passed from father to son. Here is your future czar!' And Marko pointed to Czarevitch Urosh.

Father and uncles, furious at such a decision, started to curse and abuse Prince Marko. But young Urosh stopped them by saying firmly. 'Be

silent! Marko's words were just and honest. God help you, cousin, to remain the bravest and strongest of all heroes. May your sword serve you well in every battle and may your fame spread throughout the land!'

One fine Sunday morning Prince Marko rode out to Mount Urvina. As he climbed the steep slopes, his horse Sharats suddenly stumbled, then stumbled the second time, and the third, weeping at the same time.

'What's the matter, my old friend?' Marko asked. 'We have known one another a hundred and sixty years, and your legs have always been nimble and firm. Could this be a bad omen?'

All at once he heard the well-known voice of his protector, the fairy, floating from the forest. 'Why indeed does your horse stumble? Why indeed does he weep? He sheds tears for you, Prince Marko! The loss of your head he mourns!'

Marko replied, 'I do not believe you, fairy! Why should he mourn the loss of my head, when it sits firmly upon my shoulders?' After a brief silence, the familiar voice whispered again, 'Your head may sit firmly on your shoulders, but Death is approaching at full speed.'

'This I do not believe!'

'You shall find out for yourself, when you reach the mountain top,' the fairy said. 'There between two pines lies the well of truth. Look into it and learn your destiny!'

Marko hastened to the peak of Mount Urvina, where he tied Sharats to one of the trees, and looked down into the well. Mirrored in the water he saw his own worn, wrinkled face, then all of a sudden the water rippled and the face of Death was staring at him. Now Marko knew the truth.

'How I have enjoyed my short life in this world,' he sighed, 'yet already I must bid it goodbye!' Then he drew his damascene sword and with one swift blow he cut off his faithful Sharat's head, not wishing him to fall into stranger's hands. The sword he broke into three pieces and flung it from the mountain peak down to the sea.

'When the sword rises to the surface again, let another hero, such as me, be born into this world,' he exclaimed.

Taking out a clean sheet of paper, gold inkwell and pen, he began to write, 'Whoever finds my body, let him bury it in a Christian grave. Tied to my belt he will find three purses of ducats. The first should be used to pay for my funeral, the second to decorate the chapel where I am to be buried, the third as alms to the blind

musicians, the guslars, who wander over the Serbian lands. Let them remember me in their songs, let them extol the past of Prince Marko!'

Having written it all down, Marko pinned the white sheet to a branch. He threw the gold pen and inkwell into the bushes, then spread his white cloak on the ground and lay down on it.

Three days later Abbot Vaso happened to be passing on his way to the Holy Mountain. At first he thought the prince was asleep, but when he saw and read the white sheet of paper, he realized Marko would never wake again.

Abbot Vaso carried out all Prince Marko's wishes. The prince was buried in the Hilandar church, secretly, so that his enemies would not disturb his eternal rest. And instead of being remembered by a tombstone, his fame and glory live in the songs of the blind wandering guslars, as they travel over Serbian lands.

Nasreddin, the Practical Joker

In the Turkish city of Aksehir there once lived a learned man named Nasreddin. He was not a respected priest, or even a worthy clerk. Just a nobody, who scraped by and lived by his wit as best as he could. He was a real artful dodger, full of fun, and tales about him are still circling around today.

Nasreddin was as poor as a church mouse and always suffered with a terrible thirst. It was somewhat hard to drown that thirsty worm which gnawed at his throat, when he did not have a copper to call his own. But Nasreddin always knew how to help himself.

So one fine day he went to his cupboard and brought out two identical jugs, and filled one of them with water. Then he hid them both under his kaftan and sauntered to the inn. 'Fill this jug with your very best wine,' he called to the innkeeper, passing him the empty jug. The innkeeper obliged. Nasreddin thanked him, put the jug back under his kaftan and turned to leave.

'Wait!' the innkeeper exclaimed. 'Who's going to pay?'

'I'll pay tomorow,' said Nasreddin.

'No way, mister!' the innkeeper protested. 'Pay now, or give me back the wine.'

'What's to be done,' Nasreddin sighed and returned the jug, but the one with the water, of course! The unsuspecting innkeeper emptied the water into the wine barrel. And the foxy Nasreddin toasted his health with the wine.

When he was hungry, Nasreddin again knew how to help himself. In those days there was a man who cooked and sold an excellent pilaff in the market. The delicious aroma hung round his stall and Nasreddin got into the habit of coming each day with his dish of dry rice and eating it right there. In that lovely atmosphere, the dry rice tasted like the real thing. But the pilaff vendor got annoyed and one day he said to Nasreddin, 'Listen, mister, I've watched you day after day fill your nostrils with the smell of my pilaff, yet you have not paid me even once.'

'And how much should I pay you?'

'Ten paras.'

'Very well,' agreed our joker. 'I'll pay tomorrow.'

The next day he was back with the ten paras

in his purse. Goodness knows where from he borrowed them. 'I have come to pay,' he said to the pilaff seller, jingling the coins at his ear.

'Pay up then,' snapped the man.

'I've just paid,' laughed Nasreddin.

'How's that?'

'For the smell of your pilaff I have paid with the jingle of my money!'

When things were at their very worst, Nasreddin had to use his itchy hand as an excuse. Once in the night he climbed over the fence into next door's vegetable garden, to steal some carrots. He already had a bulging sack, when the gardener caught him.

'How did you get here?' he stormed.

'The wind brought me.'

'Alright, but why are you picking my carrots?'

'I am not picking your carrots! The wind was so fierce, I had to grab hold of the carrots, or else I would have been carried goodness knows whereto. Naturally enough, I pulled out a carrot or two in the process.'

'Alright,' growled the gardener. 'But tell me, how did those carrots get into your sack? That I don't understand.'

'What sort of a man are you?' Nasreddin asked, shaking his head. 'That the wind carried me into this garden, doesn't surprise you. Yet that the carrots found their way into my sack, that you find hard to understand!'

Nasreddin decided one day that he would go into business. He tied a brace of partridges to a stick, and sauntered about the town, shouting, 'Sparrows for sale, a round dozen for a piastre!'

A passing miser chuckled and muttered, 'That Nasreddin can't tell a partridge from a sparrow!' Walking up to him, he put a piastre in his hand and said, 'I'll have a dozen of your sparrows.'

'They are all yours, you lucky man,' Nasreddin replied and, opening his sack, he handed to the shocked miser a dozen sparrows.

Some time later Nasreddin went to the neighbouring town and caught up with a couple of pot sellers, struggling to the market with huge water jugs.

'Where are you from?' they asked.

'From Aksehir,' he replied.

'Aksehir? Why, that's where that funnyman Nasreddin comes from, the one who outsmarts everyone he meets,' said one pot seller.

'He wouldn't bamboozle me,' laughed the other. 'I am no fool, like our neighbours in Aksehir.'

Nasreddin made no remark, but later on asked, 'How much do you get for such a jug?'

'A hundred piastres,' the vendors said.

'That's not much. In Aksehir you'd get at least twice that sum.'

'That I doubt,' muttered the pot sellers.

'My master pays ten paras for each pound in weight, and a jug like this must weigh twenty pounds at least,' Nasreddin insisted.

'That it does,' the potters said, nodding their heads, and they decided to go to Aksehir. 'Take us there, please,' they begged.

'With pleasure,' Nasreddin agreed, and led them, avoiding all paths, through dense thicket and bracken, over rocks, till the poor stumbling pot sellers, laden with their wares, nearly breathed their last breath. At last they arrived in the city.

'Wait here,' Nasreddin said. 'I'll ask my master how many pounds of these jugs he desires.' Wearily the pot sellers lined their jugs on the ground, whilst Nasreddin sped home. He took a set of scales and twenty paras and hastened back.

'You're in luck!' he cried. 'My master will purchase two pounds' worth.'

'What do you mean, two pounds' worth?' the potters wondered. 'Why, each jug weighs twenty pounds at least.'

'Didn't I tell you that here we buy jugs by the weight? And my master wants two pounds' worth.'

'You surely don't expect us to break our wares on account of your master!' Nasreddin turned away with a shrug of his shoulders.

'Wait a minute,' the potters snapped crossly. 'Has all our toil here been in vain? Such a whack of a way, too?'

'Oh no, not in vain,' laughed Nasreddin, 'for at least you've found out that Nasreddin outsmarts even clever potters, and not only such fools as their neighbours in Aksehir.'

A certain merchant, who was visiting Aksehir just then, heard this story, and he said to Nasreddin, 'So you've outwitted a pair of village potters, my man, but you wouldn't trick me.'

'That I would,' Nasreddin disagreed. 'Right now, in fact, if only I had my doodlesack here. Look, lend me your donkey, I'll go and fetch it and then I shall doodle you.'

The merchant lent him the donkey and Nasreddin rode home. There he put the donkey in the stable and cut off its tail. On the way back to the merchant he buried the tail in a field, leaving only the tip showing.

'You really have a crazy, scary donkey,' Nasreddin complained. 'Suddenly it began to buck till it threw me to the ground. Then it bolted into the field and sank right down in the earth, till there was nothing but its tail showing.'

'How can a donkey sink so far down?'

'Look for yourself,' said the joker, leading the merchant to the buried tail. The merchant grabbed it and started to pull.

'Don't pull so hard!' Nasreddin warned. 'You'll pull the tail right off.' But the merchant went on pulling with all his might, and the tail came out in his hand.

'See, see!' 'Didn't I tell you not to pull so hard? Now you'll never get that donkey out.'

Eventually the merchant put two and two together and sent a policeman after Nasreddin. 'I have a complaint from a merchant, that you have stolen his donkey,' the policeman growled.

'That's not true, I have no donkey.' But as he spoke, a donkey hee-hawed in the stable.

'You say you have no donkey, and yet I can hear one hee-hawing in your stable.'

'How foolish can you get, that you more notice of what a donkey says than of his master.'

Soon afterwards Nasreddin set out on the tailless donkey to the neighbouring town. It was bitterly cold and the wind was whipping through the holes of his old kaftan. Suddenly a man appeared riding towards him, dressed in a beautiful fox coat, astride a magnificent horse.

'Aren't you cold?' the man marvelled. 'Your kaftan is full of holes and yet you sing as if you did not have a care in the world.'

'I am not cold,' Nasreddin laughed. 'And only because my kaftan is full of holes. You see, the wind comes in through one hole, and goes out through the next. The warmth stays with me inside. But you, poor man, must feel the cold in that fox coat of yours!'

'I am rather cold,' the man admitted. 'Sell me your kaftan.' 'I'll give you money, and throw in my fur coat too,' the man offered.

'I tell you what,' Nasreddin said. 'Keep the money, but let's swop our coats, and also your horse for my donkey.' The man agreed. Nasreddin gave him his raggy old kaftan and the donkey, took the fox coat and the magnificent horse and rode off at full speed.

One day Nasreddin was invited to a wedding. He arrived in one of his shabby old kaftans, and nobody took the slightest notice of him. They did not even offer him a slice of bread. So our joker went off home and returned, clad in the beautiful fox coat, which he had swopped to his great advantage. Everyone present smiled and bowed, and the bridegroom himself brought him a chunk of roast lamb. Nasreddin took off his fur coat and said, 'Eat up, fur coat, for this belongs to you. To me they didn't even give a slice of bread.'

Such a fellow was our Nasreddin from Aksehir in the land of Turkey.

Doctor Faustus

Many centuries have passed since John Faustus was born on a farm in a small German village. He turned out to be a bright young lad, with a natural aptitude for learning, so his father sent him to a wealthy uncle in Wittenberg, where the boy could attend good schools and study for Holy Orders.

But John Faustus preferred to concentrate on books dealing with magic and witchcraft. When the time came for him to sit for his finals, he passed all examinations with honours, and was proclaimed a Doctor of Theology. But instead of serving the church and God, he chose to serve Satan and hell.

Once, during a witching night, he went deep into the forest and summoned the devils, which he had learned to do from the works on sorcery. The devils appeared on by one, but as Faustus has drawn a magic circle round himself, not one of them could harm him.

The last to appear was Mephistopheles, one of the most important devils, who asked, 'Why, learned sir, are you calling up devils all night? What is it you want of us?'

'I should like one of you to serve me faithfully and devotedly till I die,' Faustus explained. 'After my death he can do whatever he wishes with my soul and my body.'

'Tell me a little more what you would expect of the devil in service,' Mephistopheles continued.

'I would expect the devil to obey me in all things, to answer all my queries truthfully — and to serve only me, and no one else,' Faustus replied.

Mephistopheles then asked the third question. 'How long would such a service last?'

Faustus thought a while, then said, 'I am now twenty four years old. If I can have another twenty four years with a devil servant, I shall die content.'

Mephistopheles then remarked, 'That won't be an easy bargain for hell to keep. But as you are a brilliant doctor of theology and one fully versed in holy scriptures, I agree to serve you on your terms. But you must never demand that I appear in any visible form. I only hope Lucifer, the King of Hell, will sanction our bargain.' Mephistopheles proceeded to write it all down on a roll of parchment and Doctor Faustus had to sign in his own blood.

Doctor Faustus soon became the most powerful magician in the whole world, and his fame spread near and far.

It so happened that rumours about the remarkable doctor reached the ears of Charles V, who was staying in Innsbruck. As the ruler of the Holy Roman Empire, he was eager to meet Faustus, and invited him therefore to his court. Faustus was happy to attend and was received warmly by the emperor.

'I have already heard much about your powers of magic, dear Doctor,' Charles V said. 'I should so love to meet Alexander the Great! He was such a distinguished warrior and sovereign. I would be most obliged if you were to show him to me.'

Faustus nodded and said, 'I will let you see him, Your Majesty. But do not go too near him, or he will disappear.'

Faustus left the hall for only a moment, and already Alexander the Great was coming in, walking majestically, clad in all the finery of a Greek hero. He was followed by his lovely wife, dressed in a dazzling scarlet robe, embroidered with gold and pearls.

Charles V simply could not resist, he had to sneak up to her from behind, to see for himself if she had a wart on her neck, as was rumoured. And truly, it was right there. But he had come too close, and the beautiful lady and Alexander the Great melted away.

The exiled emperor begged Doctor Faustus to remain at his court, for such a powerful magician would do much to enhance its reputation. Doctor Faustus promised to stay, but then something happened which spoiled his visit.

One evening, as the doctor was strolling

along a passage, he noticed a sleeping knight standing by a window. He thought him a funny sight, and decided to make him funnier still by conjuring a pair of antlers on his head, making them protrude out of the window, so the knight was well and truly stuck. Then Faustus crept away.

Before long the knight woke up and realized at once he could not move his head. His cries for help brought many people who, instead of feeling sorry and helping the knight in distress, only roared with mirth. He was such a ridiculous sight! The knight screamed all the more, calming down only after doctor Faustus returned and got rid of the antlers with a few words of magic.

The knight, of course, was well aware that Faustus was responsible, and he swore to have his revenge.

One day, when Doctor Faustus was riding to a nearby wood, he saw a group of men belonging to the disgraced knight waiting to ambush him, their rifles pointing his way. Using a bit of sorcery, Faustus had himself quickly surrounded with armed cavalrymen. The very sight of them made the knight's men take to their heels.

After this little adventure, Faustus grew discontented, and left the emperor's court at the first opportunity. Laden with valuable gifts, he travelled to the count of Anholt, who was renowned for his generosity and love of enjoyment.

As Faustus approached the town of Anholt, he met a farmer driving a cart heaped with hay, pulled by horses. Faustus was travelling in the middle of the road and he had no intention to get out of the way. The same applied to the farmer, so they met face to face.

'Why don't you get out of my way?' Faustus asked.

'Why don't you?' smirked the farmer. 'It is easier for a mere rider than for me with my load.'

'If you don't get out of my way, I'll swallow that stack of hay, cart, horses and all,' Faustus threatened.

'Help yourself,' laughed the farmer, but the

smile froze on his face when the magician opened his mouth wide and swallowed the lot in one gulp. The farmer dived from his box only just in time, and ran cursing and yelling after Faustus, who rode on as if nothing had happened.

Not till he reached the town's gates, did Faustus turn round and spit out the stack of hay, the cart and the horses. The guards, terrified out of their minds, eyed this spectacle with amazement, but the farmer let out a cry of joy and jumped up on his box, whipped into the horses and drove off as quickly as he could, to get. away from such a dangerous magician. By the time Doctor Faustus entered the town, rumours of his incredible deed had reached the count's court.

The count welcomed his guest warmly, and held a feast in his honour. The table was laden with many special dishes, but as it was early spring, there was no fruit on the silver trays, except nuts and apples.

'We have no other fruit here at this time of the year,' the countess said in excuse.

Faustus did not comment, but picked up two empty silver trays and put them behind the window. Half an hour later they were laden with delicious, wondrous foreign fruits, oranges, apricots, grapes and strange fruits no one present had ever tasted or seen. The countess looked upon such a windfall with astonishment, whilst Faustus only smiled.

'My most gracious lady,' he said in the end, 'when it is cold and wet here, other parts of the world bask in sunshine and lovely fruits ripen there. I therefore commanded my servant spirit, who happens to be very clever and swift, to go and pick these fruits for you. It was not a difficult or an unusual task.'

Soon afterwards, Doctor Faustus held a banquet in honour of the count of Anholt and his friends.

At his request, Mephistopheles built him a beautiful castle on a hill. When the count and his party arrived, they marvelled at the exotic birds, swans and pheasants which lived there, and at the numerous animals from foreign

lands, such as monkeys, elephants and tigers, which ran freely in the yard. And when they were seated at the table, where many rare, delicious courses were lavishly spread, surrounded by bottles of selected wines, their enthusiasm and pleasure knew no bounds.

After the banquet, the count thanked the doctor for being such a perfect host and rode away, most impressed. When he was about half way home, he suddenly heard loud explosions like guns being fired. Turning round, he saw clouds of satanic black smoke rising from the direction of the castle. Soon all was quiet and the smoke was gone, but the castle was wiped from the earth. The evil spirit was carrying it back to hell.

Faustus continued his travels through Germany, and through distant, foreign lands. Wherever he went, he earned everyone's admiration with his feats of magic.

But the years sped by and Faustus' span of life was almost up. The unhappy magician grew sadder each day, afraid of the terrible hour when his soul and body would go to the devil. He journeyed back to Wittenberg, where years before he had struck the fiendish bargain with Mephistopheles. Surrounding himself with students, he tried to find in drink and merriment an escape from the fearsome terror that gripped his heart.

It so happened that one of the students fell heart and soul in love with a beautiful girl, but she did not return his love, as she already had promised herself to another.

The unhappy student was near despair and Doctor Faustus, feeling sorry for the youth, gave him a special ring.

'Put this ring on your finger,' he said. 'Tomorrow night a party will be held in the town gardens. Go there, and ask the girl you love to dance. Make sure that whilst she dances, she touches this ring. Then you will see.'

The enamoured student took the doctor's advice. Amazingly, the moment the maiden touched the ring, she was fired with such deep love for him that she forgot at once all about her previous suitor and agreed to marry the happy student.

On another occasion, one of the students found himself in difficulties. His father died, leaving him a substantial fortune. But a dishonest moneylender claimed that the deceased owed him a very tidy sum, and presented the son with false documents to that effect. And because the wordly, rotten moneylender also bribed the judge, it seemed he must win the case. During the trial, at which Doctor Faustus was present, the scales of justice did indeed tip in favour of the artful moneylender, but then Faustus exclaimed, 'Enough now, false judges!'

He clapped his hands thrice, and the spirit of the deceased man entered. Gripping the moneylender round the throat, the spirit whispered, 'Tell the truth at once, or I shall choke you to death!'

Pale as death, the moneylender owned up, admitting the documents were forged and the judge was bribed. That trial caused quite a disturbance throughout Wittenberg.

Then came the very last day of Faustus' life. The unhappy magician invited his student friends to his rooms. They were glad to come, for he was greatly loved and respected, as he was always ready with help and advice whenever any of them were in need. On this fateful day Faustus entertained them lavishly, then turned to them, a grave look on his face.

'My dear friends, brother students!' he said. 'I have asked you here not just to dine and wine and entertain you. Today we are seeing each other for the last time. I want you to know that all my power and fame spring from the fact that I sold my soul to the devil. He is coming to collect it in a moment or two. I asked you here to witness my terrible end and to make it a warning to you all.'

At first the students thought it a joke and they laughed, but when doctor Faustus went into the next room, and terrible moans were heard, they rushed after him, sober and terrified. A dreadful scene greeted them. The whole chamber was tainted with blood, yet there was no corpse to be seen. Only a gaping black hole in the ceiling showed that the devil had carried Doctor Faustus away.

Giant
Golem

During the reign of Emperor Rudolph, a rabbi named Jehuda Low ben Becalel was assigned to the Old Synagogue in Prague. He was a wise and a learned man and quite a powerful magician. As the leader of the Prague Jews, rabbi Low did his best to apply all he knew to ease the burden of the members of his race, who were often persecuted not only by their Christian fellow citizens, but by the emperor himself.

What use was all the wisdom, knowledge and ability to practise sorcery! Rabbi Low could not stop all the sufferings of his people, though he spent a lot of time trying to find a solution. Then, one night, an angel appeared before him, and told him to make the giant figure of Golem

out of clay, to help him against enemies. Rabbi Low then spent many long hours bent over old manuscripts, till at last he found the information he needed.

The next day he summoned his son-in-law and also his most loyal pupil, and asked them to prepare for seven days for their hard task. On the seventh day they all put on white cloaks and went to the River Vltava. There, in torch light, they fashioned from clay giant Golem. When the work was completed, the rabbi said to his son-in-law, 'You have the character of fire, therefore embrace Golem seven times, and chant words of magic.'

The son-in-law obeyed, and the clay figure

dried instantly and glowed like red hot iron. Then the rabbi turned to his pupil. 'Your nature is like water, therefore you too must embrace Golem seven times, chanting holy words.'

The pupil also obeyed. Golem cooled down and human skin appeared over his face and body.

Last of all the rabbi paced seven times round Golem, then opened the giant's mouth and placed under his tongue a piece of parchment called shem, bearing a sacred inscription. Immediately Golem rose, dressed himself in the suit which the rabbi had prepared, and followed him obediently.

'I have brought a new servant for the syn-agogue,' the rabbi said to his wife. 'His name is Joseph, but you must not use him for domestic duties.'

Golem settled down well, dozing most of the time on the bench and saying nothing; more-over, he obeyed the rabbi to the letter. Except for Friday evenings, when he always grew restless and his eyes started to gleam menacingly. Then the rabbi had to insert a new shem under his tongue, to stop him from turning wild and causing some calamity.

Before long, Golem was known all over Prague. With his heavy, slow step he walked the streets, pausing at markets, dawdling in taverns. He showed no mercy when seeing an injustice, punishing the guilty one, whether he was a nobleman or a pauper—Golem feared no one. The Jewish Town could breathe freely at last, for there was not a soul who was not wary of the giant. But keeping Golem had its problems.

The rabbi's wife, who, in spite of her husband's instructions, now and then used the giant for domestic work, was the one most to suffer. She bade him once to fill a tub with water, and he flooded the whole street. Another time she sent him to the Fruit Market for apples, and he brought back the whole stall, including the furious market woman.

'Didn't I tell you not to use Joseph for domestic purposes,' the rabbi scolded his wife. 'One must not use the urn designed for sacred service for everyday duties.'

After this, the rabbi's wife did not look upon Golem so kindly. But he soon made peace with her and earned the respect of the whole Jewish town.

Shortly before Easter, a Christian servant suddenly disappeared in the Old Town. The word spread that she had been killed by the Jews, so they could use her blood when making matzos, their Easter biscuits. Golem was accused of her murder. The rumours of his vile deed travelled through the city and the Jews feared that the maddened mob would break into their houses to plunder, kill and burn.

Rabbi Low was filled with apprehension and he ordered Golem to find the missing maid, come what may. So Golem went away.

Three days went by, and the tension in Prague grew and grew. Some people swore even that they had seen Golem creeping near the house where the girl was a servant. A few said that they heard him admit he was the murderer. They did not care that Golem was dumb and could not speak.

Then suddenly Golem appeared in the Jewish town with the missing maid. He led her to the rabbi, where she confessed that she had ran away from service back home to a tiny village in southern Bohemia. There Golem found her, seized her and carried her back to Prague, before the startled parents realized what was happening.

So the Jewish town was saved, and people began to marvel at Golem's cunning and alertness.

Soon afterwards he proved how wise he was too.

Two merchants lived in the Jewish town at that time. They were both wealthy and highly respected, but one had children who were all

frail and thin, whereas the children of the other man were healthy and strong. It happened that a son was born to both families on the very same day, at the very same hour. The midwife pitied the mother of the weak children, and swopped the two newlyborns.

The babes grew into boys, the boys into youths, and then one fell in love with the daughter of the other merchant. No one dreamed they were brother and sister. The midwife had died, taking her secret to the grave.

Then came the day of the wedding. During the ceremony, the chalice holding the wine suddenly slipped from the rabbi's hand, and the wine spilled on the floor. The rabbi sent Golem to fetch another bottle from the cellar, but Golem wrote instead with his heavy hand, 'The bride and groom are sister and brother.'

When the rabbi saw these words, he gasped in horror, and asked those present to postpone the ceremony.

Afterwards he had a long discussion with Go-

lem. Though the latter could not talk, the wise rabbi guessed from his gestures what had happened.

The next day the rabbi invited both the families to come to the synagogue. He asked other wise, respected men to attend, and when they were all present, he said to Golem, 'Go, Joseph, to the grave of the deceased midwife. Strike her grave with a stick, and ask her soul to come to us.'

Golem obeyed and returned a few moments later. He pointed in silence to a drape. The rabbi said, 'Listen to me, soul of the deceased midwife! In the name of the happiness of these two young people, I order you to tell me truthfully what you have done.'

From behind the drape, came a weak, aged voice. Between sobs, the midwife related how she had swopped the newlyborn babes. She begged the rabbi for forgiveness and told him she could find no peace. Bad conscience plagued her even after death.

'Can you prove that this is the truth?' rabbi Low asked.

'My daughter's chest contains all the written entries,' the soul of the deceased said a while later. 'Read them. I entered the name of each child I helped into this world.'

The chest was brought, and the rabbi examined all the entries. Among them he found the names of both the boys and the proof that they had been swopped.

'You spoke the truth,' the rabbi then said to the midwife's soul. Now beg the engaged couple, whom you have harmed, for their forgiveness. You shall find peace in eternity only if they forgive you.'

Now the young people realized they were brother and sister, they forgave the midwife and thanked Golem for saving them from committing a great sin.

One day, however, Golem gave the rabbi an awful headache. The week was just nearing its end, when the rabbi's young daughter fell ill. It was early Friday evening, and the rabbi left for the synagogue in a somewhat agitated state, forgetting completely that it was time to change Golem's shem.

Whilst he was gone, Golem's strength grew and grew. No longer could he keep still, but he ran wildly through the streets, ripping out windows and doors, hurling out furniture, trampling on it, smashing crockery, tearing roofs off houses. It was a real disaster.

The rabbi had just finished reading the ninety second psalm, when some men burst into the synagogue and begged him to intervene. But the service was in progress and the holy day had begun, and any activity was forbidden. All the same, the rabbi ran outside and shouted to the maddened giant, 'Stop, Joseph!'

Golem obeyed, and the rabbi placed a fresh shem under his tongue, then returned to the synagogue to restart the service. Ever since then, the ninety second psalm has always been sung twice in the Prague Old Synagogue.

After this disturbance, the rabbi asked his son-in-law and his most loyal pupil to come and see him again. They took Golem to the synagogue attic and there changed him back into the clay figure.

But Golem was not destined to find peace in the attic. After some years a vagrant student appeared in the Jewish Town, and he unearthed in some ancient manuscript the secret of how to bring Golem back to life. He climbed into the attic, placed the shem into the giant clay figure's mouth, and it truly came to life. But the figure grew and grew, towering above the terrified student. It lost its human form and turned into an enormous heap of clay, which kept on swelling and growing as if it were to bury the entire world. Realizing that he had made a terrible mistake, the student jumped upwards and plucked the shem from the clay. Immediately the soil poured downwards and completely covered him. In the clay the inquisitive student found his grave.

Narti Sosruko

Once upon a time the Narti nation lived in the Caucasus mountains. The men were great heroes, who fought bravely against their cruel neighbours—the one-eyed giants Inyds, the tiny, vicious Isps and the savage Chints. Sosruko, the son of beautiful Satanea, was the most famous Narti hero.

One day the lovely Satanea with delicate brows and slender arms took her washing to the river. On the opposite bank she saw Psytch the shepherd tending a herd of cattle. When he noticed the beautiful maiden, his heart flared with great love. Satanea too gazed at the handsome youth with admiration. She sat down on a boulder, unable to utter a word. Psytch also remained silent. The roar of the turbulent river would have in any case drowned his voice. So they parted without speaking.

Satanea placed the stone she had sat on in her laundry basket. She had no idea why she did so. When she came home, she placed the stone in a trunk and forgot all about it.

Some time later she heard strange noises coming from the trunk. Satanea raised the lid and realized the sounds came from the stone. 'What a strange stone,' she muttered and closed the trunk.

But something inside the stone kept on creaking and bubbling; the stone grew in size and in warmth, till it almost set the trunk on fire. So Satanea put the stone in the fireplace.

There the stone stayed for nine months and nine days. It grew and grew and got hotter and hotter, till sparks flew from it.

Satanea ran to the heavenly blacksmith Tlepsh and asked, 'Can I, dear god, tell you a secret?'

'Most certainly,' said the god. 'I am here, after all, to help people with my trade, so they can trust me.'

'I cannot tell you about it, but, on the other

burst open. Splinters flew in all directions, and a little fiery boy fell out of the stone. His body was aflame, sparks flew from it and smoke surrounded him.

Satanea yearned to grasp the newborn babe to her heart, but she cried out in pain. As soon as she touched the boy, she burned her hands. As she dropped him, he burned a hole in her skirt.

Tlepsh seized the baby with his tongs and plunged him in water. The water sizzled and hissed, then steam poured from it. Eventually the boy's body turned to steel, with the exception of his hips, which were held by the tongs.

'Take your steel son,' the heavenly blacksmith said. 'He will become a great hero.'

The boy grew, it was a joy to behold.

When one month old, he was as big as those one year old, and at the age of one he could sit firmly astride a horse. Everyone in the whole country talked about him. They named him Sosruko, which means the son of a stone.

One day Sosruko paid Tlepsh a visit.

'Come and help me, boy,' the blacksmith said. 'Work the bellows, but not too hard!'

Sosruko thought he blew gently, but he brought down the whole forge. Only the anvil stayed put, for it was firmly wedged deep in the earth.

'What a strong man you are!' the blacksmith cried. 'Now pull the anvil up too!'

Sosruko tried with all his might, but it did not budge.

'You must grow stronger still,' Tlepsh remarked, and Sosruko sadly turned for home.

Early the next morning Sosruko returned to the forge, seized the anvil and managed to tear it out of the earth. He carried it outside, then went back home.

When Tlepsh arrived, he was most surprised. 'I wonder who tore that anvil out of the ground? No man can have such strength.'

Three men entered the forge just then. The eldest carried a scythe, and he asked, 'Please help us, god! We have this magic scythe, which works on its own. We cannot agree which one of us should be its owner.'

The blacksmith examined the scythe and recognized it immediately. His teacher Lobech had made it for the god of harvests.

'This scythe belongs to none of you,' he said. 'But I shall use it to make a magic sword. The one who carries this anvil back where it belongs, will get the sword.'

The brothers were real muscular fellows,

hand, I cannot remain silent about it,' Satanea said. 'Whatever shall I do?'

The heavenly blacksmith smiled. 'A true woman of the human race! She seeks advice and yet is afraid of hearing my advice. Tell me your secret and I shall help you.'

Satanea took Tlepsh by the hand and led him to the strange stone.

On seeing it, the blacksmith cried, 'Heavens above, what miracle is this? I have seen many things in my life, but never anything like this.'

Tlepsh then gripped the fiery stone with a pair of tongs and carried it to the forge. Satanea went with him.

The blacksmith pounded into the stone with a hammer for seven days and nights. Satanea felt as if each blow was aimed at her heart and her heart hurt and trembled. At last the stone

quite confident that they would manage easily. So they agreed to Tlepsh's terms.

The blacksmith turned the scythe into a magic sword, but not one of the brothers was able to move the anvil. Sosruko entered just then. Without saying a word, he picked the anvil up and carried it back to its rightful place. There he thrust it into the ground.

The brothers eyed the young man with the gigantic strength with amazement. The eldest cried, 'He should have the magic sword!'

'That is true,' the heavenly blacksmith agreed. And he gave the sword to Sosruko.

'Now I have a sword,' Sosruko remarked. 'But I do not have a horse fit for a hero to go with it.'

'Your mother will give you a horse,' Tlepsh said. 'Go to her.'

So Sosruko hastened home.

But Satanea did not want to give her son a horse fit for a hero.

'Oh, my son, the light of my life! The horse you want is so wild, that the best riders are thrown from the saddle. And you are only a child.'

Sosruko then told her how he tore the anvil out of the earth, then thrust it back again, and how he had been given the magic sword. Satanea gave in and led her son to a high rock.

'First you must roll aside this enormous boulder. It hides the entrance to the cave, which is the home of your horse.'

Sosruko rolled away the stone and entered the cave. A magnificent mount stood inside. His hooves kicked the soil, till sparks flew, and he neighed so crossly and fiercely, that the earth trembled.

Yet Sosruko was not afraid. He jumped into the saddle, and the horse shot out of the cave, rising swiftly beyond the clouds. They did not return to earth till seven days later. By then the horse obeyed Sosruko's every word. He had found his master.

Sosruko carried out many heroic deeds on his faithful mount, with his magic sword always at the ready. His neighbours, the one-eyed giants Inyds, the tiny, vicious Isps and the savage Chints trembled with fear at the very mention of his name. He was always a welcome guest on Mount Charama, where the Narti council met.

He happened to come there one day, and as usual received a warm welcome. He was led to the seat of honour, and tournaments were held for his pleasure. Sosruko won as always, and the following day he won the dance competition too. On the third day, when the council sat, Sosruko proved himself the wisest man present.

He was returning home in a happy frame of mind, when a rider shot towards him on a mountain meadow. He was all in black, wearing a black steel helmet and black steel gloves. Without uttering a sound, the mysterious rider attacked and knocked Sosruko to the ground as if he were a sheaf of corn.

Sosruko was startled. He had no idea there was a hero living more valiant and stronger than he. Fear kept him on the ground.

'Rise, brave hero!' cried the black rider, roaring with laughter. 'Rise, unconquerable hero! I don't want to finish you off whilst you lie helpless on the ground!'

Sosruko was now terrified and he began to beg, 'Don't kill me, brave hero! I have spent the last three days on Mount Charama, fighting in

tournaments, dancing and councelling. I am terribly weary. Wait till I have rested, then let us fight!'

'Very well,' the rider laughingly agreed. 'Come back here in one week's time. If you don't, I'll spread the word what a coward you are.'

Sosruko sadly rode home.

'What has happened to you, my son, the light of my life, that you are so downcast?' his worried mother asked.

'I shall tell you. I met a rider, he was all in black, with a black steel helmet and black steel gloves. This man knocked me down with his lance, as if I was a sheaf of corn. I had to plead for my life! In a week's time we are to meet again. Mother, I fear I shall die in the duel.'

'Oh, my son, my light! You afraid?' Satanea cried. 'Yet I do not blame you. The black rider is a member of the cunning Tortesh clan, the son of Albech and the witch Barymbucha. He is a wicked, evil man. So far nobody has managed to overpower him, yet he kills everybody he meets. If you slay that terrible Tortesh, you will free the Narti nation from an enemy who is more fearsome than the Inyds, Isps and Chints.'

'How can I kill the dreaded Tortesh, when he is much stronger than I?' Sosruko sighed.

'I shall ask God Tlepsh,' Satanea said and went to see the blacksmith.

After much thought, he suggested, 'Sosruko need not feel ashamed if I help him in battle. Have no fear! Tell him not to worry when he fights the duel.'

When the week ended, Sosruko rode to Mount Charama. Though he believed that Tlepsh would be there to help him, his heart was anxious. As he came to the meadow where the duel was to take place, a hundred bells suddenly appeared on the harness of his faithful horse. A hundred hungry wolves were running behind him and a hundred eagles were soaring above his head.

The terrible Tortesh turned white with fear when he heard the unbearable ringing of so many bells. His terror grew when he was pounced on by the hundred wolves and the hundred eagles, who attacked from the air. Vainly he swung his sword, vainly his horse beat with his hooves into the hungry wolves. It was then that Sosruko galloped to their side. With one mighty swipe of his magic sword, the bells stopped ringing and Tortesh's head rolled on to the green grass.

The Narti nation was now free of the fearsome black rider.

Year after year the gods used to meet on Ochromacho, the mount of happiness, to drink the heavenly liquid sano, sweet wine unknown to men. The gods always liked to invite one noted Narti hero.

When the time came for the gods to hold their feast again, they discussed which of the Narti heroes they should invite.

Sozrech, the god of home happiness, suggested, 'Let us ask Bearded Nasren, who presides at Narti banquets. He is the bravest and the strongest man.'

'I would like to invite Shaneya, the brilliant Narti hunter,' said Mazychta, the god of forests and hunts.

'What about Gormysh, the most competent Narti shepherd?' said Amysh, the god of herds.

'There is Chimish too, who is such an excellent farmer,' Tchagoledz, the god of harvest added.

'Say what you like,' Tlepsh said decisively. 'The greatest Narti hero is Sosruko.'

The other gods agreed, and so Sosruko was invited to the feast. When he arrived, the gods seemed surprised.

'Do you mean to say this is the greatest Narti hero? He is just an ordinary little fellow!' they protested.

'There is no one in the whole world who will conquer him,' Tlepsh vowed.

'In that case, litttle fellow, drink our sano! It is wine fit only for gods. When you taste it, you will know how good it is,' said Psatch, the god of life, as he handed a horn filled with the wine to Sosruko.

Sosruko downed it and his heart grew merry. 'It is indeed an excellent drink!' he cried.

'Now go, and tell everyone how tasty the heavenly wine is,' Psatch spoke once more.

But Sosruko was not anxious to leave.

'Could I please have another sip?' he asked.

'That is not possible, Psatch said shaking his head. The god of gods Tcha would be very angry.'

'No, he would not,' Tlepsh disagreed. 'Go on, give him another drink!'

Psatch only shrugged his shoulders, but the merry god of the forests and hunts went into the bushes. From a barrel which was hidden there he poured more wine into the horn.

Sosruko drank, and courage entered his heart.

'Does this excellent drink come from that barrel?' he asked.

'Yes, it contains the sano,' the god of the harvest replied. 'The most important thing is that at the bottom of the barrel are the seeds from which the grapes grow.'

The gods gasped that their secret had been revealed. Sosruko did not wait to hear more, but ran down the hill to escape from the gods.

From that day men began to grow grape vine, and make from them the sweet wine sano, which lightens the heart and gives courage.

On a different occasion, Sosruko bade his mother goodbye, jumped on to his faithful horse, and rode off to Mount Charama. As soon as they set out, the horse stumbled.

'That is a bad omen!' Satanea cried. 'My son, the light of my life, do not go to sit at the Narti council. Death awaits you there.'

Sosruko dismissed her words with a wave of the hand. 'Death awaits a hero at every turn. If I were to sit at home by the hearth, death would find me there too.'

As he rode, Sosruko saw two jugs on the path. One was filled with white sano, the other was empty. The empty jug twisted and twirled

round the full one, and the latter leaned over the empty one, yet it did not spill a single drop into it.

Sosruko was puzzled by this, but he rode on. Then he saw a rope, pulled right across the path, as if it was trying to stop the horse from riding further. When the horse jumped over the rope, it tied itself in a knot and flew over the horse's head to bar his way once more.

'What a strange rope,' Sosruko muttered, but rode on.

A little later he reached an old Narti village. This was the home of the lovely Adiuch, who loved Sosruko dearly. Sosruko returned her love, but dangerous adventures were of greater importance to him than love. Sosruko now entered Adiuch's house, and found the beautiful maiden asleep on a sofa. He embraced and kissed her, wondering why the left side of her body was hot, and the right side as cold as ice.

Adiuch woke up and welcomed the youth, asking him where he was going to.

'I am on my way to Mount Charama, to sit at the Narti council.'

Adiuch grew sad. 'Don't go there, Sosruko. You will meet your death.'

'My mother told me that too,' Sosruko said impatiently. 'But I am going on. No use talking about it. But if you are so wise, then explain the incredible things I saw on my journey here.'

Sosruko then told her about the two jugs, and about the rope. Adiuch sat deep in thought, then said, 'The full jug represents a wise man, who knows many good and useful things. The empty jug represents a foolish man. The foolish man would like to learn from the wise one, and the wise man would gladly help, but it is no use. You cannot help a fool. Just like one cannot help you, my dearest. Your mother and I have warned you not to go to the Narti council, for death awaits you there. The warning was in vain. And that rope represents your mother's anxiety. Like that rope, she too tried to stop you on your journey to death.'

Sosruko frowned and said, 'Now tell me why the left side of your body is hot, and the right as cold as ice.'

'That is because I love you, and don't love you. My heart, which is on the left side, burns for you. But my mind warns me against you, for any adventure means more to you than my love.'

Sosruko did not like what Adiuch told him. He bade her a cold farewell and rode on to Monut Charama.

Instead of the gods, only the men of the Tortesh clan had gathered on Mount Charama. They hated Sosruko, for having slain their greatest hero. At their side stood Narti's main enemies, the one-eyed giants Inyds. A strange council, to be sure.

When Sosruko appeared at the bottom of the mountain, the enemies cried in delight, 'We shall kill him! He is much too proud, and he has made us suffer many times!'

They rolled a huge wheel with sharp steel spikes at the youth, but he only threw his steel chest out, and the wheel disintegrated.

The one-eyed giants began to tremble, but the Tortesh men said, 'His chest is, after all, made of iron!'

And they rolled down another wheel.

This time Sosruko met it with his steel back, and again broke the wheel.

'His back is also made of steel,' the Tortesh men remarked and let go of another wheel. This was met by Sosruko's brow, and there was nothing left of it but splinters.

Suddenly the witch Barumbuch appeared on the mountain — the one whose son Sosruko had killed. She cried, 'Roll down one more wheel! Sosruko will meet it with his hips and they are not made of steel.'

As the last wheel rolled down the mountain, Sosruko prepared to meet it with his hips. The wheel sliced off both his legs.

'Alas!' Sosruko cried out. 'My mother Satanea was right! The beautiful Adiuch was right! I should not have come to sit at the Narti council.'

Sosruko used his remaining strength to fire arrows at his enemies on Mount Charama. Many he slew, but many more remained alive. When he had fired his last arrow, the last drop of his blood trickled to the ground, and his soul left his body.

So died the greatest Narti hero, Sosruko, the son of a stone.

The Wise Hiawatha

Once, long ago, the Indian Iroquois were scattered over prairies and forests. The Seneca tribe hunted game, whereas the Cayuga tribe grew corn. The two tribes envied one another, which often led to quarrels and attacks and thefts of food and weapons. Even when threatened by a common enemy, they were unable to unite for their joint defence. The Iroquois were weak, and lived in hiding, in fear for their possessions and lives.

This continued for many years, until the arrival of Hiawatha. No one knows from where he came. He appeared one day wrapped in a white cloak, rowing a white canoe on Tioto Lake, which lies amid deep forests. There the Iroquois used to meet to exchange their wares, grain for furs, meat for arms. But even here they failed to agree. Someone wanted beaver furs for an old worn cover, another a sack of salt for a little bag of grain. Everyone tried to cheat, so instead of bartering with the goods, they shouted abuse and often fought amongst themselves.

Hiawatha watched the Red Indians arguing, then raised his hand and cried, 'Do not quarrel like a lot of old women! Listen to me, and I shall help you to agree.'

The Indians grew silent and gazed at the stranger with wonder and interest. He continued, 'Pull your canoes as far as you can from the water's edge!' Surprisingly no one objected and they all obeyed.

Hiawatha then raised his hands towards the heavens and in that moment the sky darkened with a huge black cloud. But it was no ordinary cloud, it was a gigantic flock of wild ducks. They dived to the surface of the lake and drank greedily. When they flew away, the lake was half empty. Hiawatha then called more and more ducks, till all the water was gone.

Hiawatha then said, 'I am Hiawatha and I have come to help and unite you. Can't you agree how many arrows you should give for a bag of salt, and how much salt for a beaver skin? Can't you agree how much grain you should give for a cover and how many covers

for earthenware pots? Then look at the lake!' On the lake bed gleamed thousands upon thousands of shells. 'These shells will be your money. Divide them fairly among yourselves; file them, so they are nicely rounded, then thread them on strings. I shall then determine how many shells you must give for salt, furs, weapons, mats, earthenware and all other goods.'

The Indians followed his advice. Before water flooded back into Tioto Lake, they were trading with whatever wares they had. Hiawatha put up his wigwam on the hill above the lake.

As the days passed, the narrow, hardly visible track which led to the wigwam turned into a wide path. The Indians sought out the wise Hiawatha whenever they had a problem. Hiawatha knew everything, understood everything. He taught the Indians many useful things, yet there was one thing he was unable to teach them: how to live in unity and harmony.

'Men can learn everything of their own accord. But only disaster will teach them how to live in peace with their fellow brothers.'

It so happened that the lakeland region was attacked by wild enemy tribes from the North. They destroyed camps, slaughtered women and children. The Iroquois fled from them to wise Hiawatha. They camped under trees and in the shade of rocks, anxious for his advice.

He entered their circle and said, 'The enemy has forced you to flee, because you are not united. But if you join forces against him, you will be successful in your defence. Then great peace will reign in this land. There are so many of you! You speak the same language, yet you do not trust one another. But now, when death is

206